A Research Agenda for Neolibe

Elgar Research Agendas outline the future of research in a given area. Leading scholars are given the space to explore their subject in provocative ways, and map out the potential directions of travel. They are relevant but also visionary.

Forward-looking and innovative, Elgar Research Agendas are an essential resource for PhD students, scholars and anybody who wants to be at the forefront of research.

Titles in the series include:

A Research Agenda for Management and Organization Studies
Edited by Barbara Czarniawska

A Research Agenda for Cities
Edited by John Rennie Short

A Research Agenda for Entrepreneurship and Context
Edited by Friederike Welter and William B. Gartner

A Research Agenda for Neoliberalism
Kean Birch

A Research Agenda for Neoliberalism

KEAN BIRCH

Senior Associate, Innovation Policy Lab, University of Toronto, Canada

Elgar Research Agendas

 Edward Elgar
PUBLISHING

Cheltenham, UK • Northampton, MA, USA

Published by
Edward Elgar Publishing Limited
The Lypiatts
15 Lansdown Road
Cheltenham
Glos GL50 2JA
UK

Edward Elgar Publishing, Inc.
William Pratt House
9 Dewey Court
Northampton
Massachusetts 01060
USA

Paperback edition 2018

A catalogue record for this book
is available from the British Library

Library of Congress Control Number: 2017936583

This book is available electronically in the **Elgar**online
Social and Political Science subject collection
DOI 10.4337/9781786433596

ISBN 978 1 78643 358 9 (cased)
ISBN 978 1 78643 359 6 (eBook)
ISBN 978 1 78897 618 3 (paperback)

Typeset by Servis Filmsetting Ltd, Stockport, Cheshire

Printed and bound by CPI Group (UK) Ltd, Croydon, CR0 4YY

For Sheila and Maple

Contents

Figures

Tables

Acknowledgements

Thanks to all the publishers for permission to reproduce previously published work in this book. Chapter 3 draws and significantly expands on my blog post published on *Discover Society* and called 'How to think like a neoliberal' (1 July 2015); Chapters 4 and 5 draw on my journal article, Birch, K. (2015), 'Neoliberalism: The whys and wherefores . . . and future directions', *Sociology Compass* 9(7), 571–84; Chapter 6 draws on my book chapter, Birch, K. (2016), 'Financial economics and business schools: Legitimating corporate monopoly, reproducing neoliberalism?', in S. Springer, K. Birch and J. MacLeavy (eds), *The Handbook of Neoliberalism*, London: Routledge, pp. 320–30; and Chapters 6 and 8 draw on my journal article, Birch, K. (2016), 'Market vs. contract? The implications of contractual theories of corporate governance to the analysis of neoliberalism', *ephemera: theory & politics in organization* 16(1), 107–33.

I would like to thank a number of people who have directly and indirectly influenced my thinking on neoliberalism over the last few the years – not that they are in any way responsible for the contents of this book. I take full responsibility for that alone. Thanks to Larry Busch, Peggy Chiappetta, Brett Christophers, Steve Fuller, Bob Jessop, Les Levidow, Julie MacLeavy, Philip Mirowski, Vlad Mykhnenko, Sean Phelan, Matti Siemiatycki, Simon Springer, Katherine Trebeck, and David Tyfield. I would also like to thank Matthew Pittman at Edward Elgar for his editorial advice and help, the anonymous reviewers for their suggestions, and the various people who made comments on Academia.edu. A special thanks to my cousin Sam who showed unstinting support during my 'writing' of this book. Finally, and as always, I owe most to Sheila and Maple for making life fun again after long days staring at the computer screen, sometimes in confusion, but mostly in a daze.

1 Introduction

Introduction

Ever since the global financial crisis, a range of people have been trying to understand how we have ended up where we are, who or what is responsible, and how we might change things for the better. As I am writing this book, in late 2016, it seems as though there is a major political-economic shift underway in which several decades' worth of technocratic "free market" rhetoric and strong-arming are about to be swept away by the combined, if not allied, forces of a resurgent, racist, and right-wing nativism and a wobbling, defensive, and left-wing assault on financial globalization. Where the world will end up, no one knows. What we do know, though, is that the coming decade will define our future in that it will determine whether countries around the world can address a series of pressing global challenges like climate change, the refugee crisis, rising inequalities and poverty, disease threats, inter-generational conflict, and so on. A return to neoliberalism as a way to understand, let alone solve, these challenges no longer seems viable; even the International Monetary Fund (IMF) – a rabid flag-bearer for many years – has rejected the cookie-cutter implementation of market liberalization for which it, and other international financial institutions, has been so well-known. With all this in mind, it is an appropriate time to reflect on where debates about neoliberalism have been, where they might go next, and what else we might turn to in our desire to understand our futures.

It is important for me to be upfront about something from the start. This book is not *about* neoliberalism per se; rather, it is about how we *understand* neoliberalism. And by "*we*", I mean people both critical of a certain perspective of the world – namely a pro-market approach that erases any other, non-economic principles – *and* the people often disparagingly defined as "neoliberal", the promoters of a pro-market approach. It is also about the contradictions inherent in how both those neoliberals and the scholars who criticize them understand etition, and social order. As such, this book is not pri- ... attempt to argue that neoliberalism is this or that, or ...mpt to critique the transformative effects of neoliberalism, or ...n attempt to develop and synthesize the multitude of viewpoints on neoliberalism; others have got there long before me (e.g. Turner 2007; Mudge 2008; Centeno and Cohen 2012; Davies 2014; Dean 2014; Flew 2014; Springer 2016; Chiapello 2017). Rather, my aims in this book are to provide the following: an introduction to the intellectual history of "neoliberal" thought and the sort of worldview this engenders; an introduction to a range of critical approaches to understanding neoliberalism and the analytical ambiguities in these approaches; and a new way of understanding and analysing neoliberalism derived from three core contradictions at play in both neoliberal thought and the criticisms of those ideas.

Now, any reader will quickly get the sense from reading this book that I am increasingly ambivalent about the usefulness of neoliberalism as a concept in my analytical toolkit. I struggle, and increasingly so, with neoliberalism. I struggle with even basic questions like what is it? What does it mean? And how should I use it? I have been writing about neoliberalism for at least a decade now (e.g. Birch 2006, 2015a, 2015b, 2016; Birch and Mykhnenko 2009, 2010; Springer et al. 2016), so it seems strange to find myself at this theoretical impasse. It might be the fact I have read so much about how different people, from a number of different perspectives, understand, analyse, and criticize neoliberalism that has led me to this point. I find it difficult to reconcile all these (mostly critical) perspectives with one another, or find commonalities across them that enable me to identify, satisfactorily, something we can all call neoliberalism. In the end I find myself left with only one very basic commonality, namely neoliberalism, at its base, involves the infiltration or installation of "markets" as the organizing principle for our economies, politics, *and* societies. It is on this issue that I focus my attentions in this book.

My aims as mentioned earlier mean that I have split the book into three sections. In the first section, comprising Chapters 2 and 3, I discuss the intellectual history of neoliberal thought as well as the epistemic basis of the neoliberal view of the world. I do this in order to outline where neoliberal ideas have come from, how they have changed over time, and how the assumptions about the market underpinning them shape the way people think about the world. In the second section, comprising Chapters 4 and 5, I examine several critical perspectives of neoliberalism and the problems with those different perspectives. These chapters provide an introduction to the varied ways that people analyse and understand neoliberalism, and the struggle I now have with the use of the concept. In the final section, comprising Chapters 6, 7, and 8, I present my own take on neoliberalism by engaging with three core contradictions in the way contemporary capitalism is currently understood by neoliberals and their critics. These include the need to understand (1) the corporation and corporate monopoly in an era supposedly dominated by markets; (2) the forms of rentiership that are increasingly replacing entrepreneurship in the economy, despite the idea that we are becoming more entrepreneurial as the result of neoliberalism; and (3) the distinction between a market-based order and a contract-based order where the former is dependent on the latter.

Neoliberalism, neoliberalism everywhere . . .

Neoliberalism is in the air! It seems like no end of commentators, academics, journalists, politicians, and activists use the term "neoliberalism" nowadays to describe a particular set of ideas (and their implementation) in which markets are elevated above all other social principles and institutions (see Treanor 2005; Klein 2007; Monbiot 2016). I will forswear the use of scare quotes every time I use the word neoliberalism from now on, but I do want readers to bear in mind that I am critical of the concept, as will become evident. With that caveat in mind, it is worth stressing that there seems to be enormous interest in something we define as neoliberalism. Over the last few years, it appears as though neoliberalism has entered the popular consciousness as a useful term to describe the current configuration of our societies, polities, and economies. This year alone it has been used in the following stories and commentaries, drawn from *Google News*, across a range of media outlets:

- "George Monbiot says we're to blame for everything. Perhaps he's even right", *The Adam Smith Institute* (blog), Apr 16;
- "Neoliberalism: The Ideology at the Root of All Our Problems", *Truth-Out*, Apr 19;
- "Neoliberalism Is Destroying Almost Everybody's Lives", *AlterNet*, Apr 27;
- "You're witnessing the death of neoliberalism – from within", *The Guardian*, May 30;

the IMF Now Admits Neoliberalism Has Failed", *Fortune*, Jun 3;

- "This is our neoliberal nightmare: Hillary Clinton, Donald Trump, and why the market and the wealthy win every time", *Salon*, Jun 6;
- "Nobel prize-winning economist Stiglitz tells us why neoliberalism is dead", *Business Insider*, Aug 19;
- "Trump's victory and the ignoble death of "progressive" neoliberalism", *Red Flag*, Nov 9;
- And so on.

A more nuanced look at the past few years, however, illustrates a more complicated engagement with the term. In particular, it shows that neoliberalism is really a word predominantly, if not exclusively, used in left-wing or centre-left circles. For example, in a recent article for the journal *Capital & Class* the Australian political economist Bill Dunn (2016) collected data on the number of times "neoliberalism" was used in a range of leading daily newspapers in the UK and USA. According to his data, neoliberalism has been used over 285,000 times in *The Guardian*, a left-leaning British newspaper, but only 110 times in the *New York Times* and 119 times in the *Washington Post*, and only 115 times in *The Daily Telegraph*, 23 times in the *Daily Mirror*, and eight times in the *Daily Mail* (see Dunn 2016, Table 1, p.9). As this should illustrate, it is difficult to tell how commonplace a word like neoliberalism is. On the one hand, it is almost pervasive in one media outlet, but on the other hand it barely appears in others. Having written a "popular" – by which I do not mean bestseller! – book about neoliberalism myself (Birch 2015a), I am often asked by family and friends what it means and what it represents. It is not, even now, part of most people's daily lexicon.

Although there is increasing interest in what neoliberalism means and represents amongst a particular section of the population, it is primarily used as a derogatory or pejorative term to refer to someone who holds certain beliefs. Namely, that markets with no or very limited government intervention in restricting competition or shaping prices are the best – or "natural" – way to organize our economies and also our societies. This is based on the claim that markets are efficient, in that they lead to the lowest cost and resource use, and also moral, in that they support individualism, autonomy, and choice (e.g. Friedman 1962). This does not mean, however, that governments are not important, since they provide and enforce the framework conditions (e.g. property and contract law) necessary to ensure that markets function properly, but rather that there is always the possibility that governments and the state will lead down the slippery slope to totalitarianism (e.g. Hayek 1944 [2001]). Consequently, governments need to be kept in check, presumably meaning that so must the populations who elect them.

. . . But not a concept to think (with)?

The intellectual history of neoliberalism is a fascinating one – trust me! I outline its evolution in detail in Chapter 2, but it is also worth looking at how it has been used as a concept here, even if only briefly. A lot of commentaries on and analyses of neoliberalism start with an intellectual history of sorts, linking a range of (neoliberal) ideas to an array of (neoliberal) thinkers. Generally speaking, these tend to highlight a number of key events, people, and disseminator organizations, campaigns, and movements (e.g. Harvey 2005; Turner 2007; Mirowski and Plehwe 2009; Peck 2010; Burgin 2012; etc.). First, neoliberalism is often described as originating at the *Colloque Walter Lippmann* held in Paris in 1938 and organized by the French philosopher Louis Rougier. It was at this meeting that the term "neo-liberalism" was supposedly first proposed, although not necessarily adopted by the participants (Burgin 2012); however, this claim is debated. Second, neoliberalism is often associated with a range of thinkers from a range of liberal schools of thought, including well-known figures, especially economists, like Friedrich Hayek and Ludwig von Mises from the Austrian School; Milton Friedman and Gary Becker from the Chicago School; Wilhelm Röpke and Alexander Rüstow from the Freiburg or Ordoliberal School, and many others. Third, neoliberalism is linked to a huge expansion of centre-right and right-leaning think tanks, policy groups, and dissemination networks that arose in response to the dominance of Keynesian thinking after World War II. These include the Institute of Economic Affairs (est. 1955) and Adam Smith Institute (est. 1977) in the UK; the Heritage Foundation (est. 1973) and Cato Institute (est. 1974) in the USA; and the Fraser Institute (est. 1974) in Canada. According to many neoliberal critics, these think tanks and other organizations, often funded by corporate foundations, helped to spread neoliberal ideas into mainstream public discourse, thereby influencing and transforming political debate to such an extent that the electorates in these three countries ended up voting neoliberal politicians into power by the 1980s (e.g. Thatcher, Reagan, Mulroney).

esting to note that up until this time – that is the 1980s – the liberalism" was largely used by so-called neoliberals to define themselves (Friedman 1951; Friedrich 1955; Boas and Gans-Morse 2009; Brennetot 2014, 2015), although by no means universally, and that this usage reversed as it became a pejorative term in the 1980s (Boas and Gans-Morse 2009). After the 1938 *Colloque*, for example, a number of French intellectuals used the term *néoliberalisme* as a way "to designate the intellectual movement launched on the occasion of the Lippmann Colloquium" (Brennetot 2014: 6). At this time, there was already an existing "new" liberal intellectual movement in Germany, which is now generally called *Ordoliberalism* but is otherwise known as the Freiburg or German School of neoliberalism. According to Brennetot (2014), the term neoliberal – or *neoliberalismus* – was used to refer to Ordoliberals after World War II (see Friedrich 1955), as well as similar movements in other countries like Italy and France. This was the case even after the Mont Pèlerin Conference in 1947 organized by Hayek, which many see as the epicentre and fount of the forthcoming neoliberal hegemony after it led to founding of the Mont Pelerin Society (e.g. Mirowski and Plehwe 2009; Mirowski 2013). As the French movement faded, the German movement became the primary centre of "neoliberalism". After the 1960s, however, the term was gradually taken up to refer to intellectual movements in other parts of the world, even as a self-description, including and especially in Latin America (Boas and Gans-Morse 2009; Brennetot 2014). After the Chile *coup d'état* of Augusto Pinochet in the early 1970s, neoliberalism was increasingly used to define the implementation of Chicago School-inspired policies like monetarism in Latin America, becoming tarnished by association. By the 1980s it had therefore taken on an almost wholly negative hue used by critics to refer to a pro-market and anti-state movement.

Today, neoliberalism is used analytically in a number of ways, which I discuss in detail in Chapter 4. Almost all uses of the concept are pejorative or negative, providing a critical take on a specific set of ideas and policies that are generally set in opposition to post-war Keynesianism, especially government planning and intervention in the economy (e.g. Harvey 2005; Peck 2010, 2013; Mirowski 2013). Some, like Storper (2016), argue that this is a knee-jerk form of anti-market sentiment on the part of critics, whilst others, like Barnett (2009), argue that it reflects the creation of a straw-boogeyman against whom critical thinkers can orient themselves – unreflexively, according to Barnett. It almost does not matter anymore how neoliberalism is defined as a concept, or what it is meant to represent empirically; as one of the concepts key framers and users, the economic geographer Jamie Peck (2013: 133), states: "Neoliberalism has always been an unloved, rascal concept, mainly deployed with pejorative intent, yet at the same time apparently increasingly promiscuous in application". Nevertheless, that statement did not stop Peck outlining exactly why neoliberalism was and still is a useful concept to deploy in our analysis of the world. It seems like neoliberalism has come to a crossroads as a concept – is it still fit for purpose, is it in need of a serious reboot, or should it be set aside for something else?

Untangling three contradictions of neoliberalism

My own position is that neoliberalism is no longer useful as a concept because it has come to mean whatever anyone wants it to mean, leading to a state of affairs in which almost anything nowadays – from university rankings through to pet food advertising – can be theorized as "neoliberal". I see this as a result of several contradictions in the way neoliberalism is defined as a concept by its critics and used to analyse contemporary capitalism, all the time reflecting the claims of supposed neoliberals about the ascendance and importance of markets. The last section of this book addresses these contradictions head-on. Over three chapters I discuss three core contradictions that I think need untangling in our analyses of contemporary capitalism. As mentioned already, these include (1) the relationship between the corporate entity and corporate monopoly in an era supposedly dominated by markets; (2) the increasing propensity towards rentiership rather than entrepreneurship in the economy; and (3) the importance of contract and contract law in the organization of capitalism.

These contradictions provide a fruitful ground for further research on neoliberalism that could, in my view, motivate researchers and others to address and unpick an array of tricky questions that are increasingly important to our futures. In particular, this book might re-open questions about the role and impacts of corporate power in relation to promoting or stymieing much-needed societal transformations, whether this be in promoting sustainability or democracy or equality. It might also help identify the issues with popular and policy expectations about techno-scientific innovation as the solution to the global, national, and local challenges we are facing (e.g. climate change) by problematizing the idea that innovation is, by definition, a productive activity (i.e. entrepreneurship), rather than a potentially parasitic process of appropriation (i.e. rentiership). Finally, it provokes a rethinking of contemporary liberal–capitalist society as a market-based order in which freedom, liberty, and autonomy are supported and encouraged; instead, it outlines the ways that contractual arrangements and configurations have evolved to transform people and their ability to act. Hopefully what I write here provides readers with something interesting to think about with regards to these issues and more.

Bibliography

Barnett, C. (2009), "Publics and markets: what's wrong with neoliberalism?", in S. Smith, R. Pain, S. Marston and J.-P. Jons III (eds), *The Sage Handbook of Social Geography*, London: Sage, pp. 269–96.

Birch, K. (2006), "The neoliberal underpinnings of the bioeconomy: the ideological discourses and practices of economic competitiveness", *Genomics, Society and Policy*, 2(3), 1–15.

Birch, K. (2015a), *We Have Never Been Neoliberal: A Manifesto for a Doomed Youth*, Winchester, UK: Zero Books.

Birch, K. (2015b), "Neoliberalism: the whys and wherefores . . . and future directions", *Sociology Compass*, 9(7), 571–84.

Birch, K. (2016), "Market vs. contract? The implications of contractual theories of corporate governance to the analysis of neoliberalism", *ephemera: theory & politics in organization*, 16(1), 107–33.

Birch, K. and Mykhnenko, V. (2009), "Varieties of neoliberalism? Restructuring in large industrially-dependent regions across Western and Eastern Europe", *Journal of Economic Geography*, 9(3), 355–80.

Birch, K. and Mykhnenko, V. (eds) (2010), *The Rise and Fall of Neoliberalism: The Collapse of an Economic Order?*, London: Zed Books.

Boas, T. and Gans-Morse, J. (2009), "Neoliberalism: from new liberal philosophy to anti-liberal slogan", *Studies in Comparative International Development*, 44(2), 137–61.

Brennetot, A. (2014), "Geohistory of 'neoliberalism': rethinking the meanings of a malleable and shifting intellectual label", *Cybergeo: European Journal of Geography*, article 677, accessed 1 October 2016 at http://cybergeo.revues.org/26324.

Brennetot, A. (2015), "The geographical and ethical origins of neoliberalism, the Walter Lippmann Colloquium and the foundations of a new geopolitical order", *Political Geography*, 49, 30–39.

Brown, W. (2015), *Undoing the Demos*, New York, NY: Zone Books.

Burgin, A. (2012), *The Great Persuasion*, Cambridge, MA: Harvard University Press.

Centeno, M. and Cohen, J. (2012), "The arc of neoliberalism", *Review of Sociology*, 38, 317–40.

Chiapello, E. (2017), "Critical accounting research and neoliberalism", *Critical Perspectives on Accounting*, 43, 47–64.

Crouch, C. (2011), *The Strange Non-Death of Neoliberalism*, Cambridge: Polity Press.

Dardot, P. and Laval, C. (2014), *The New Way of the World*, London: Verso.

Davies, W. (2014), *The Limits of Neoliberalism*, London: Sage.

Dean, M. (2014), "Rethinking neoliberalism", *Journal of Sociology*, 50(2), 150–63.

Dunn, B. (2016), "Against neoliberalism as a concept", *Capital and Class*, doi: 10.1177/0309816816678583.

Flew, T. (2014), "Six theories of neoliberalism", *Thesis Eleven*, 122(1), 49–71.

Foucault, M. (2008), *The Birth of Biopolitics*, New York, NY: Picador.

Friedman, M. (1951), 'Neo-liberalism and its prospects', *Farmand*, 17 February, pp. 89–93, accessed 1 October 2016 at http://0055d26.netsolhost.com/friedman/pdfs/other_commentary/Farmand.02.17.1951.pdf.

Friedman, M. (1962), *Capitalism and Freedom*, Chicago, IL: University of Chicago Press.

Friedrich, C. (1955), "The political thought of neo-liberalism", *The American Political Science Review*, 49(2), 509–25.

Harvey, D. (2005), *A Brief History of Neoliberalism*, Oxford: Oxford University Press.

Hayek, F. (1944 [2001]), *The Road to Serfdom*, London: Routledge.

Hayek, F. (1960 [2011]), *The Constitution of Liberty*, Chicago, IL: Chicago University Press.

Jones, D.S. (2012), *Masters of the Universe: Hayek, Friedman, and the Birth of Neoliberal Politics*, Princeton, NJ: Princeton University Press.

Klein, N. (2007), *Shock Doctrine*, Toronto, ON: Vintage Canada.

Mirowski, P. (2013), *Never Let a Serious Crisis Go to Waste*, London: Verso.

Mirowski, P. and Plehwe, D. (eds) (2009), *The Road from Mont Pèlerin: The Making of the Neoliberal Thought Collective*, Cambridge, MA: Harvard University Press.

Monbiot, G. (2016), "Neoliberalism – the ideology at the root of all our problems", *The Guardian*, 15 April, accessed 1 October 2016 at https://www.theguardian.com/books/2016/apr/15/neoliberalism-ideology-problem-george-monbiot.

Mudge, S. (2008), "What is neo-liberalism?", *Socio-Economic Review*, 4, 703–31.

Peck, J. (2010), *Constructions of Neoliberal Reason*, Oxford: Oxford University Press.

Peck, J. (2013), "Explaining (with) neoliberalism", *Territory, Politics, Governance*, 1(2), 132–57.

Springer, S. (2016), *The Discourse of Neoliberalism: An Anatomy of a Powerful Idea*, Lanham, MD: Rowman & Littlefield.

Springer, S., Birch, K. and MacLeavy, J. (eds) (2016), *The Handbook of Neoliberalism*, London: Routledge.

Storper, M. (2016), "The neo-liberal city as idea and reality", *Territory, Politics, Governance*, 4(2), 241–63.

Thorsen, D.E. and Lie, A. (n.d.), "What is neoliberalism?", accessed 1 October 2016 at http://folk.uio.no/daget/What%20is%20Neo-Liberalism%20FINAL.pdf.

Treanor, P. (2005), "Neoliberalism: origins, theory, definition", accessed 1 October 2016 at http://web.inter.nl.net/users/Paul.Treanor/neoliberalism.html.

Turner, R. (2007), "The 'rebirth of liberalism': the origins of neo-liberal ideology", *Journal of Political Ideologies*, 12(1), 67–83.

Part I

What is neoliberalism?

2 An intellectual history of neoliberal thought

Introduction

As anyone who has started reading about neoliberalism should realize pretty quickly, there is an enormous literature on the origins of neo-liberalism, on its sometimes quite diverse schools, and on the various ideas promulgated by different "neoliberal" thinkers and organizations. It is not easy, therefore, to answer the seemingly simple question, "but, what *is* neoliberalism?". Some scholars have given it a go (e.g. Thorsen and Lie n.d.; Treanor 2005; Mudge 2008). Despite asking that very question here, I am probably not going to be able to answer it – or at least not satisfactorily for every reader. That is not for want of trying. I do think, however, my inability to answer that very simple question is for one simple reason, namely neoliberalism is not easy to define. It has many meanings depending on who we identify as neoliberal, depending on when we start looking for the origins of neoliberalism, and depending on how we ourselves seek to theorize neoliberalism as an explanatory concept. In my case, these issues are the very reasons for writing a book such as this.

I imagine that the bookshelves of most readers are groaning under the weight of papers, articles, and books on neoliberalism, of what-ever definition and in whatever manifestation of the moment. Recent events like the 2007–2008 global financial crisis – itself not so recent anymore, I guess – sparked an upsurge in interest in the political-economic common sense that drove us to where we are today, nearly ten years later. More immediate events like the British referendum decision to leave the European Union (EU) – or Brexit for those with short attention spans – and the face-off between Hillary Clinton and Donald Trump over who becomes leader of the "free world" are signals of a growing malaise with the current state of our political economies. If Will Hutton (1995) was writing today and asking the same question he did in the mid-1990s, he would surely have to conclude that we are all in "a pretty sorry state indeed". As noted, the cause of this sorry state of affairs is frequently laid at the door of neoliberalism by critical thinkers and scholars, from well-known journalists like Naomi Klein (2007) and George Monbiot (2016) to big name academics like David Harvey (2005), Jamie Peck (2010), Philip Mirowski (2013), and Mark Blyth (2013).

We therefore really do need to understand this thing called neoliberalism. What is it? Where did it come from? Why has it been so influential around the world? My aim in this chapter is to provide a brief intellectual history of neoliberalism – or, more accurately, *neoliberalisms* in the plural. In order to achieve my aims, I have to start with an outline of the most commonly recounted story of neoliberalism's birth and evolution. It is a tale told in a number of books, to which I turn later, and then frequently recounted by anyone who applies the neoliberal label to their analysis of the world. After this conventional story, my aim is to complicate things by untangling the diversity in neoliberal thought, unpacking the intellectual history as a way to illustrate the differences between neoliberal schools of thought – for example, Chicago School versus Ordoliberalism – and problematize the notion that there is *one* neoliberalism. I finish the chapter with a discussion of the intellectual legacies of different neoliberalisms.

Neoliberal birth pangs: the conventional narrative

There are a range of helpful histories of neoliberalism worth reading by anyone interested in understanding what it is and why it matters. I will suggest a few here, without wishing to suggest that one or another is any better than the others. Some are more specific; some try to cover everything; others focus on one particular country or another. As a caveat, in this chapter I focus specifically on the Global North as my own knowledge only goes so far.

A number of histories read like narratives of neoliberal ascendancy. For example Richard Cockett's (1995) *Thinking the Unthinkable*, which provides a detailed history of neoliberalism in Britain; Johan van Overtveldt (2007) and his book *The Chicago School*, which provides an in-depth look at the Chicago School of Economics; *Masters of the Universe* by the barrister Daniel Stedman Jones (2012), which focuses on the shifting centre of neoliberal ideas from Europe to the USA; and Angus Burgin's (2012) *The Great Persuasion*, which examines the importance of Chicago academics like Milton Friedman in aligning neoliberal ideas with the rise of neo-conservatism in America. Other histories are more conceptual, inserting a different analytical lens in their scouring of the rise of neoliberalism. Examples range across Mirowski and Plehwe's (2009) *The Road from Mont Pèlerin*, which showcases the global influence of the "neoliberal thought collective" brought into being by Mont Pelerin Society (MPS) after its first meeting in 1947; Jamie Peck's (2010) geographical analysis of the uneven and hybrid manifestations of neoliberalism; and Mark Blyth's (2013) more focused book, *Austerity*, dealing with the aftermath of the global financial crisis.

Even mentioning a few books like these leaves out an enormous range of literature that is worth reading, including a lot of "up-and-coming" scholars, such as Edward Nik-Khah and Robert van Horn's (2012) work on the "other" Chicago Schools (e.g. Law, Business); as well as William Davies (2014) who dissects the insertion of economics in political judgement in *The Limits of Neoliberalism*; the work of Arnaud Brennentot (2014, 2015) on the geo-historical spread of neoliberal ideas; Simon Springer (2016) whose book *The Discourses of Neoliberalism* seeks to meld Marxist and Foucauldian perspectives on neoliberalism (see Chapter 4); and, shameless self-promotion aside, my own attempts to rethink neoliberalism as a concept (e.g. Birch 2015a, 2016a). While this might be a rather eclectic and (very) partial list, it is meant to encourage the reader to avoid the tendency only to read the "big names" and ignore everyone else writing about neoliberalism, an all too common occurrence in analyses and discussions of neoliberalism (e.g. di Palma 2014; Brown 2015; etc.). I could go on (and on), but at some point I have to stop citing things you, the reader, could go and read – if for no other reason than to stop you putting down this book.

For the rest of this section, I want to outline the usual story that is told about the rise and ascendancy of neoliberalism, drawing on the previously mentioned works as well as others. It generally starts with the epistemic and moral bankruptcy of 19th century liberalism, or *laissez-faire* capitalism. In a famous 1926 essay, John Maynard Keynes proclaimed "The end of *laissez-faire*" in an attempt to shake off popular economic assumptions prevalent at the time, which, he argued, economists had found more than wanting (Burgin 2012). As such, Keynes reflected – or even prefigured – a range of critical voices of capitalism, from social democrats through socialists to communists, whose arguments were greatly strengthened by events like the 1929 Great Crash and subsequent Depression, which left millions of people unemployed and living in poverty. The inability of various governments to resolve these sorts of crises discredited many of those same governments and their political-economic system, especially those still clinging to 19th century ideas (Cockett 1995). Liberalism was supplanted by different forms of collective planning, including, at the one extreme, fascism and, at the other extreme, forms of Keynesian government management of demand. Liberal ideas were abandoned and liberal thinkers found themselves marginalized and ridiculed.

Most scholars of neoliberalism therefore point to the 1920s and 1930s as the era of its birth (e.g. Bockman 2013). The stimulus for its emergence from the ashes of *laissez-faire* was the perception of liberal thinkers that collective thought and planning represented a threat to the world, whether in the totalitarian forms of Nazi Germany or Soviet Russia or the democratic form of America's New Deal. Neoliberalism started as an intellectual response to these perceived threats to the liberal tradition, bringing together a range of liberal schools of thought. These included the Austrian School of people like Ludwig von Mises and Friedrich Hayek; Edwin Cannan and Lionel Robbins from the British School, largely centred on the London School of Economics; Louis Rougier and others in the French School; Henry Simons and Frank Knight at the Chicago School of Economics; and Wilhem Röpke and Alexander Rüstow from the Freiburg School, also known as the Ordoliberal School (Birch 2015a; Brennetot 2015). Others orbited around these groups, sometimes settling in one tradition or another, and sometimes moving away again – examples include Austrian–British scientists and philosophers like Michael Polanyi and Karl Popper.

In most accounts, the birth of neoliberalism is usually placed at the *Colloque Walter Lippmann* held in Paris in 1938 (e.g. Cockett 1995; Harvey 2005; Turner 2007; Denord 2009; Jackson 2010; Peck 2010; Burgin 2012; Brennetot 2014, 2015; Dardot and Laval 2014; Birch 2015b). The French philosopher Louis Rougier organized the event in order to discuss the American commentator Walter Lippmann's 1937 book *The Good Society*, which was a restatement of liberalism for the 20th century and an attack on collective planning as the precursor to state tyranny (Brennetot 2014). As such Lippmann's book reflected the arguments of many European liberals at the time and, more specifically, foreshadowed much of what Hayek (1944 [2001]) subsequently argued in *The Road to Serfdom*. The Colloque itself was attended by 25 participants, mainly French academics, civil servants, and business people as well as a smattering of well-known European liberals like Hayek, von Mises, Röpke, and Rüstow (Denord 2009; Brennetot 2014). More generally, participants at the Colloque also sought to develop recommendations for how to reinvigorate liberal ideals and their policy relevance. While some people, like Brennetot (2014), argue that "neoliberalism" was coined at the meeting as a term to reflect this "new" liberalism, others argue that the participants did not come to agreement on how to define themselves, whether as "neoliberals" or not (Burgin 2012: 72–3).

With the outbreak of World War II in 1939, any plans made at the *Colloque Walter Lippmann* were put on hold. In particular, Louis Rougier had sought to establish an international network of liberal scholars, but this did not get off the ground. A couple of years earlier, Rougier had established a French language publishing house – *La Libraire de Medicis* – which published a number of works by participants at the Colloque over the following years (Brennetot 2014). Although World War II stopped any further international meetings of neoliberal thinkers, it had an unintended side effect, namely it led to the dispersal of European liberal thinkers around the world. Often fleeing persecution from fascist authorities, people like von Mises, Röpke, and Rüstow followed Hayek who had left Austria in 1931 to take up a post at the London School of Economics (LSE) (Jackson 2010). This *neoliberal diaspora*, as we might dub it, helped to spread their ideas across the Atlantic, in particular, and also to other parts of the world. As a result, by the time Hayek travelled to the USA to promote *The Road to Serfdom* in 1945 he attracted a great deal of popular and, more importantly, business attention. According to Jamie Peck (2010), for example, the popularity of Hayek's ideas led the American Harold Luhnow, director of the William Volker Fund, to support the organization of a conference in Switzerland in 1947. In most histories of neoliberalism Harold Luhnow plays an important role, although his role is often obscured behind the greater interest in the ideas of neoliberal thinkers like Hayek and Milton Friedman. However, Michael McVicar (2011: 192) points to the importance of people like Luhnow in the intellectual history of neoliberalism:

> After Volker's death in 1947, the Volker Fund was reborn under the management of Harold W. Luhnow, who led it in a distinctly libertarian direction, using carefully placed grants to support scholars, organizations, and publications that rejected government interference in the economy and favored an aggressive anticommunist and pro-Christian philosophy.

I will come back to the influence of Luhnow, the Volker Fund, and its ilk later. For now, it is important to note Luhnow's role in financing the 1947 Mont Pèlerin Conference, as well as financing the salaries of Hayek and von Mises in the USA (Burgin 2012).

By 1947, and in the aftermath of World War II, there was a resurgent interest in establishing an international network in support of a "new" liberalism. Hayek organized a meeting in Switzerland at the village of Mont Pèlerin. This conference is frequently cited as another foundational moment in the intellectual histories of neoliberalism (e.g. Turner 2007; Mudge 2008; Mirowski and Plehwe 2009; Peck 2010; Burgin 2012; Mirowski 2013). The meeting was slightly bigger than the *Colloque Walter Lippmann* and had a far more international flavour. It included the following participants from the following countries or schools of thought (Turner 2007), amongst others:

●   Britain: Lionel Robbins, John Jewkes, Michael Polanyi
●   Austrian diaspora: Ludwig von Mises, Friedrich Hayek, Karl Popper, Fritz Machlup
●   Americans: Frank Knight, Milton Friedman, Henry Hazlitt (journalist), George Stigler, Aaron Director
●   Germans: Walter Eucken, Wilhelm Röpke, Ludwig Erhard (government minister)
●   French: Maurice Allais, Bertrand de Jouvenel

One key figure was missing, Louis Rougier. He had been accused of collaboration with the French Vichy regime during World War II and was not invited to the meeting (Burgin 2012: 77). At the meeting, the participants established the MPS, which still exists today, and laid out its statement of aims – drafted by Lionel Robbins (see Box 2.1). Initially headed by Hayek, the MPS became a major centre of neoliberal thought, and for some critical scholars it can be characterized as the centre of a neoliberal "thought collective" that dominates contemporary political-economic thinking (Mirowski and Plehwe 2009; Mirowski 2013).

In the following decades, the influence of neoliberalism gradually spread through the establishment of other national and international organizations, think tanks, policy networks, and groups like the MPS (e.g. Plehwe et al. 2006; Peck and Tickell 2007; Birch and Tickell 2010; Miller 2010). A few individuals played key roles here, including Harold Luhnow who I mentioned earlier. Others like the British businessman

---

BOX 2.1   MONT PELERIN SOCIETY STATEMENT OF AIMS

1. The analysis and exploration of the nature of the present crisis so as to bring home to others its essential moral and economic origins.
2. The redefinition of the functions of the state so as to distinguish more clearly between the totalitarian and the liberal order.
3. Methods of re-establishing the rule of law and of assuring its development in such manner that individuals and groups are not in a position to encroach upon the freedom of others and private rights are not allowed to become a basis of predatory power.
4. The possibility of establishing minimum standards by means not inimical to initiative and functioning of the market.
5. Methods of combating the misuse of history for the furtherance of creeds hostile to liberty.
6. The problem of the creation of an international order conducive to the safeguarding of peace and liberty and permitting the establishment of harmonious international economic relations.

Source: Mont Pelerin Society website, https://www.montpelerin. org/statement-of-aims/ (accessed 1 October 2016).

Antony Fisher were pivotal in promoting neoliberalism. In particular, Fisher helped to establish think tanks like the Institute of Economic Affairs (IEA), set up in 1955, and international networks like the Atlas Economic Research Foundation, set up in 1981, to promote "free" market ideas (Miller 2010). Supposedly inspired by meeting Hayek at the LSE in 1947, Fisher took to heart Hayek's comment that "the decisive influence in the battle of ideas and policy was wielded by intellectuals whom he characterised as the 'second-hand dealers in ideas'" (Cockett 1995: 123). Other pro-market or pro-business supporters followed suit in the following decades, especially in the USA where the Heritage Foundation (est. 1973), American Legislative Exchange Council (est. 1973), Manhattan Institute (est. 1978 with help of Fisher), and others were founded in quick succession. Often supported by corporate or business foundations like the Volker Fund and Olin and Scaife Foundations (Harvey 2005), these think tanks helped to promote a suite of "neoliberal" policies across the Anglo-American world (Peck and Tickell 2007). Although they obviously played a crucial role in promoting neoliberal ideas, it is important to note the fact that neo-liberal ideas were part of a broader "New Right" or neoconservative agenda, especially in the USA, promoting both pro-business policies and American hegemony (Birch and Tickell 2010). In this context, it is often difficult to separate the "neoliberal" from the "neoconservative".

As such, most narratives about the intellectual development of neo-liberalism highlight the importance of (mostly) conservative political movements and politicians; in particular, governments run by Margaret Thatcher (UK, 1979–1990), Ronald Reagan (USA, 1981–1989), David Lange (New Zealand, 1984–1989), and Brian Mulroney (Canada, 1984–1993) are often represented as the epitome of the neoliberal ascendancy (Swarts 2013). The emergence of this wave of so-called "neo-liberal" politicians in the 1980s was accompanied by the transformation of international financial institutions (IFI) as well. Organizations like the World Bank and International Monetary Fund (IMF) adopted what John Williamson (1993) called the "Washington Consensus", involving support for policies like the privatization of state assets; liberalization of trade and capital mobility; deregulation, or private re-regulation; infla-tion control; and marketization of public services (Mudge 2008; Birch and Mykhnenko 2010; Birch and Siemiatycki 2016; Springer et al. 2016). As this conventional story of the rise of neoliberalism reaches its apogee in the years before the global financial crash, neoliberalism is generally aligned with a range of "third way" politics and policies. Associated with politicians like Bill Clinton (USA, 1993–2001), Tony Blair (UK, 1997–2007), and Gerhard Schroder (Germany, 1998–2006), these poli-cies were supposed to support the continuing extension of markets, as well as ameliorate their worst side-effects through directed state interventions in areas like education and training, *active* welfare policy, research and development support, market development policies, and so forth (Tickell and Peck 2003). After the global financial crisis, there is little left of the intellectual validity of neoliberal ideas aside from a turn to austerity politics outlined by Mark Blyth (2013) and others (e.g. Jessop 2016; Whiteside 2016).

Untangling the history of neoliberal thought

Although there is nothing necessarily wrong with this conventional narrative of the emergence, spread, dominance, and (perhaps) fall of neoliberalism, there are several places where any rigorous analysis of neoliberalism needs to tread lightly, and perhaps turn over a few more stones. I want to highlight a few examples here in order to problematize any quick and easy readings of the rise of neoliberalism – these have implications for its use by critical thinkers as a concept to explain the world around us.

First, there are some questions about whether the term "neo-liberal" was coined at the *Colloque Walter Lippmann*. In fact, "neo-liberal" was used much earlier than the Colloque, suggesting that the idea *of* and *for* a "new" liberalism preceded the Paris meeting by some years. For example, Thorsen and Lie (n.d.) and Brennetot (2014) illustrate a number of cases where "neo-liberal" was used long before 1938, including:

- R.A. Armstrong (1884): used the term "neo-liberal" in an article for *The Modern Review* to refer to "liberals" who actually promote government interventions in the economy, which he described as a "prodigious catalogue of anti-liberal acts and aspirations on the part of Liberals falsely so-called" (p.736).
- Charles Gide (1898): described a "Neo-liberal school" associated with the Italian economist Maffeo Pantaleoni, which is premised on an: "hedonistic world . . . in which free competition will reign absolutely; where all monopoly by right or of fact will be abolished; where every individual will be conversant with his true interests, and as well equipped as any one else to fight for them; where everything will be carried on by genuinely free contract . . . [etc., etc.]" (pp.494–5).
- H.E. Barnes (1922): used the term "neo-liberal" to describe the sociologist Leonard Hobhouse, as a contrast to the *laissez-faire* attitudes of Herbert Spencer.

Another example, not picked up by either Thorsen and Lie or Brennetot is the following:

- Arthur R. Burns (1930, p.490): used "neo-liberal school" in a review of Georg Halm's book, *Die Konkurrenz* to describe Halm and others who argued that socialism "lacks an adequate basis for economic calculation and, therefore, any means of directing production or limiting the demand for capital". As such, this terminological use reflects the "socialist calculation debate" that people like von Mises and Hayek engaged in during the 1920s and 1930s.

I am sure there must be other, earlier examples of the use of "neo-liberal" as a term by one person or another, but I will leave that intellectual excavation to others. Of the ones highlighted earlier, Gide's and Burns's use of the term "neo-liberal" comes closest to the modern usage and understanding, reflecting a school of thought in which competition, markets, economic rationality, free contract, and so on are valued over and above any other form of social organization (e.g. collective planning). Armstrong and Barnes use the term in a more prosaic fashion, to represent people who no longer adhere to dominant forms of 19th century British liberalism.

Second, as a definitional term neoliberalism is rarely used nowadays by the people castigated by critical thinkers to describe themselves. Neoliberals like Hayek (1960 [2011]), for example, referred to himself as a classical liberal – and specifically not a conservative. Today there are few instances where neoliberals actually call themselves "neoliberal". One rare example is Sam Bowman (2016), an executive director at the Adam Smith Institute (ASI), who calls himself a neo-liberal, although defining it in a very specific way. This was not always the case, as Friedman (1951), Friedrich (1955), and Brennetot (2015) demonstrate. In the early 1950s, Milton Friedman (1951) wrote an essay "Neoliberalism and its prospects" for the Norwegian magazine *Farmand* in which he described his perspective as "neo-liberal". In it, he argued that the state needs to adopt a "positive function" to support "the competitive order". Friedman (1951, n.p.) explained that this:

> doctrine sometimes called neo-liberalism which has been developing more or less simultaneously in many parts of the world and which in America is associated particularly with the name of Henry Simons is such a faith.

Despite this essay, Friedman dropped the moniker "neo-liberal". Instead, the term was generally associated with a range of European liberal intellectuals, especially German and French liberals. More recent work by Brennetot (2015) shows how "neoliberalism" was used as a term in France from about 1939 until the early 1950s to refer to French and other liberals associated with the *Colloque Walter Lippmann* and authors published by *La Libraire de Medicis*. However, by the 1950s, the likes of Carl Friedrich (1955) defined the Ordoliberal German School as the original "neo-liberal" approach, largely ignoring the French roots although he did identify Italian and French intellectuals as neoliberals too. Friedrich argued that these neoliberals "see the political as primary" and "want the state to be strong" (p.512), contrasting somewhat with later Chicago School perspectives and with Austrians like Hayek and von Mises, who are described as "paleo-liberals". Subsequent use of the term became increasingly negative as neoliberalism was associated with Latin American dictatorships (Boas and Gans-Morse 2009; Brennetot 2014), especially Chile's dictatorship under Augusto Pinochet (1973–1990), to such an extent that neoliberals stopped using the term to describe themselves altogether (see Robin 2013).

Finally, there is often confusion about the role of business and business financing in the rise of neoliberalism. Business people and business foundations played an important role at the birth of the MPS and other like organizations. As mentioned already, Harold Luhnow of the Volker Fund helped finance the 1947 Mont Pèlerin Conference, as did the Swiss businessman Albert Hunold (Burgin 2012). Generally, the financiers of neoliberalism are left in the background, but it is worth emphasizing the influence of business and business leaders on the direction of intellectual debate in the mid- to late-20th century, especially in the conservative movement. Two examples will have to suffice here, the latter of which I return to later in the book. First, in her book *Invisible Hands* Phillips-Fein (2009) traces the US conservative movement's long-running campaign against the state. This anti-state and pro-business position contrasts markedly with the "strong state" notions of some European neoliberals, and yet ends up enrolling American neoliberals from the Chicago and Virginia Schools in support (see later). Second, American neoliberals diverged significantly from their European brethren in attitudes to business and especially business monopoly during the 1950s and 1960s (Birch 2016b). This divergence has been traced to two major research projects – the Free Market Study (1946–1952) and the Antitrust Project (1953–1957) – undertaken at the University of Chicago, funded by the Volker Fund, and supported by Hayek, both before and after he moved to the University in 1950 (van Horn 2009, 2011; van Horn and Mirowski 2009). As a result of these research projects, the position of Chicago School adherents totally reversed from criticizing corporate monopoly towards supporting large corporations on the basis of claims that economies of scale are efficient and increase consumer welfare (van Overtveldt 2007: 297; Crouch 2011). As such, the Chicago brand of neoliberalism became a cheerleader of corporate monopoly, distinguishing itself from the European brands (see Chapter 6) and a strident critic of government in whatever form (Nik-Khah and van Horn 2016).

Schools of neoliberal thought and their legacies

As this untangling of the intellectual history of neoliberalism should demonstrate, there is a need to be far more nuanced in our treatment of neoliberalism, avoiding the assumption that there is *one* intellectual school or tradition. In fact, I would instead stress the need, as mentioned in the introduction, to consider neoliberalism in the plural, as an array of neoliberal schools of thought (Birch 2015a). It is important to consider and specify their differences so that they are not simply equated or conflated with one another.

As anyone reading about neoliberalism soon realizes, there are several major strands of neoliberal thought. Generally speaking, most writers distinguish between the Austrian, Chicago, and Ordoliberal schools (e.g. Foucault 2008; Peck 2010; Burgin 2012; Dardot and Laval 2014). However, neoliberalism comes in all sorts of shapes and sizes, meaning that it is possible to identify several other major schools of neoliberal thought alongside these ones. In my previous book on neoliberalism, *We Have Never Been Neoliberal*, I identified seven main traditions (Birch 2015a: 27), but I would now add an eighth to that list – the French school (Brennetot 2015). I have outlined these intellectual traditions in Table 2.1, including a reference to their perspective on the role of the state and their attitude towards corporate monopoly, along with more basic information. As Table 2.1 illustrates, there are commonalities and differences between the various schools of neoliberal thought, some significant enough to problematize the idea that one term (i.e. "neoliberalism") can reflect all of them. The most obvious differences are between the European and American schools, although the Austrian School – primarily in relation to Hayek – provides a bridge of sorts between the two sides of the Atlantic.

It is helpful to provide an outline of the overlapping influences and legacies of these schools of thought with one another – and more widely. Although details of the major neoliberal schools are probably well-known, some of the others are not. I am therefore going to go through each in turn, in order to provide a basic introduction to their origins and legacies.

- As one of the earliest intellectual traditions, the Austrian School comes from marginalist thinking in classical economics developed by Carl Menger and others – like the British economist William Stanley Jevons – in the 19th century. It stands in contrast to the

Table 2.1 Schools of neoliberal thought

School	Main period	Key people	Key idea	Role of state	Corporate monopoly
Austrian	Late 19th to mid 20th	Ludwig von Mises, Friedrich Hayek (plus students like Fritz Machlup, Israel Kirzner)	Subjectivism	Limited (to law)	Negative
British	Early to mid 20th	Edwin Cannan, Lionel Robbins, Arnold Plant (plus Ronald Coase)	Liberalism	Limited	Negative
Chicago (1st)	Early to mid 20th	Frank Knight, Henry Simons, Jacob Viner	New liberalism	Strong	Negative
Chicago (2nd)	Mid 20th to early 21st	Aaron Director, Milton Friedman, George Stigler	Libertarian	Anti-state	Positive
French	Early to mid 20th	Louis Rougier, Jacques Rueff	New liberalism	Strong	Negative
Italian/Bocconi	Early 20th (plus early 21st)	Maffeo Pantaleoni, Luigi Einaudi (plus recent austerity advocates)	Hedonism / Austerity	Strong	Negative
Ordoliberal/Freiburg	Early 20th to early 21st	Walter Eucken, Wilhelm Ropke, Alexander Rustow	Ordoliberalism	Strong	Negative
Virginia	Late 20th to early 21st	James Buchanan, Gordon Tullock	Public choice	Anti-state	Positive (except rent-seeking)

Source: Adapted from Birch (2015a: 27).

German Historical School of people like Werner Sombart, Max Weber, and even Joseph Schumpeter. According to Shand and Shackle (1980: 13), marginalism was based on subjective notions of value, in that "value is not a property inherent in goods but constitutes a relation between appraising minds and objects appraised". The later theories of von Mises and Hayek – in terms of their emphasis on choice, economizing actions, and market order – come directly from this root, even if they disagree with some of the foundational notions like market equilibrium and perfect competition (Gane 2014). The emphasis on markets is inherited as a result of subjectivist tenets. The particular neoliberal Austrian School of von Mises, Hayek, and their students probably represents one of the main intellectual origins of (modern) neoliberalism. It is notable, however, that although the Austrian perspective was influential across other schools, especially in laying the foundations for the second Chicago School (van Horn 2015), its influence waned significantly as Hayek and von Mises went their own ways. After Hayek moved to the University of Chicago in 1950 – his appointment was to the Committee on Social Thought, not the Department of Economics, and was funded by the Volker Fund – his work veered off from the type of economic research undertaken at Chicago at that time. In particular, Hayek spent much of his time writing *The Constitution of Liberty*, published in 1960 and concerned more with law than orthodox economics.

Other early schools of neoliberalism included:

- The Italian School, which eventually morphed into the more well-known Bocconi School founded by Luigi Einaudi, which is associated with public choice theories and then theories of fiscal consolidation used to justify austerity policies (Blyth 2013). Rarely discussed in conventional accounts of neoliberalism, the Italian School arose from the work of economists like Maffeo Pantaleoni – see Gide (1898) for a detailed discussion – and Luigi Einaudi, both early supporters of Italian fascism (Gorenewegen 1998; Faucci 2004). When the government of Benito Mussolini turned towards corporatist policies in the mid-1920s, people like Einaudi started to criticize the government. After World War II, Einaudi became governor of the Bank of Italy and then Italian president.
- The British School, like the Austrian, arose from the marginalist ideas of people like William Stanley Jevons. Key exponents

included Edwin Cannan, a professor at the LSE, and his students and younger colleagues like Lionel Robbins and Arnold Plant – the latter was Ronald Coase's teacher, who is an important later figure to whom I return in Chapter 6. As liberal economists, they sought to oppose the dominance of Keynesianism in the UK, and were joined by Hayek after he moved to the LSE in 1931 (Cockett 1995). Although other figures like Michael Polanyi or Karl Popper might be considered as part of this British School, they were much more peripheral. After Hayek left for the USA in 1950, some of the British School, like Robbins, made their peace with mainstream Keynesian economics. Subsequently, the British School largely dissipated, with the remnants finding a home in think tanks rather than universities (ibid.).

- The first Chicago School was another early centre of liberal thought, again pivotal in the intellectual history of neoliberalism. As several commentators note, it is necessary to distinguish between two Chicago Schools in order to capture the differences between their adherents (e.g. van Overtveldt 2007: 5). The first Chicago School is associated with people like Frank Knight, Henry Simons, and Jacob Viner, whose focus included the negative impacts of monopolistic practices on capitalism. As van Horn (2009, 2011) and Jackson (2010) point out, early Chicagoans like Henry Simons were highly critical of corporate monopoly and thought that there needed to be a strong state, which could and should play a positive role in ensuring a competitive, liberal order. For example, in his 1934 *A Positive Program for Laissez Faire*, Simons stressed the need to strengthen anti-trust laws and break up corporate monopolies. Simons was a key figure tying Hayek to Chicago, attempting to get Hayek a job there and trying to establish an American version of *The Road to Serfdom*. According to Peck (2010), the suicide of Simons in 1946 represented a significant break between the first and second Chicago Schools.

- The French School is one of the least well-known, despite the fact that France was an important centre of liberal thought before World War II, as the location of the *Colloque Walter Lippmann* in Paris demonstrates (Brennetot 2014, 2015). In his account of French neoliberalism, Denord (2009) argues that the French School split predominantly between members who resisted Nazi occupation and those who collaborated with the Vichy regime, while others left France altogether. In particular, the downfall of Louis Rougier meant the loss of an important lynchpin. Subsequent engagement in the MPS by French intellectuals became spotty, with significant disagreements over the rightward shift in the MPS (Brennetot 2015).

It is worth considering the two major schools of neoliberalism together at this point: Ordoliberalism and second Chicago. Although they emerged at different points in time, they are often contrasted with one another, for the simple reason that they take quite distinct approaches to the promotion of market competition.

- The German, Frieburg, or Ordoliberal School represents another early neoliberal tradition, although this time centred on a "state-first" approach in which the goal is to create the framework conditions under which market competition can flourish (Friedrich 1955; Gerber 1994; Dardot and Laval 2014; Siems and Schnyder 2014). A strong state is meant to create order so that market economy, which is not natural or spontaneous, can emerge and function. As Friedrich (1955) pointed out in the 1950s, Ordoliberalism is based on the idea of a "social market economy" in which economic power is regulated so that competition can work. Like the Italian School, Ordoliberals had significant influence over the political-economic structure and direction of their national economy after World War II (Peck 2010). For example, Ludwig Erhard, a Minister of Economic Affairs and then Chancellor, was influenced by Ropke to enact a radical restructuring of Nazi-era price and wage controls in 1948. The fact that the German "economic miracle" and success of its supposed social democratic economy rests on neoliberal ideas and their implementation needs further analysis. This is especially the case in relation to studies of the European Union because Ordoliberal ideas and policies, especially the idea of "framework conditions", underpin much of the Single European Market (Gerber 1994).
- Perhaps the most well-known neoliberal tradition is the second Chicago School. Generally associated with the Department of Economics, some highlight Milton Friedman (e.g. Peck 2010) and others Gary Becker (e.g. Foucault 2008) as the leading stars in this school. However, a recent and growing body of work is shedding light on the role and importance of Chicago's Law School and Business School in promoting a particular form of neoliberal thinking. In particular, work by Nik-Khah and van Horn illustrates that academics like Aaron Director and George Stigler played as important – if not more so – a role as Friedman and Becker (e.g. Nik-Khah 2011; Nik-Khah and van Horn 2012,

2016). I have sought to outline the importance of business education in this regards myself (e.g. Birch 2016b), although mainly by drawing on the work of others. In their work, Nik-Khah and van Horn draw on archival material to show how Director and Stigler helped to shape the second Chicago School, especially through things like the Free Market Study and Antitrust Project. As Colin Crouch (2011) notes elsewhere, much of the work in new fields like law and economics – pioneered at Chicago Law School – helped to redefine perceptions of corporate monopoly and, subsequently, antitrust policies in the USA. I come back to these issues in Chapter 6. For now, though, it is important to stress the ascendancy of the second Chicago School as the "ideal type" of neoliberalism in many people's eyes, especially the libertarian and anti-state positions that dominated after the 1950s and 1960s. Examples of this included Friedman's (1962) book *Capitalism and Freedom*, which was, for many people, the American version of Hayek's *The Road to Serfdom*.

The final school I highlight here is the most recent one, the Virginia School.

- The Virginia School is predominantly associated with the likes of James Buchanan and Gordon Tullock. Both these economists worked at universities in Virginia, particularly at George Mason University, and were trained at the University of Chicago. Their major contribution to neoliberalism was public choice theory, which applied the theory of utility maximization to political systems and organization (van Overtveldt 2007). For example, Tullock (1967) developed the notion of "rent-seeking" to theorize businesses that seek legislative changes that favour them, rather than engage in product or services competition. According to Sonja Amadae (2016), Buchanan's position is built on the notion that each individual has an incentive to cheat when engaged in exchange (cf. Hayek), which thereby necessitates some form of legal system to prohibit cheating. However, the problem is that everyone has an incentive to get government to create rules that benefit them. Public choice was influenced by the Italian School.

Although there are several schools of neoliberal thinking, each with its own legacy and impacts, it is generally safe to assume that when most people talk or write about neoliberalism, what they mean is either the second Chicago School or Virginia School version. Almost a caricature of free market fundamentalism, these schools expound, on the one hand, utopian visions of free market societies and, on the other hand, the market(-like) characteristics of the behaviour we engage in everyday life. These views, and those of Hayek, have come to represent what it means to be neoliberal, as I discuss in Chapter 3.

Conclusion

Hopefully this chapter has demonstrated that it is difficult, if not impossible, to identify or agree on one all-encompassing and definitive version of neoliberalism. I started the chapter by outlining the common narrative around its emergence as a particular set of political-economic ideas and policies, starting with the 1938 *Colloque Walter Lippmann* and culminating with election of several pro-market politicians in the late 1970s or early 1980s. Although this account provides a helpful narrative arc for people unfamiliar with neoliberalism, it is problematic if taken at face value. Neoliberalism has a complex, shifting, and contradictory intellectual history, not only stretching back to the late 1930s but beyond that to earlier, inchoate versions. It would be better to think of the 1930s as a time in which several disparate strands of liberalism came together in an attempt to rethink liberalism for the 20th century, in the face of the discrediting of *laissez-faire* and the ascension of government planning as the dominant political-economic system.

In order to untangle this mess, I outlined eight schools of neoliberal thought, ranging from the more well-known ones like the Chicago, German, and Austrian schools to the less well-known ones like the British, Italian, and French. This helps to illustrate where the schools of thought diverge from one another, and perhaps help identify issues that might explain this divergence. For example, many critics of neoliberals outline the differences between the German (or Ordoliberal) and Chicago schools (e.g. Foucault 2008; Peck 2010). It is possible, in this instance, to identify quite significant differences when it comes to their analytical treatment of things like the role of the state, market competition, and corporate monopoly. On the one hand, the German School places an emphasis on the role of a strong state in creating the framework conditions for market competition; whereas on the other hand, the Chicago School places greater emphasis on removing the influence of the state in order to promote market competition. In this regard, it is interesting to note the influence of the German School on the founding of the German social market economy – the epitome of coordinated capitalism – and the influence of the Chicago School on Anglo-American capitalism (Gerber 1994; Siems and Schnyder 2014). Considering that the roots of several current political economies can be traced back to these different schools, it is important to tease out their differences as much as it is important to understand their similarities.

Bibliography

Amadae, S.A. (2016), *Prisoners of Reason*, Cambridge: Cambridge University Press.

Armstrong, A. (1884), "Liberal or socialist?", *The Modern Review*, 5, 731–47.

Barnes, H.E. (1922), "Some typical contributions of English sociology to political theory", *American Journal of Sociology*, 27(4), 442–85.

Birch, K. (2015a), *We Have Never Been Neoliberal: A Manifesto for a Doomed Youth*, Winchester, UK: Zero Books.

Birch, K. (2015b), "Neoliberalism: the whys and wherefores . . . and future directions", *Sociology Compass*, 9(7), 571–84.

Birch, K. (2016a), "Market vs. contract? The implications of contractual theories of corporate governance to the analysis of neoliberalism", *ephemera: theory & politics in organization*, 16(1), 107–33.

Birch, K. (2016b), "Financial economics and business schools: Legitimating corporate monopoly, reproducing neoliberalism?", in S. Springer, K. Birch and J. MacLeavy (eds), *The Handbook of Neoliberalism*, London: Routledge, pp. 320–30.

Birch, K. and Mykhnenko, V. (eds) (2010), *The Rise and Fall of Neoliberalism: The Collapse of an Economic Order?*, London: Zed Books.

Birch, K. and Siemiatycki, M. (2016), "Neoliberalism and the geographies of marketization: the entangling of state and markets", *Progress in Human Geography*, 40(2), 177–98.

Birch, K. and Tickell, A. (2010) "Making neoliberal order in the United States", in K. Birch and V. Mykhnenko (eds), *The Rise and Fall of Neoliberalism*, London: Zed Books, pp. 42–59.

Blyth, M. (2013), *Austerity*, Oxford: Oxford University Press.

Boas, T. and Gans-Morse, J. (2009), "Neoliberalism: from new liberal philosophy to anti-liberal slogan", *Studies in Comparative International Development*, 44(2), 137–61.

Bockman, J. (2013), "Neoliberalism", *Contexts*, 12(3), 14–15.

Bowman, S. (1996), *The Modern Corporation and American Political Thought*, University Park, PA: Pennsylvania State University Press.

Bowman, S. (2016), "I'm a neoliberal. Maybe you are too", accessed 1 October 2016 at https://medium.com/@s8mb/im-a-neoliberal-maybe-you-are-too-b809a2a588d6#.ffj5mgbbo.

Brennetot, A. (2014), "Geohistory of 'neoliberalism': rethinking the meanings of a malleable and shifting intellectual label", *Cybergeo: European Journal of Geography*, 677, accessed 1 October 2016 at http://cybergeo.revues.org/26324.

Brennetot, A. (2015), "The geographical and ethical origins of neoliberalism, the Walter Lippmann Colloquium and the foundations of a new geopolitical order", *Political Geography*, 49, 30–39.

Brown, W. (2015), *Undoing the Demos*, New York, NY: Zone Books.

Burgin, A. (2012), *The Great Persuasion*, Cambridge, MA: Harvard University Press.

Burns, A. (1930), "Review: *Die Konkurrenz (Untersuchungen über die Ordnungsprinzipien und Entwicklungstendenzen der Kapitalistischen Verkehrswirtschaft)* by Georg Halm", *Journal of Political Economy*, 38(4), 490–91.

Cockett, R. (1995), *Thinking the Unthinkable: Think-Tanks and the Economic Counter-Revolution, 1931–1983*, London: Harper Collins Publishers.

Crouch, C. (2011), *The Strange Non-Death of Neoliberalism*, Cambridge: Polity Press.

Dardot, P. and Laval, C. (2014) *The New Way of the World*, London: Verso.

Davies, W. (2014), *The Limits of Neoliberalism*, London: Sage.

Denord, F. (2009), "French neo-liberalism and its divisions: from the Colloque Walter Lippmann to the 5th Republic", in P. Mirowski and D. Plehwe (eds), *The Road from Mont Pèlerin: The Making of the Neoliberal Thought Collective*, Cambridge, MA: Harvard University Press, pp. 45–67.

di Palma, G. (2014), *The Modern State Subverted*, Colchester, UK: ECPR Press.

Faucci, R. (2004), "From corporative 'Programmed Economy' to Post-War planning: some notes on the debate among Italian economists", in R. Arena and N. Salvadori (eds), *Money, Credit and the Role of the State*, Aldershot, UK: Ashgate, pp. 413–30.

Foucault, M. (2008), *The Birth of Biopolitics*, New York, NY: Picador.

Friedman, M. (1951), "Neo-liberalism and its prospects", *Farmand*, 17 Feb, pp. 89–93, accessed 1 October 2016 at http://0055d26.netsolhost.com/friedman/pdfs/other_commentary/Farmand.02.17.1951.pdf.

Friedman, M. (1962), *Capitalism and Freedom*, Chicago, IL: University of Chicago Press.

Friedrich, C. (1955), "The political thought of neo-liberalism", *The American Political Science Review*, 49(2), 509–25.

Gane, N. (2014), "Sociology and neoliberalism: a missing history", *Sociology*, 48(6), 1092–106.

Gerber, D. (1994), "Constitutionalizing the economy: German neoliberalism, competition law and the 'new' Europe", *American Journal of Comparative Law*, 42, 25–84.

Gide, C. (1898), "Has co-operation introduced a new principle into economics?", *The Economic Journal*, 8, 490–511.

Gorenewegen, P. (1998), "Maffeo Pantaleoni", in F. Meacci (ed.), *Italian Economists of the 20th Century*, Cheltenham, UK and Northampton, MA, USA: Edward Elgar Publishing.

Harvey, D. (2005), *A Brief History of Neoliberalism*, Oxford: Oxford University Press.

Hayek, F. (1944 [2001]), *The Road to Serfdom*, London: Routledge.

Hayek, F. (1960 [2011]), *The Constitution of Liberty*, Chicago, IL: Chicago University Press.

Hutton, W. (1995), *The State We're In*, London: Vintage.

Jackson, B. (2010), "At the origins of neo-liberalism: the free economy and the strong state 1930–47", *Historical Journal*, 53(1), 129–51.

Jessop, B. (2016), "The heartlands of neoliberalism and the rise of the austerity state", in S. Springer, K. Birch and J. MacLeavy (eds), *The Handbook of Neoliberalism*, London: Routledge, pp. 410–21.

Jones, D.S. (2012), *Masters of the Universe: Hayek, Friedman, and the Birth of Neoliberal Politics*, Princeton, NJ: Princeton University Press.

Keynes, J.M. (1926), "The end of *laissez-faire*", accessed 1 October 2016 at http://www.panarchy.org/keynes/laissezfaire.1926.html.

Klein, N. (2007), *Shock Doctrine*, Toronto, ON: Vintage Canada.

Lippmann, W. (1937), *The Good Society*, Boston MA: Little, Brown and Company.

McVicar, M. (2011), "Aggressive philanthropy: progressivism, conservatism, and the William Volker Charities Fund", *Missouri Historical Review*, 105(4), 191–212.

Miller, D. (2010), "How neoliberalism got where it is: elite planning, corporate lobbying and the release of the free market", in K. Birch and V. Mykhnenko (eds), *The Rise and Fall of Neoliberalism*, London: Zed Books, pp. 23–41.

Mirowski, P. (2013), *Never Let a Serious Crisis Go to Waste*, London: Verso.

Mirowski, P. and Plehwe, D. (eds) (2009), *The Road from Mont Pèlerin: The Making of the Neoliberal Thought Collective*, Cambridge, MA: Harvard University Press.

Monbiot, G. (2016), "Neoliberalism – the ideology at the root of all our problems", *The Guardian*, 15 April, accessed 1 October 2016 at https://www.theguardian.com/books/2016/apr/15/neoliberalism-ideology-problem-george-monbiot.

Mudge, S. (2008), "What is neo-liberalism?", *Socio-Economic Review*, 4, 703–31.

Nik-Khah, E. (2011) "George Stigler, the Graduate School of Business, and the pillars of the Chicago School", in R. van Horn, P. Mirowski and T. Stapleford (eds), *Building Chicago Economics*, New York, NY: Cambridge University Press, pp. 116–47.

Nik-Khah, E. and van Horn, R. (2012), "Inland empire: economics imperialism as an imperative of Chicago neoliberalism", *Journal of Economic Methodology*, 19(3), 259–82.

Nik-Khah, E. and van Horn, R. (2016), "The ascendancy of Chicago neoliberalism", in S. Springer, K. Birch and J. MacLeavy (eds), *The Handbook of Neoliberalism*, London: Routledge, pp. 27–38.

Peck, J. (2010), *Constructions of Neoliberal Reason*, Oxford: Oxford University Press.

Peck, J. and Tickell, A. (2007), "Conceptualizing neoliberalism, thinking Thatcherism", in H. Leitner, J. Peck and E. Sheppard (eds), *Contesting Neoliberalism*, New York, NY: Guilford Press, pp. 26–50.

Phillips-Fein, K. (2009), *Invisible Hands*, Cambridge MA: Harvard University Press.

Plehwe, D., Walpen, B. and Neunhöffer, G. (eds) (2006), *Neoliberal Hegemony: A Global Critique*, London: Routledge.

Robin, C. (2013), "Nietzsche's marginal children: on Friedrich Hayek", *The Nation*, 27 May, accessed 1 October 2016 at http://www.thenation.com/article/174219/nietzsches-marginal-children-friedrich-hayek#axzz2Z8oBQeqB.

Shand, A. and Shackle, G. (1980), *Subjectivist Economics*, Exeter, UK: Pica Press.

Siems, M. and Schnyder, G. (2014), "Ordoliberal lessons for economic stability: different kinds of regulation, not more regulation", *Governance*, 27(3), 377–96.

Simons, H. (1934), *A Positive Program for Laissez Faire*, Chicago, IL: University of Chicago Press.

Springer, S. (2016), *The Discourse of Neoliberalism: An Anatomy of a Powerful Idea*, Lanham, MD: Rowman & Littlefield.

Springer, S., Birch, K. and MacLeavy, J. (eds) (2016), *The Handbook of Neoliberalism*, London: Routledge.

Swarts, J. (2013), *Constructing Neoliberalism*, Toronto, ON: University of Toronto Press.

Thorsen, D.E. and Lie, A. (n.d.), "What is neoliberalism?", accessed 1 October 2016 at http://folk.uio.no/daget/What%20is%20Neo-Liberalism%20FINAL.pdf.

Tickell, A. and Peck, J. (2003), "Making global rules: globalisation or neoliberalisation", in J. Peck and H. Yeung (eds), *Remaking the Global Economy*, London: Sage, pp. 163–82.

Treanor, P. (2005), "Neoliberalism: origins, theory, definition", accessed 1 October 2016 at http://web.inter.nl.net/users/Paul.Treanor/neoliberalism.html.

Tullock, G. (1967), "The welfare costs of tariffs, monopolies, and theft", *Western Economic Journal*, 5(3), 224–32.

Turner, R. (2007), "The 'rebirth of liberalism': the origins of neo-liberal ideology", *Journal of Political Ideologies*, 12(1), 67–83.

van Horn, R. (2009), "Reinventing monopoly and corporations: the roots of Chicago Law and Economics", in P. Mirowski and D. Plehwe (eds), *The Road from Mont Pèlerin*, Cambridge, MA: Harvard University Press, pp. 204–37.

van Horn, R. (2011), "Chicago's shifting attitude toward concentrations of business power (1934–1962)", *Seattle University Law Review*, 34, 1527–44.

van Horn, R. (2015), "Hayek and the Chicago School", in R. Leeson (ed.), *Hayek: A Collaborative Biography*, Basingstoke, UK: Palgrave Macmillan, pp. 91–111.

van Horn, R. and Mirowski, P. (2009), "The rise of the Chicago School of Economics and the birth of neoliberalism", in P. Mirowski and D. Plehwe (eds), *The Road from Mont Pèlerin*, Cambridge, MA: Harvard University Press, pp. 139–78.

van Overtveldt, J. (2007), *The Chicago School: How the University of Chicago Assembled the Thinkers Who Revolutionized Economics and Business*, Chicago, IL: Agate Publishing.

Whiteside, H. (2016), "Neoliberalism as austerity: the theory, practice, and purpose of fiscal restraint since the 1970s", in S. Springer, K. Birch and J. MacLeavy (eds), *The Handbook of Neoliberalism*, London: Routledge, pp. 361–69.

Williamson, J. (1993), "Democracy and the 'Washington Consensus'", *World Development*, 21, 1329–36.

3 How to think like a neoliberal

Introduction

Although many people find it a problematic assumption, neoliberalism is usually equated with "free markets" or "free market" fundamentalism in popular, and often scholarly, discourse. In part, this probably reflects the fact that the terminology of "free markets" provides an easy shorthand for writers to represent neoliberalism – an often misunderstood or unheard of term – which is evident in reviews of books like Block and Somers's (2014) *The Power of Market Fundamentalism*. Even in a book like this one I am writing, where I am seeking to unpack and problematize the concept of neoliberalism, it is still easy to fall into the habit of framing neoliberalism in these terms – that is, as a free market order, rationality, restructuring process, etc. I have sought elsewhere to get away from this tendency analytically (e.g. Birch 2015, 2016), but also think it is worthwhile to avoid it politically or normatively. By this I mean that it is important to take back or rehabilitate "the market" from so-called neoliberal thinkers, politicians, policy-makers, and others for at least two reasons. On the one hand, to highlight and stress the disjuncture between (neoliberal) claims about supposedly "free" market ideas, policies, and politics and the metaphorical goodness of associated abstractions like "freedom", "liberty", "choice", etc. On the other hand, it is important to analyse whether it makes any sense even to equate neoliberalism with markets at all, free or otherwise. I come back to this in later chapters, especially Chapters 6 and 8.

If neoliberalism is a market-based approach to understanding and living in the world, as argued by most critical commentators, it is therefore important to get a better grasp on what we mean by "market" before going any further. What does it mean to say that neoliberalism concerns the extension of markets? Or, even, *the* market? What does it mean to say that neoliberalism involves the installation of markets (or the market) as the central organizing institution in society? What does it mean to say that neoliberalism involves the spread of market rationality? And subjectivity? What does it mean to say that neoliberalism involves replacing democracy or politics with markets or economics? In order to answer these sorts of questions, it is important to unpack the term "market", especially any framing of markets as "the market". However, to do this requires disentangling neoliberalism from neoclassical economics; they are not the same things, as Mirowski (2013) and others note. It is therefore important to understand how markets are represented in economics and how they are represented in "neoliberal" thought.

My goal in this chapter is to show the reader how to think like an neoliberal. In order to do this, I have to introduce you to two things. First, I want to look at how markets are conceptualized in economic thought. Second, I want to discuss how markets are conceptualized in neoliberal thought. These two things are related, but they are not the same – and it is important to remember that. In what follows, I argue that markets are (at least) three-dimensional, in that they involve a set of *conditions* (neoclassical perspective), set of *transactions* (new institutional perspective), and set of *signals* or *outcomes* (contemporary neoliberal perspective). Different neoliberals, however, have distinct and different understandings of markets in their arguments, which I highlight with a discussion of how Friedrich Hayek, Milton Friedman, Gary Becker, and Richard Posner – as key represents of neoliberalism – deploy the market in their thinking. As neoliberal thought evolved, it has largely come to adopt Becker's and Posner's approach, namely that everything (e.g. marriage, crime, etc.) is and can be considered as already a market. As such, it is possible to apply this market-based approach to almost any subject matter, which I then do in the final section when I consider the thought experiment of a market for undergraduate grades.

Markets in economic thought

A number of academics and others argue that economics is *performative* rather than simply *descriptive* (e.g. Callon 1998; MacKenzie 2009; Muniesa 2014). By this they mean that economics – as a discipline – does not simply involve the production of descriptive knowledge, telling us how the world works. Instead, in economics – like in many other forms of knowledge, including natural sciences – the production of knowledge directly affects how the world works. For example, Ferraro et al. (2005) argue that the ontological basis of economics – that is, societies are comprised of individual, rational, and self-interested humans – comes to affect the way the world works because it affects how people then understand and act in the world. In particular, Ferraro et al. detail various research showing that people who are taught economics become more individualistic and selfish, thereby confirming the initial theoretical assumptions. As such, like many other forms of knowledge, economics is rife with self-fulfilling claims about the world and our actions in it. It is, therefore, pertinent to consider how economics, as a discipline, represents "the market", as a starting point for then analysing how neoliberalism can be conceived as a "market-based" perspective, or social order, or rationality . . . or what-have-you.

The performativity of economics need not be considered as indirect or accidental – that is, no-one is actively trying to make us think like economists. In fact, the explosion of popular economics over the last decade – especially since the publication of *Freakonomics* (Levitt and Dubner 2005) – provides an important illustration of how economists have sought actively to shape and configure the way we think about and act in the world. It is no coincidence that a book like *Freakonomics* was published by a professor at the University of Chicago, especially one so influenced by the work of Gary Becker (see later). Other examples of popular economics include books like:

- *Naked Economics* (Wheelan 2003)
- *Undercover Economist* (Harford 2006)
- *Happiness* (Layard 2006)
- *The Economic Naturalist* (Frank 2008)
- *Nudge* (Sunstein and Thaler 2009)
- *SuperFreakonomics* (Levitt and Dubner 2009)
- . . . and many more

The purpose of these books is to tell the rest of us, as economic lay-people, how to think like an economist, presumably so that we can start making better decisions in our lives. As with *Freakonomics*, though, it is notable that these books often focus on individual incentives, preferences, behaviours, and emotional outlooks as mediated by a market (see Gelman and Fung 2011 for critique). According to Harford (2006), for example, markets are a coordinating mechanism for satisfying *individual* preferences through the generation of *aggregate* information on individual choices. Such popular books end up representing markets as ways to understand the incentives that underpin all sorts of different actions, even all our actions. Moreover, it is also notable that these sorts of books frequently castigate experts and their claims to insight, representing *other* experts as if they are simply another voice in the "marketplace" we can choose to listen to or ignore if we so choose. It is implied that the latter choice – ignoring experts and thinking on our own two feet – actually makes us more autonomous and more rational, ensuring that our decisions are actually more beneficial to us. Finally, it is interesting that such a significant popular economics book like *Freakonomics* does not really define "market" anywhere; rather, the very idea of a market is taken for granted as a basic foundational concept for the rest of the argument in the book. This leaves the question "what is a market?" largely unanswered.

Although it might be useful to analyse and dissect the arguments in popular economics books, most people who learn economics do so in formal educational settings like schools and, especially, colleges and universities. In fact, most people learning economics do so from reading economics textbooks where the information they read is presented as the product of economics experts who know better than the students. In his work, Peter-Wim Zuidhof (2014) specifically considers how such economics textbooks teach college and university students how to "think like an economist" – a reframe that comes out most clearly in Greg Mankiw's (2014) textbook *Principles of Economics*, which is now in its seventh edition. According to Zuidhof, other textbooks make similar claims, stressing the idea that economics is increasingly defined by its "approach" – as with popular economics – rather than its "object" of study. Zuidhof claims that this switch in defining economics is relatively recent, suggesting that in more recent economics teaching – or at least its representation in popular and educational texts – economics is increasingly framed as the best way to understand the world, which, Zuidhof argues, reflects a "neoliberal" rationality. All that being said, it is interesting to look at how these economics textbooks conceptualize markets because neoliberalism is supposedly defined by its market orientation. As one of the most well-known economics textbooks, a good starting point for doing this is to look at how Mankiw (2014: 66) defines markets:

> A market is a group of buyers and sellers of a particular good or service. The buyers as a group determine demand for the product, and the sellers as a group determine the supply of the product.

Immediately following this brief definition, Mankiw goes on to outline the relationship between supply and demand in a market, but does not do much else to expand on what he means by market. All of this is important for the simple reason that so many people acquire their perception of what a market is from these sorts of textbooks. For example, Zuidhof (2014) states that between 1 million and 1.5 million university students in the USA use introductory economics each year, and that 750,00 economics textbooks are sold each year. Although these sorts of texts, both popular and educational, are influential, it is important to remember that they do not necessarily reflect neoliberal definitions of markets. It is therefore critical to unpack how neoliberal thinkers theorize markets and what this means for understanding how neoliberals think as they do.

Neoliberalism and the market

Across a diverse array of critical accounts and conceptions of neoliberalism (see Chapter 4), the one defining feature of neoliberalism that keeps cropping up is that it is a market-based or -centred *thing*, whether that be a social order, rationality, epistemology, process, policy suite, or something else entirely. Consequently, it is important to look at how neoliberals define the market in order to analyse and understand neoliberalism in whatever sense we use it. Although these sorts of definitional issues may seem pedantic, they are important for understanding concepts like neoliberalism. For example, Hodgson (1999: 269) argues that there is a difference between "market" and "exchange" in that the latter represents "the agreed contractual transfer of a property right to a good or service, in return for money or a bartered good or service", while the former represents "a set of institutionalised and recurrent exchanges of a specific type". It therefore makes sense to think carefully about what we mean when we talk about markets. In order to get a better sense of what a "market" entails, it is helpful to turn to the work of Colin Crouch (2011). In his book *The Strange Non-Death of Neoliberalism*, Crouch outlines five conditions for "pure markets", which include:

- All prices are comparable, everything is traded;
- Market entry is without barriers, with multiple providers and purchasers;
- Maintenance of a high volume of transactions;
- Market participants are perfectly informed;
- Economy and polity are separated. (ibid.: 30)

As should be evident from this list, the idea that a pure market does, or even can, exist is problematic. It would entail, if Crouch is right, the wholesale erosion and eradication of all other social, cultural, political, and religious rationales for life itself – the only thing that could inform and drive our decisions would be individualized and entirely monetary measurements, incentives, and choices. Since Crouch provides a thorough critique of this perspective in his book, I am not going to do the same here, but I come back to some of these problematic assumptions later in the chapter and later in the book. For now, though, it is important to highlight that there is a distinction in the way neoliberal thinkers and neoclassical economists define and understand the market.

According to Dardot and Laval (2014), markets and competition are framed as a "condition" in neoclassical economics, which is the result of the influence of marginalist ideas. As such, a competitive market is "the framework in which the rational action of agents can ideally lead to equilibrium" (p.102), primarily resulting from a situation in which there are lots of buyers and sellers – see the Mankiw definition mentioned earlier. Where a situation fails to meet these conditions – by having too few buyers or sellers – then competition cannot be perfect or pure, leading to a disruption of market equilibrium. In making these sorts of claims, Geoffrey Hodgson (1999: 103–5) argues that neoclassical economics asserts the universality of markets as standing outside of historical context or social relations, that is, they claim that the market is and has always been mechanism for "rational action" that leads to "equilibrium" in whatever era or in whatever society markets operate. In conceptualizing markets as a set of conditions, it is easy to see why 19th century *laissez-faire* liberals supported the removal of state intervention in market relations because markets are idealized as a set of necessary conditions in which interference would simply disrupt their operations. The market, in this framing, does not require the state except in its "nightwatchman" role because the market is necessarily comprised of individual and autonomous buyers and sellers.

In contrast to neoclassical economics, Dardot and Laval (2014: 106) argue that neoliberal thinkers in the Austrian School, like Hayek and von Mises, framed markets and competition as a "subjective process" of price discovery, in contrast to a set of contextual conditions. As such, Austrian thinkers – and other neoliberals – claim that markets are price-generating mechanisms that provide information to market participants as long as participants are competing when they make their choices. If competition is restricted, then markets cannot function properly. Moreover, any restrictions on competition mean that individuals cannot make choices properly – because markets would not provide proper information – and, therefore, they cannot learn how to conduct themselves properly. As such, Dardot and Laval argue, this Austrian/neoliberal conception of markets entails "a process of self-formation of the economic subject" in which the "market process constructs its own subject" (p.106). This is why neoliberals like von Mises and his students (e.g. Israel Kirzner, see Hanlon 2014) place such a stress on *entrepreneurship* because each person is meant to learn how best to achieve their goals through attention to market price signals (see Chapter 7). In contrast to the position of markets in neoclassical economics, this implies that the state is necessary in order to stop the "manipulation" of prices – a commonality Austrians share with Ordoliberals – *and* to ensure that people are forced into market-like thinking and conduct. This is why Foucault (2008) – and those who draw on his work – stressed the need to think of neoliberalism as a form of governmentality (see Chapter 4).

In contrasting neoclassical and Austrian/neoliberal conceptions of the market, it is possible to argue – perhaps a little simplistically – that neoclassical economics emphasizes market inputs (i.e. number of buyers and sellers), while the Austrian/neoliberal position emphasizes outputs such as prices, although always from the perspective that prices play a dynamic role as signals informing future choices. At this point, I would also add a third framing of markets as mechanisms for *transacting*, which necessarily entails some form of cost (e.g. bargaining, negotiating, monitoring, enforcing, etc.). This conception of markets refers specifically to the work of Ronald Coase (1937, 1960) and others on *transaction costs*. Associated with "contractual" relations, especially long-term contracts (see Chapter 8), this form of transacting overcomes the costs "that would be absolutely insufferable for the individuals" in Foucault's (2008) words. As Davies (2010, 2014) notes, Chicago neoliberals were particularly influenced by the work of Coase in the way they conceived the social costs of things like regulation or government action. Rather than assume that government regulation was efficient, Coase argued that "it may be more efficient (in the aggregate) to let one agent impose 'social costs' on a rival, and leave them to work out the damages or redress between themselves" (Davies 2014: 50). Alongside this anti-government perspective, however, Coase's (1937) work has also been influential in suppressing the role of market price in neoliberal thinking (see Chapters 7 and 8). According to Hodgson (1999: 169, 175), the theory of the firm propounded by Coase – in which Coase theorized organizational production as equivalent to market relations – meant that later theorists of the firm, like

Armen Alchian and Harold Demsetz, "imagined markets all around them, including within firms". This perspective, however, depended on conceptualizing contractual relations as if they were market relations without specifying the types of contract or engaging with contracts as legal agreements (see Chapter 8). From this transactional perspective, markets can be viewed as already everywhere and, therefore, the state as basically unnecessary.

This sort of discussion of markets is important because critics of neoliberalism do not always do a very good job of distinguishing between neoclassical (or orthodox) economics and neoliberalism – see Mirowski (2013) for criticism of this conflation. For example, David Harvey (2005) treats them as largely the same thing in his book *A Brief History of Neoliberalism* and Wendy Brown (2015) defines neoliberalism as the "economization" of society. As a result, it is sometimes hard to understand what is specifically egregious about neoliberal ideas of market society. For example, are markets themselves problematic? Are certain kinds of markets problematic? Are certain conceptions of markets problematic? Or, even, do critics of neoliberalism themselves assume, problematically, that anything relating to markets is wrong (Storper 2016)?

Four ways to think like a neoliberal

Having discussed markets in neoliberal thought, I now want to consider what this means for understanding the world *as a neoliberal*. In this section I am going to go through the epistemic arguments of four leading neoliberal thinkers regarding markets. Before I do so, however, it is probably a good idea to introduce each protagonist, starting with Friedrich Hayek, then Milton Friedman, Gary Becker, and finally Richard Posner. In what follows I draw on Cockett (1995), van Overtveldt (2007), Peck (2010), Dardot and Laval (2014), and Amadae (2016) in order to provide a brief background of these four characters.

Background: Hayek, Friedman, Becker, and Posner

Most people identify Friedrich Hayek as a central figure in the emergence of neoliberal thought. Born in 1899 in Vienna, Austria, Hayek was strongly influenced by another Austrian economist, Ludwig von Mises, especially after he joined a seminar group organized by von Mises in 1924 in Vienna. At the time, von Mises was engaging in the "socialist calculation" debate. Although Hayek joined the University of Vienna in 1929, the liberal perspective propounded by Hayek (and von Mises) was at odds with wider Austrian opinion at the time, leading him to accept a position at the London School of Economics (LSE) in 1931. He got the position after a recommendation from Lionel Robbins, whose German language skills meant he was aware of Hayek's work, and the work of other German speaking liberals. Although he had found a conducive intellectual environment, Hayek did not dominate British or European public or academic debate in the 1930s; instead, he was generally in the shadow of John Maynard Keynes during that decade. In 1938, Hayek attended the *Colloque Walter Lippmann* in Paris (see Chapter 2), and after the start of World War II he moved to Cambridge temporarily. In 1940 Hayek began writing *The Road to Serfdom*, which was then published in 1944 in the UK (Hayek 1944 [2001]). With the help of fellow Austrian Fritz Machlup and Chicago professors Frank Knight and Aaron Director, Hayek's book was published by the University of Chicago Press for an American audience. In 1945 *Reader's Digest* published an abridged version. By the time Hayek came over to the USA in 1945 for a book tour, he garnered considerable public interest. As mentioned in Chapter 2, Hayek also attracted the attention of businesspeople like Harold Luhnow of the Volker Fund, who then went on to financially support events like the 1947 Mont Pèlerin Conference and foundation of the Mont Pelerin Society (MPS). A few years later, in 1950, Hayek moved to the University of Chicago where he was appointed to a position in the Committee of Social Thought (after being turned down by the Department of Economics); the position was funded by the Volker Fund. According to a number of sources, Hayek did not fit in with economists at Chicago, which perhaps explains why his major work in the 12 years he was there was *The Constitution of Liberty* (Hayek 1960), a book more about politics and law than economics. By 1962, Hayek was ready to return to Europe and took a post at the University of Freiburg in Germany and then retired in 1968. He subsequently worked at the University of Salzburg and returned to Freiburg in the late 1970s. In 1974 Hayek was awarded the *Swedish National Bank's Prize in Economic Sciences in Memory of Alfred Nobel* (aka Nobel Prize in Economics), shared with the Swedish social democratic economist Gunnar Myrdal. Hayek died in 1992.

Hayek probably has the most interesting personal history of the four people I discuss here. Others, like Milton Friedman, have a much less well-travelled life. Friedman was born in New York in 1922 and went to the University of Chicago in 1932 as a graduate student, where he met his future wife Rose Director – sister of Aaron Director. After moving around for a few years, Friedman got an appointment at the University of Wisconsin-Madison in 1940 and completed his PhD at the University of Columbia. He did not last long in Madison, and was appointed to the University of Chicago in 1946 and remained there until retirement. Another attendee at the first meeting of the future MPS in 1947, Friedman subsequently began work on *A Monetary History of the United States, 1867–1960* in 1948 at the behest of Arthur Burns, who was then chair of the National Bureau of Economic Research and later became Chair of the Federal Reserve. Collaborating with Anna Schwartz, the two economists produced the empirical support for monetarism (Friedman and Schwartz 1963). Around the same time that *A Monetary History* was published, Friedman also published *Capitalism and Freedom* (Friedman 1962), which has been described as the American version of Hayek's *The Road to Serfdom*. In 1976, a year before retirement, Friedman received the *Swedish National Bank's Prize in Economic Sciences in Memory of Alfred Nobel*. At the time it caused controversy, including protests, because of Friedman's involvement in training the "Chicago Boys", a group of Chilean economists appointed by the dictator Augusto Pinochet to convert Chile into a free market wonderland (Dezalay and Garth 2002). An enthusiastic proselytiser, Friedman also played an important public role as advisor to presidents (e.g. Ronald Reagan) and popularizer of neoliberal ideas through TV programs like *Free to Choose* (1980) and a weekly column in *Newsweek* magazine (1966–1984). Friedman died in 2006.

A slightly less well-known, but no less influential figure than Friedman in the Chicago School is Gary Becker. Another American, born in 1930, he received a PhD from Chicago in 1955 – being taught by Friedman – and then taught in Chicago until moving to Columbia University in 1957 and returning to Chicago in 1968 until his death in 2014. As outlined in his 1992 "Nobel" lecture, Becker's work applied price theory – the building block of Chicago economics – to a range of non-economic phenomena, like discrimination, marriage, crime, addiction, etc. (Becker 1992). However, he is most well-known for his work on human capital, especially in critical circles. In part, Becker's reputation resulted from Michel Foucault's (2008) analysis in *The Birth of Biopolitics* of Becker's work on human capital. Interestingly, in a conversation with François Ewald and Bernard Harcourt in 2012 called "Becker on Ewald on Foucault on Becker", Becker generally agreed that Foucault had not misconstrued his ideas (Becker et al. 2012). He published his key work, *Human Capital*, in 1964 and based his arguments on the idea that training and schooling can be thought of as the same as any other investment (see Chapter 7). Before his death, Becker blogged regularly with Richard Posner, another Chicago alumni, and the final character is this drama.

Even less well known than Gary Becker is Richard Posner, who is, nevertheless, a key player in the roll-out of supposedly neoliberal ideas in the USA, especially as they relate to "law and economics". More specifically, his role as a judge in the United States Court of Appeals for the Seventh Circuit – appointed in 1981 by Ronald Reagan – has meant that he has had significant influence on legal thinking and decision-making. Born in 1939 and hailing from New York, Posner joined the Chicago Law School in 1969 after Aaron Director convinced him of the important role played by economics in law. Posner focused on issues like antitrust and took a critical approach to antitrust suits, seeing them as a mechanism for inefficient firms to stymie their more efficient competitors (van Overtveldt 2007: 306). In 1973, his key work, *Economic Analysis of Law*, was published, and it has provided the basis for much of the thinking on the relationship between law and economics ever since (Davies 2010). According to Amadae (2016), Posner built on but moved beyond the work of earlier law and economics scholars (e.g. Ronald Coase) in using game theory to understand things like economic value. Amadae goes on to argue that Posner basically "asserts that the justification of owning property is the ability to generate wealth" meaning that "a reassignment of property rights can be as effective as an actual market exchange in realizing surplus value" (p.211). Hence, Posner's ideas actually violate key notions about the inalienability of private property and have significant implications around notions of consent (ibid.), to which I return later. Posner is still alive.

The place of markets in neoliberal epistemologies

Having introduced each thinker to the reader, it is now time to outline their basic epistemic understanding of markets. I would stress "basic" here and suggest that anyone interested in a more detailed understanding would need to explore the work of the authors themselves in more depth.

Starting with Hayek, there is some ambiguity in how he conceived of the market. From books like *The Road to Serfdom* (1944) and *The Constitution of Liberty* (1960), it is evident that Hayek saw markets and collective planning as irreconcilable, politically, ethically, and socially. According to Hodgson (1999: 106), Hayek sometimes adopted the neoclassical approach to markets, conceiving them as a set of universal conditions (see earlier). However, Hodgson points out that Hayek also saw markets as institutions that have evolved over time; they are not, in this sense, the evolutionary context in which firms operate, but rather a structure that evolves over time. It is the latter view that is now most associated with Hayek, as Dardot and Laval (2014) illustrate. According to them, Hayek viewed markets as a subjective process of discovery that reveals the prices of goods and services through an array of socio-economic interactions, which also shapes the subjectivity of participants. Hayek (1944 [2001]) framed markets as an information processor mechanism that generates an aggregate "spontaneous order" from a diversity of individual decisions and choices, which he termed "catallaxy" (Aldridge 2005). As such, perfect information or knowledge prior to market interaction makes no sense, nor does it make sense subsequently because markets are dynamic and always evolving. Market participants are constantly learning and adapting, as are markets. However, Mirowski (2013) argues that Hayek's perspective means that there is therefore no reason for anyone to acquire or develop knowledge beyond our own preferences and desires because that is all we can ever actually know, or need to know. Ultimately, Hayek emphasized the evolution of markets and their underpinnings (e.g. common law) as the progressive and, in Hayek's view, socially beneficial expansion of private rules and laws. As such, his evolutionary epistemology reflects a conservative view – despite denials to the contrary – that we are building on the past and moving towards a future, and therefore better, market society.

Although Hayek adopted an historical and evolutionary perspective in his approach to markets, Milton Friedman stressed the foundational importance of universal markets. As such, he adhered more to the neoclassical position, assuming that there is – or can be – such a thing as a "pure market" (Crouch 2011). As Dardot and Laval (2014: 170–1) argue, Friedman's approach to markets was driven by work establishing the stable, certain rules needed for markets to work "properly", that is, as pure markets – and hence why he was so interested in monetarism. Friedman's more popular work like *Capitalism and Freedom* (1962) was premised on the idea that freedom originates in "free markets" because it "minimize[s] the extent to which government need participate directly in the game" (p.15). According to Friedman, government therefore represents an external constraint on our decisions and, in the end, on our ability to find and develop cohesive social relations with one another (p.23). This depends, however, on creating certain market conditions (e.g. "stable" money) and forcing individuals to adapt to free markets so that they do not learn inappropriate patterns of behaviour – e.g. anticipating interest rate rises or falls (Dardot and Laval 2014). In reading Friedman, and analyses of his views, it is evident that his perspective is based on the idea that "society" – and Friedman was mostly concerned with American society – was and probably still is not currently underpinned by free markets because it does not have the right market conditions, which are distorted by government interference. As an epistemology, this perspective is based on a normative assumption that there is such a thing as a pure or free market, that we do not have the right conditions for it at the minute, and that our social goal should be to install and adapt to a pure market as soon as possible. In summary, for Friedman, markets were a utopian reference point for making epistemic and normative claims about the world.

It is not surprising that neoliberalism as we know it – or, better yet, as we conceive it – is so closely aligned with the Chicago Schools of Economics, Business, and Law because so many influential figures emerged from these sites. I now want to turn to Gary Becker, another Chicagoan. Although following in the footsteps of Friedman, Becker developed a distinct epistemic approach in which he largely conceived of all social life *as if* it was already a market. This is most evident in his Bank of Sweden Award lecture in which he argued that "individuals maximize welfare *as they conceive it*, whether they be selfish, altruistic, loyal, spiteful, or masochistic" (Becker 1992). In Becker's approach, all life, from marriage to crime to health, can be conceived in market terms as the calculation of costs and benefits. Bernard Harcourt (2012) notes that this perspective could even be seen as progressive at the time Becker started publishing it in the 1960s. For example, Harcourt notes that Becker's argument meant that "We are all potential criminals . . . Each and everyone one of us would commit a crime if the price were right" (p.134). It is possible, perhaps, to argue that Becker represents the epitome of neoliberalism that most critics take issue with. His perspective has serious epistemic and normative implications, namely that we no longer need to assume there is something like a pure or free market, which means that (so-called) neoliberals can simply ignore the criticisms of the contradictions entailed by this ideal type. Moreover, neoliberals no longer have to spend time trying to institute pure or free markets (without success), nor do they have to wait for market society to arrive at some point in the undefined future. As such, Becker's position moves neoliberals on from Hayek's and Friedman's positions by positing that markets are already everywhere. There are problems with this view, which I come back to later (see Birch 2016).

The final perspective is that of Richard Posner, another alumnus of Chicago. He builds on Becker's approach – treating everything as already a market – and generally focuses on the relationship between law and economics. However, according to Harcourt (2012: 136), Posner takes the view that things like crime are "market bypassing" activities because they are attempts "to go around the free market". This differentiates his position from that of Becker who did not attempt to define crime. Here, Harcourt argues that Posner is also building on the work of Coase, especially the notion of social cost, emphasizing that low transaction costs reflect efficient markets and that crime creates "costly legal transactions" (quoted in Harcourt 2012: 139). As such Posner is really asserting the idea that private individuals should determine the costs of transactions themselves because this is the most efficient outcome and that transactions actually involve a transfer of rights, such as property rights, rather than things. From this perspective, Amadae (2016: 211) notes that "a reassignment of property rights can be as effective as an actual market exchange in realizing this surplus value", and therefore efficiency. Moreover, she goes on to argue, that this means from a Posnerian perspective "it is self-evident that the promotion of self-interest is indistinguishable from consent", which means "Individuals inherently consent to that state or action that makes them better off" (p.213). The upshot of this is that there is no actual need for any market signals or transaction actually to take place because rights can be reassigned to ensure that resources are used efficiently – and by efficiently, Posner means by those who can receive the most value from them (i.e. the wealthiest). In sum, it is as if markets are altogether irrelevant from Posner's perspective.

Having discussed four neoliberal viewpoints of markets in this section, it is worth summarizing the evolution of neoliberal thinking that they represent. Hayek started with a natural rights approach to markets, arguing that markets and societies are dynamic and evolving (progressively in his view) towards a fully market society. Friedman, in contrast, adopted the more neoclassical view that free markets are a reference point which help to define what we should do now in order to make society more like the utopian pure market of neoclassical theory. This was taken a step further by Becker in his approach to treating everything as already a market, before Posner simply did away with the need for markets altogether by arguing that a particular conception of efficiency – in which the "justification of owning property is the ability to generate wealth" (Amadae 2016: 211) and therefore the most efficient outcome – can be used to determine the assignment or reassignment of property rights. I address a number of contradictions with these perspectives throughout the rest of the book, but for now wanted to provide a simple example of how these sorts of neoliberal definitions of markets can be applied in practice.

Putting on neoliberal-tinted glasses

It is a useful mental exercise to try and think like people we want to criticize. It provides an insight into the perspective of those people and, more importantly, forces us to look at our own assumptions about the world. In thinking like a neoliberal in this chapter, I force myself out of my comfort zone. In general, I write for an audience of like-minded people; they usually share the same epistemic, normative, and political assumptions I have. Mostly this means thinking "neoliberalism is bad". As such, it is helpful to think about neoliberalism in less negative terms as a way to understand why it is so attractive to so many people, without falling into simplistic notions that it is merely an ideological façade for an elite power grab, or corporate takeover of society.

Putting on those neoliberal-tinted spectacles, however, only allows me to go so far. Although anyone can understand the epistemic and normative basis of neoliberal ideas, it is also helpful to illustrate how those ideas can shape the real world. As a teacher, one way I have found to do this is through a game. I regularly teach courses on neoliberalism, and at the start of each course I create a market in grades by "selling" the students their final grade. The purpose is to show them how a market-based logic could – and often does – inform their lives and their choices. I auction off the course grades to students by offering the top 20% of bidders A-grades, the next 20% B-grades, the next 40% C-grades, and everyone else receives a failing grade. I split the auction into two rounds as a way to create a dynamic market; consequently, students have an opportunity to see what other people are bidding and to spread their bets. At the start of each round, each student writes down their bid in secret and I then reveal the results. The only limitation I place on students is that they can only use the cold, hard cash in their pockets; no cards, no credit, no IOUs.

Now, obviously, I do not actually sell the students their grades, but I use the game to show students how a market might be created for pretty much anything, as long as we configure it right. This contrasts somewhat with Becker and, to a lesser extent perhaps, Posner who argue that everything is already a market because I am creating certain market conditions, rules, and outcomes, but it helps students to think about how to turn things into markets. This is important because so many people are trying to do just that, as markets for greenhouse gas emissions, reducing deforestation, and other new-fangled market mechanisms demonstrate (Lohmann 2010; Felli 2014). Taking Becker too literally means that we ignore the immense human social and technical effort that needs to go into constructing new markets. Adopting Posner's perspective means looking at how certain rights – property or otherwise – are instituted, assigned, and traded through (constructed) markets.

The point of my exercise in the classroom is that it demonstrates to students how a market can be created for (almost) everything and anything; how easy it is to create new property (i.e. grades) and (re)assign them according to the value the students (i.e. market participants) put on them, leading to the most efficient (i.e. highest spending) outcome for society – at least in Posner's terms. There are significant problems with this undertaking: first, in the game, the rule that students can only use the money they have in their pockets illustrates the differing capacities people have in market systems, from birth or otherwise; and second, the actual act of buying their grades leads the students to realize that such monetary transactions can destroy the very value of the thing they want. If we all know that students can buy their grades then there is little reason to consider their degrees as nothing less than worthless, and hence we would treat them as such. Contradictions abound in this exercise.

Conclusion

The purpose of this chapter was to introduce readers to a neoliberal viewpoint in order to illustrate how neoliberal ideas about markets can come to inform how we think about and act in the world. I started from the premise that neoliberalism is a market-based *something*, whether political project, restructuring process, policy suite, subjectivity, epistemology, and so on. This meant I needed to examine what markets are and how they are understood in neoliberal thought. I started by looking at markets in economic thought, including popular economics, before turning to the conceptualization of markets in neoliberal thought. In discussing neoliberal notions of markets, I identified four different conceptions associated with four key neoliberal figures: Hayek, Friedman, Becker, and Posner. The epistemic claims of each of these individuals reflects a different framing of "the market". For example, Hayek stressed the evolution of markets (and societies) as an institution, while Posner largely argues away the relevance of markets.

In discussing these neoliberals in this chapter, brief as it must be, I hoped to have introduced the reader to a range of neoliberal epistemic and normative assumptions about the world. In my view, it is necessary to approach the topic with a modicum of self-awareness so that we do not simply reject everything that neoliberal thinkers argue. This is important because it helps us better understand neoliberal ideas and their implementation, but it is also important because it might help us, by which I mean people critical of neoliberalism, to rehabilitate the market as a social institution, rather than reject it outright because of its association with a particular creed (Storper 2016). There is an opportunity here, especially in light of events in 2016 (e.g. Brexit referendum, Donald Trump election), to start to take back markets as social institutions that can be amenable to a range of underlying principles, if we work how to configure them as we desire. Knee-jerk rejection of markets and economics, evident in the work of people like Wendy Brown (2015), do not do much to get us beyond the current state of affairs.

Bibliography

Aldridge, A. (2005), *The Market*, Cambridge: Polity.

Amadae, S.A. (2016), *Prisoners of Reason*, Cambridge: Cambridge University Press.

Becker, G. (1964), *Human Capital*, Chicago, IL: The University of Chicago Press.

Becker, G. (1992), "The economic way of looking at life", *nobelprize.org*, accessed 20 December 2016 at http://www.nobelprize.org/nobel_prizes/economic-sciences/laureates/1992/becker-lecture.pdf.

Becker, G., Ewald, F. and Harcourt, B. (2012), "Becker on Ewald on Foucault on Becker: American neoliberalism and Michel Foucault's 1979 *Birth of Biopolitics* lectures", University of Chicago, Coase-Sandor Institute for Law & Economics Working Paper No. 614.

Birch, K. (2015), *We Have Never Been Neoliberal: A Manifesto for a Doomed Youth*, Winchester, UK: Zero Books.

Birch, K. (2016), "Market vs. contract? The implications of contractual theories of corporate governance to the analysis of neoliberalism", *ephemera: theory & politics in organization*, 16(1), 107–33.

Block, F. and Somers, M. (2014), *The Power of Market Fundamentalism*, Cambridge, MA: Harvard University Press.

Brown, W. (2015), *Undoing the Demos*, New York, NY: Zone Books.

Callon, M. (ed) (1998), *Laws of the Markets*, Oxford: Wiley Blackwell.

Coase, R. (1937), "The nature of the firm", *Economica*, 4(16), 386–405.

Coase, R. (1960), "The problem of social cost", *Journal of Law and Economics*, 3(1), 1–44.

Cockett, R. (1995), *Thinking the Unthinkable: Think-Tanks and the Economic Counter-Revolution, 1931–1983*, London: Harper Collins Publishers.

Crouch, C. (2011), *The Strange Non-Death of Neoliberalism*, Cambridge: Polity Press.

Dardot, P. and Laval, C. (2014), *The New Way of the World*, London: Verso.

Davies, W. (2010), "Economics and the 'nonsense' of law: the case of the Chicago antitrust revolution", *Economy and Society*, 39(1), 64–83.

Davies, W. (2014), *The Limits of Neoliberalism*, London: Sage.

Dezalay, Y. and Garth, B. (2002), *The Internationalization of Palace Wars: Lawyers, Economists, and the Contest to Transform Latin American States*, Chicago, IL: University of Chicago Press.

Felli, R. (2014), "On climate rent", *Historical Materialism*, 22(3–4), 251–80.

Ferraro, F., Pfeffer, J. and Sutton, R. (2005), "Economics language and assumptions: how theories can become self-fulfilling", *Academy of Management Review*, 30(1), 8–24.

Foucault, M. (2008), *The Birth of Biopolitics*, New York, NY: Picador.

Frank, R. (2008), *The Economic Naturalist*, London: Virgin Books.

Free to Choose Media (1980), *Free to Choose*, accessed 19 October 2016 at http://freetochoosemedia.org/broadcasts/index.php.

Friedman, M. (1962), *Capitalism and Freedom*, Chicago, IL: University of Chicago Press.

Friedman, M. and Schwartz, A. (1963), *A Monetary History of the United States, 1867–1960*, Princeton, NJ: Princeton University Press.

Gelman, A. and Fung, K. (2011), "Freakonomics: what went wrong?", *American Scientist*, 100(1), accessed 19 October 2016 at http://www.stat.columbia.edu/~gelman/research/published/freakwww.pdf.

Hanlon, G. (2014), "The entrepreneurial function and the capture of value: using Kirzner to understand contemporary capitalism", *ephemera: theory & politics in organization*, 14(2), 177–95.

Harcourt, B. (2012), *The Illusion of Free Markets*, Cambridge, MA: Harvard University Press.

Harford, T. (2006), *Undercover Economist*, New York, NY: Little Brown.

Harvey, D. (2005), *A Brief History of Neoliberalism*, Oxford: Oxford University Press.

Hayek, F. (1944 [2001]), *The Road to Serfdom*, London: Routledge.

Hayek, F. (1960), *The Constitution of Liberty*, Chicago, IL: University of Chicago Press.

Hodgson, G. (1999), *Economics and Utopia*, London: Routledge.

Layard, R. (2006), *Happiness*, London: Penguin.

Levitt, S. and Dubner, S. (2005), *Freakonomics*, New York, NY: William Morrow.

Levitt, S. and Dubner, S. (2009), *SuperFreakonomics*, New York, NY: William Morrow.

Lohmann, L. (2010), "Neoliberalism and the calculable world: the rise of carbon trading", in K. Birch and V. Mykhnenko (eds), *The Rise and Fall of Neoliberalism*, London: Zed Books, pp. 77–93.

MacKenzie, D. (2009), *Material Markets*, Oxford: Oxford University Press.

Mankiw, G. (2014), *Principles of Economics*, Independence, KY: Cengage Learning.

Mirowski, P. (2013), *Never Let a Serious Crisis Go to Waste*, London: Verso.

Muniesa, F. (2014), *The Provoked Economy*, London: Routledge.

Peck, J. (2010), *Constructions of Neoliberal Reason*, Oxford: Oxford University Press.

Posner, R. (1973), *Economic Analysis of Law*, New York, NY: Little, Brown and Company.

Storper, M. (2016), "The neo-liberal city as idea and reality", *Territory, Politics, Governance*, 4(2), 241–63.

Sunstein, C. and Thaler, R. (2009), *Nudge*, London: Penguin.

van Overtveldt, J. (2007), *The Chicago School: How the University of Chicago Assembled the Thinkers Who Revolutionized Economics and Business*, Chicago, IL: Agate Publishing.

Wheelan, C. (2003), *Naked Economics*, New York, NY: W.W. Norton & Co.

Zuidhof, P.-W. (2014), "Thinking like an economist: the neoliberal politics of the economics textbook", *Review of Social Economy*, 72(2), 157–85.

PART II

Current conceptions of neoliberalism

4 Different conceptions of neoliberalism

Introduction

As the previous two chapters should demonstrate, neoliberalism is a term rife with ambiguity – if one is willing to accept that it is a useful concept at all. I need to stress here that many, many people do think it is a useful concept – and not only academics. After the global financial crisis, for example, neoliberalism has been increasingly adopted by commentators in popular debate and discourse as a way to characterize the political economy of the last three to four decades. It is used in mainstream British media outlets like *The Guardian* newspaper, which is an admittedly left-leaning media outlet, as well as in more right-leaning newspapers like *The Times* and *The Daily Telegraph* where there have been attempts to rehabilitate the term (Pirie 2016). It has even led to "twitterstorms" (Sherman 2016), presumably in "twitter teacups". There is an ongoing debate in such mainstream venues about its usefulness, showing the extent to which it has come to represent a boogeyman word of sorts – used by some as a pejorative to denounce others (Monbiot 2016), decried by yet others as useless and "mythic" (Talbot 2016). Some right-leaning think tanks have even decided to "come out as neoliberal" (Bowman 2016). In many ways, neoliberalism has come of age in the last few years; and it is perhaps wise now to ask whether we have reached "peak neoliberalism" – a point to which I return later.

With so much attention, it might seem odd for someone like me – who has used the concept of neoliberalism quite prolifically – to raise questions about the usefulness of the term (Birch 2015a). It is perhaps for the very reason it has become so popular that I now find myself scratching my head whenever I see it in use. As will become obvious in later chapters, I do think the concept needs to be rethought and that this rethinking is a helpful exercise. I provide more detail on why I increasingly struggle with the term in the following chapter, and so will not write any more here. That being said, I think one of the reasons I find the concept of neoliberalism to be problematic is that it has come to mean so many different things to many different people. Rather than clarify its meaning, academic debate has seemingly contributed to this proliferation of meaning. In this chapter, for example, my aim is to outline a range of critical perspectives of neoliberalism, noting here that most – if not all – theoretical analyses of neoliberalism are essentially critiques of "neoliberal" principles, policies, and adherents. It is not, as many people point out, a term used by its adherents (Mirowski 2013a) so much as a term – often pejorative – used by its opponents (e.g. Bourdieu 1998). There is nothing necessarily wrong with this because other terms are used in a similar fashion (e.g. racism, sexism, etc.). However, the sheer diversity in critical conception of neoliberalism does create an issue.

In introducing the reader to a range of analytical perspectives of neoliberalism, I want to problematize the notion that neoliberalism is or can be an easily deployed concept that applies to everything "bad" in contemporary societies. In order to do this, I start with an outline of the popularity of the term in academic circles by asking whether we have seen a peak in its popularity, before then turning to its increasing use in popular discourse, especially amongst journalists and other social commentators. I then outline the seven key perspectives on neoliberalism in academic debate: Foucauldian, Marxist, ideational, thought collective, institutional, state theory, and processual. After outlining their main characteristics, I then conclude, leaving my discussion of the ambiguities in each perspective to Chapter 5.

Peak neoliberalism?

As Chapter 2 shows, the term neoliberalism has been in use since the late 19th century, although whether it meant the same thing we use it for today is debatable. The popularity – if not ubiquity – of the concept has been highlighted by several scholars already, including Boas and Gans-Morse (2009) and Peck (2010). In their research, these authors illustrate the growth in popularity since 1980. First, Boas and Gans-Morse (2009: 138) show that the use of neoliberalism as a concept in academic debate started its intellectual ascent around about 1992 – pretty much after the fall of the Berlin Wall and collapse of the Socialist Bloc in Eastern Europe. Since then there has been a steady rise in its use until the early 2000s when it plateaued, although their data ends in 2005. Second, Peck's (2010: 13) data updates Boas and Gans-Morse somewhat, showing a continuing rise in usage of neoliberalism up to 2009. As both these analyses show, the concept of neoliberalism became very popular in the 1990s and afterwards.

In order to update these authors, I collected data myself on the use of neoliberalism in articles indexed by Web of Science, an academic database service provided by the company Thomson Reuters (see Figure 4.1 for details). From these data, it is possible to see a few key trends over time. First, throughout the 1980s neoliberalism was barely used as a term, despite the fact this was the era of supposed neoliberal politicians like Margaret Thatcher, Ronald Reagan, Brian Mulroney, and others. For example, the term was used on average 5.3 times per year during the 1980s. Second, the concept started to become popular from 1992 with 30 mentions, but then took off from the late 1990s, at which point it hit 161 mentions in 1999 alone. From a personal perspective, this growing use of the term is interesting to note because I was at university during the second half of the 1990s studying sociology. At the time I do not recall anyone using the term, although one of my professors did recommend reading Shand and Shackle (1980) on

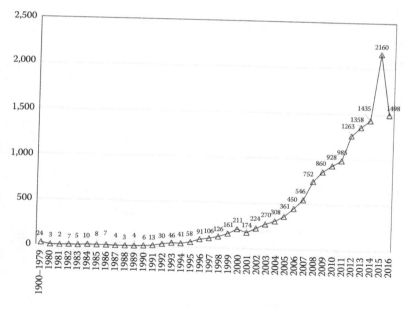

Source: Web of Science; data collected using "neoliberal* AND neo-liberal*" as Topic search term. Data for 2016 only up to 24 October.

Figure 4.1   The popularity of neoliberalism in academic debate

"subjectivist economics". Third, the concept becomes increasingly popular in the 2000s, a decade that saw the publication of several key works (e.g. Peck and Tickell 2002; Harvey 2005) and the English translation of Foucault's (2008) lectures on *The Birth of Biopolitics*. Finally, the 2010s has consolidated the use of the term, leading to an all-time high of over 2000 mentions in 2015. Evidently, neoliberalism has become a major analytical term used across the social sciences and humanities, although it is unclear whether 2016 will witness a slight drop from the 2015 peak (I only collected data up until 24 October 2016).

While it might look like neoliberalism is now a major, even dominant, concept in the social sciences (and humanities), it is worth comparing its use with other, similar concepts. In order to do that, I also collected data on the use of "globalization" in articles indexed by Web of Science. I used the search term "globali*" in order to capture the diverse ways people use "globalization" analytically – e.g. "globalizing", "globalize", etc. – but also to avoid uses of more definitional terms like "global" or "globally". As can be seen from Figure 4.2, the concept of

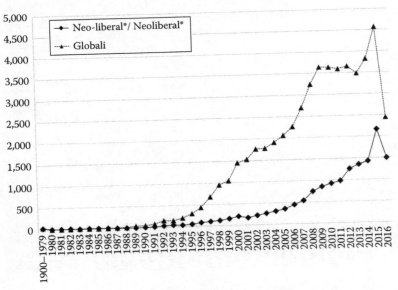

Source: Web of Science; data collected using "globali*" as Topic search term. Data for 2016 only up to 24 October.

Figure 4.2   The popularity of globalization and neoliberalism in academic debate

globalization is far more widespread than neoliberalism, although it has a fairly similar trendline. A few things are worth pointing out here. First, globalization starts out quite similarly to neoliberalism in terms of its usage in academic debate, in that it is rarely used in the 1980s, at least until 1987. Second, globalization becomes popular earlier than neoliberalism, starting its intellectual ascent in the late 1980s. Third, by the 1990s globalization takes off, which is something I remember from my time at university when globalization was a major new concept; it is as popular in the 1990s as neoliberalism is in the 2000s. Fourth, by the 2000s globalization is about five-times as popular a concept as neoliberalism, although it starts to plateau in the late 2000s. This plateau might be explained by the rising popularity of neoliberalism supplanting globalization in debate. Finally, globalization remains a popular concept and one that over-shadows neoliberalism, at least until late 2016.

All these data can only provide a sense of the academic trends around the use of neoliberalism (and globalization) as a concept. It is helpful to remember that there are other popular concepts, like globalization, still at play and that neoliberalism is not, in a general sense at least, on the tips of everyone's pens and fingers as they type (despite what it might feel like sometimes). It is, however, pertinent to look at how the concept of neoliberalism has been taken up outside academia in order to see how it is being applied more widely and in broader social discourse.

Criticizing neoliberal straw men?

Many non-academics are increasingly using the concept neoliberalism to describe contemporary capitalism or society. As data collected by Brennetot (2014) shows, the term "neoliberal" has shown up in the title of more and more books published worldwide since the early 1990s, reflecting the more specific trends I identified in academic journal articles earlier (see Figure 4.1). Although the data Brennetot uses does not necessarily demonstrate a clear pattern of use in popular discourse, because the books include academic works as well, it does show that there is a more general audience for the discussion of neoliberalism. This is also evident when using Google's Ngram Viewer program, which searches for words in published books. I used Ngram to search for "neoliberal", "neoliberalism", and "free market" as terms that would likely return popular trends in published books – see Figure 4.3 for

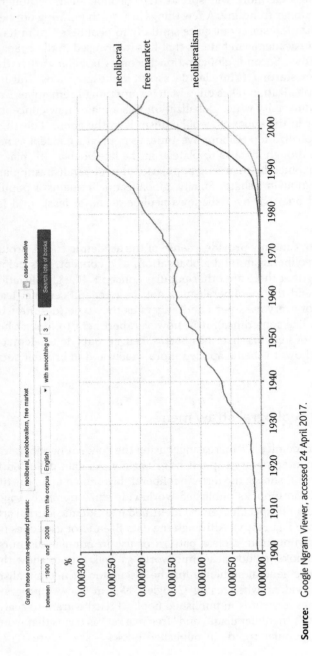

Source: Google Ngram Viewer, accessed 24 April 2017.

Figure 4.3 Books with "neoliberal, neoliberalism, free market" in them (1900–2008)

details of this search. As the data show, "free market" was a preferred term until around the mid-1990s when it started to decline in usage. Speculating on this decline is difficult, but it might reflect the shift in preference of critical writers of "free market" policies and politics to using "neoliberal" or "neoliberalism" as a way to define and analyse the world. By the mid-2000s, "free market" was superseded by "neoliberal" altogether, while "neoliberalism" was in increasing use as well. It is possible to explore this data in more detail, but I do not want to become bogged down at this stage of the book; rather, what I want to do next is discuss a few key examples of how neoliberalism is used in popular discourse.

Some of the main writers to introduce neoliberalism to a wider audience are journalists, especially people like Naomi Klein (2007), Paul Mason (2015), and George Monbiot (2016) who have done most to introduce the public to the individuals, ideas, and policies generally identified with neoliberalism. Other less well-known writers and commentators have also discussed neoliberalism, including bloggers like Richard Seymour (leninology.co.uk) and Thomas Clark (anotherangryvoice.blogspot.ca).

Starting with her book *The Shock Doctrine*, Klein (2007) uses "neo-liberalism" to refer to a range of conservative and neo-conservative ideas, think tanks, and policies. She specifically references a "policy trinity" that includes "the elimination of the public sphere, total liberation for corporations and skeletal social spending" and writes about neoliberalism as an "ideology" which is "a shape-shifter, forever changing its name and switching identities" (p.17). Nevertheless, Klein identifies neoliberalism as a form of corporatism, rather than market-centred order. In a slightly different vein, Paul Mason (2015: xi) argues that neoliberalism "is the doctrine of uncontrolled markets". Again, he provides a list of characteristics, including "the state should be small", "financial speculation is good", "inequality is good", and "that the natural state of humankind is to be a bunch of ruthless individuals, competing with each other". However, despite the association of neoliberalism with "uncontrolled markets", Mason also emphasizes the role of the state in pushing neoliberal-friendly policies and stifling economy-saving innovation. A final journalist who is worth considering is George Monbiot because he has written a lot about neoliberalism in his columns for *The Guardian* newspaper. In particular, he has described neoliberalism as "the ideology at the root of all our problems" (Monbiot 2016). In defining the term, Monbiot argues that:

Neoliberalism sees competition as the defining characteristic of human relations. It redefines citizens as consumers, whose democratic choices are best exercised by buying and selling, a process that rewards merit and punishes inefficiency. It maintains that "the market" delivers benefits that could never be achieved by planning.

Again, like Klein and Mason, Monbiot associates a particular form of free market fundamentalism with the erosion of the state as an institution of governance and its subversion into an appendage of corporate power.

Although these journalistic accounts have brought neoliberal ideas and policies to the attention of a wider readership than academic writing could ever do, they are also – at least partially – problematic when trying to understand how to use neoliberalism as a concept to explain the world. They create a problem because they end up turning neoliberalism into some form of "straw-man" responsible for all sorts of egregious and nefarious actions and effects. On the one hand, rising corporate monopoly can be blamed on neoliberalism (e.g. Klein); while on the other hand, neoliberalism is defined by an adherence to free market relations (e.g. Monbiot). I return to this sort of contradiction in Chapter 6, but it helps to illustrate the way that neoliberalism can come to mean almost anything to anyone. Without identifying the specific characteristics that make neoliberalism distinct as a form of political economy, it ends up turning into another buzzword. It is, therefore, vital to carefully unpack the different conceptions of neoliberalism in order to understand how it is used and how it can end up being abused as a concept. I turn to the first part of this task next, and leave the second part to the next chapter.

Analysing neoliberalism: how many critical perspectives?

Anyone who is new to thinking about neoliberalism – or anyone who has been at it for some time – needs to appreciate the different ways that different people understand and define it. A number of people have written about the range of different critical perspectives of neoliberalism (e.g. Springer 2010; Dean 2014; Flew 2014; Birch 2015a, 2015b; Chiapello 2017), and it is worth looking at these attempts to synthesize the analytical trends. Generally speaking, though, these writers differentiate between a few main analytical perspectives, including Marxist, Foucauldian, and Gramscian traditions. My main aim in this chapter is to provide a brief introduction to a range of different perspectives, largely drawing on my own intellectual background in political economy, broadly speaking. I write "introduction" very deliberately because what I do here can only ever represent a starting point for others in their research. It is not, I want to stress, a comprehensive overview of a field that is expanding almost by the hour – as Figure 4.1 should demonstrate. I start with the work of Foucault and go from there, covering Marxist, ideational, processual, institutional, and other perspectives afterwards. It is important to remember that I am *not* providing an overview of neoliberalism per se, but rather an overview of different critical understandings of neoliberalism and its use as a concept or analytical term.

Foucault and governmentality

Michel Foucault was one of the first people to try and conceptualize neoliberalism. His analysis formed part of a series of lectures he did in 1978 and 1979 at the College of France called *The Birth of Biopolitics* (Foucault 2008). These lectures were not published in French until 2004 and in English only in 2008, although they had been discussed prior to these dates (e.g. Lemke 2001). It is worth noting that the publication of the lectures in French coincides with a surge of interest in neoliberalism in the mid-2000s (see Figure 4.1). In these lectures, Foucault aimed to excavate the histories of liberalism, which led him to examine modern versions of liberalism as part of his analysis of governmentality, or the art of government. The modern forms of liberalism that Foucault focused on were the German Ordoliberal tradition and the American "neoliberal" tradition represented by the Chicago School, especially the work of Gary Becker. According to Foucault, these two schools of thought can be distinguished from one another as a result of their approach to market competition. Both are underpinned by similar political rationalities – in this case, the importance of market competition – but they also entail distinct technologies of power – including things like laws and regulations. It is the combination of these rationalities and technologies that constitutes particular governmentalities, by which Foucault meant the ways that governments seek to shape their citizens and the conduct of their citizens as members of society. According to Foucault, for example, German Ordoliberalism is characterized by the idea that market competition rests on a strong state that creates and reinforces the framework conditions for markets. In contrast, American neoliberalism is underpinned by the idea of extending market competition throughout society, into all areas of social life, including our own personal lives. As a result of these forms of governmentality, Foucault argued, people end up changing themselves so that they adopt competitive behaviours and attitudes (see Chapter 2).

A number of scholars have built upon Foucault's work over the years, with some of the most well-known being Nikolas Rose (1993, 1999), Wendy Larner (2000), Thomas Lemke (2001), Mitchell Dean (2014), Pierre Dardot and Christian Laval (2014), and Wendy Brown (2015). For example, in his book *Powers of Freedom*, Rose (1999) adopted and developed Foucault's notion of governmentality, although with a broader object in mind than neoliberalism. More recently, Dardot and Laval (2014) have built on Foucault's analysis of neoliberalism by updating it for the 21st century. Their general argument is that neoliberalism is *productive* in the Foucauldian sense that it generates new "kinds of social relations, certain ways of living, certain subjectivities" (p.3). In particular, they argue that the emphasis on market competition "even transforms the individual, now called on to conceive and conduct him- or herself as an enterprise" (ibid.). Similarly, Brown (2015) seeks to update Foucault for the 21st century in her book *Undoing the Demos*. Here, she seeks to frame neoliberalism as the "economization" of everything, especially individual decisions and choices, which she argues are restructured as a series of investment decisions. In referencing Foucault, she notes that Foucault (2008: 61) claimed certain forms of neoliberalism, namely the Ordoliberal version, are based on "generalizing the 'enterprise' form within the social body or social fabric". As such, neoliberalism is premised on the conversion of people into enterprises – a topic I return to in Chapter 7. Although Foucault has been highly influential, his analytical approach can be criticized for several reasons, which I come back to in the next chapter.

Marxism and class analysis

Perhaps the second most influential strand of research on neoliberalism comes from the Marxist analysis of people like Duménil and Lévy (2004, 2011), Harvey (2005, 2006), and others (e.g. Laclau and Mouffe 1985; van Apeldoorn 2002; Peet 2007; Hall 2011; van Apeldoorn and Overbeek 2012; Cahill 2014). This Marxist perspective tends to frame neoliberalism as a project to restore elite class power in which neoliberal ideas and principles (e.g. free market competition) represent the ideological icing on the underlying class struggle. As Harvey

(2005: 19) points out, when the former (i.e. principles) come up against the latter (i.e. class interests) "then the principles are either abandoned or become so twisted as to be unrecognizable". Consequently, neoliberalism, at least as a set of ideas, represents "a system of justification and legitimation" for things like tax cuts for high earners, rising unemployment and inequality, stagnant median wages, etc. (ibid.). In their critical takes on neoliberalism, Duménil and Lévy (2004) and also Harvey (2005), who draws heavily on Duménil and Lévy's empirical research, argue that this project to restore elite class power starts in the 1970s when the wealth of the top 1 percent fell. As a result, Duménil and Lévy (2011) argue that neoliberalism represents a project in which capitalist classes ally with managerial classes to restore the incomes of the top 1 percent. Since the 1970s, things like rising inequality and the reversal of welfare gains made by workers after World War II are generally cited as evidence of this elite class restoration, as is the growing financialization of the economy (e.g. Harvey 2005; Duménil and Lévy 2011). In this sense, neoliberalism is not necessarily manifested as envisioned in neoliberal theories of the market, or competition, or entrepreneurship.

Others in this Marxist tradition take a slightly different approach to thinking about neoliberalism as a political-economic project. Academics like Bastian van Apeldoorn (2002) and Damien Cahill (2014), for example, argue that neoliberalism can be thought of as a policy regime characterized by policies like privatization, fiscal austerity, deregulation, and hollowing out of labour rights. In both cases, though, they analyse the role of key class interests in the pursuit of neoliberalism; for example, van Apeldoorn stresses the role of elite transnational classes in establishing and supporting neoliberal policy regimes, while Cahill emphasizes the political power of corporations in mobilizing the power of capitalist states in the pursuit of business interests. As such, they are still broadly class-based perspectives, although with greater focus on the suite of policies that reflects neoliberal notions of market competition, rather than simply being an ideological justification à la Harvey (2005). Interestingly, both van Apeldoorn and Cahill take a Polanyian-esque turn by arguing that neoliberalism is embedded in a broader set of social relations, rather than representing the disentangling of the market from society (cf. Polanyi 1944 [2001]). In this sense, they provide a more grounded perspective than Harvey and Duménil and Lévy, stressing that neoliberalism is bound up with an array of institutional arrangements. This then helps to explain the variety and diversity in neoliberalism evident around the world. However, the Marxist perspective does not do enough to unpack these institutional differences (see later).

Ideational analysis

Before looking at the institutional perspective on neoliberalism, it is worth considering forms of ideational analysis. Unlike the Marxist perspective, this approach is based on the assumption that ideas have causative power. Moreover, unlike notions of hegemony, ideational analysis does not conceptualize discourse as necessarily limited to a justificatory or legitimating function; rather, it stresses the role played by ideas in shaping policies, politics, and political economy. It is most closely associated with scholars in political science, especially the likes of Andrew Gamble (1986), Mark Blyth (2002, 2013) and Colin Hay (2004), although others are also relevant (e.g. Cerny 2008; Swarts 2013). One of the main proponents of this ideational perspective is Blyth (2002), especially in his book *Great Transformations* – an updating of Polanyi's major work. In this book, Blyth analyses the rise of neoliberalism as a set of powerful economic ideas. He argues that economic ideas help to frame political-economic policy problems, help to identify possible solutions to those problems, and help to establish the effects of those solutions. As such, ideas come to represent a series of goals or objectives to which social actors orient themselves and their understandings of the world.

Ideational analysis is meant to help people explain why institutions change. In his attempt to demonstrate the causative power of ideas Blyth therefore looks at institutional transformations in Sweden and the USA during and after the 1970s as they moved from Keynesianism to neoliberalism. Blyth identifies, for example, a confluence of economic theories in the rise of neoliberalism, including monetarism (linked to Milton Friedman), supply-side economics (linked with Arthur Laffer), and rational expectations (linked with James Buchanan). This confluence provided a powerful driver of institutional change because it combined a range of complementary ideas that redefined social problems, their solutions, and policy objectives. The ideational perspective is a social constructivist approach, emphasizing that political economy as we know and experience it is a social construction of our actions, behaviours, and assumptions. As such, it helps to explain the fact that different countries with very different material and institutional starting points converged on a very similar policy direction (i.e. "neoliberalism") around the same time. This is perhaps best illustrated by the work of Jonathan Swarts (2013), who adopts the ideational perspective to look at neoliberalism in four Anglo-American countries – UK, Canada, Australia, and New Zealand. As Swarts notes, political or social imaginaries can have significant impacts on political-economic institutions because they help to establish the "proper relationship between the state, society, and the economy" (p.10).

History and philosophy of economics

A second perspective centred on ideas has emerged from scholars in the history and philosophy of economics. However, unlike the ideational perspective, these scholars emphasize the need for in-depth study of neoliberalism as an epistemology – or way of knowing the world – and as an epistemic community. Key writers in this perspective include people like Philip Mirowski (2013a) and his collaborators (e.g. Mirowski and Plehwe 2009; van Horn 2009, 2011; van Horn and Mirowski 2009; Nik-Khah and van Horn, 2012; also Davies 2010). According to Mirowski (2013a), neoliberalism is not a static or even necessarily coherent set of ideas, principles, assumptions, or theories – hence, why it is difficult to analyse the causative power of ideas alone. Rather, neoliberalism is better conceptualized as a "thought collective" centred especially on the Mont Pelerin Society (MPS) (e.g. Mirowski and Plehwe 2009). Mirowski (2013a: 42) argues that this "neoliberal thought collective" (or NTC) comprises a range of often competing but also cross-fertilizing viewpoints, predominantly split between Austrian–Hayekian and Chicagoan–Friedmanite. These were brought together in the MPS but have also proliferated in a series of satellite organizations (e.g. university departments, think tanks, foundations, policy networks, media, etc.) in ever widening circles from the centre, all of which have signed up to the epistemic assumptions in neoliberalism and all of which have sought to promulgate a diluted – and even distorted – version of neoliberalism to the public masses.

It is therefore important to understand the (ever-mutating) epistemological basis of neoliberal political-economic thought, as this informs the policy prescriptions and popular politics they develop and promote. Mirowski (2013a, 2013b) identifies "13 Commandments" of neoliberal doctrine, including the arguments that markets are social constructions, not a naturally emergent order, which means that they need protection by a strong state; the market has to be represented as a natural order (and even natural right) to the public; the distinction between market, state and society needs erasing; the role of the state needs to be redefined, but not hollowed out or eradicated, even if – again – the latter can be represented as the aim to the public; politics is better thought of as a marketplace in which citizens can "buy" democracy; personhood and the meaning of humanity have to be thoroughly re-imagined as human capital (see Chapter 3); freedom is the highest virtue, although this does not necessarily mean personal liberty; and more besides. As Mirwoski points out, these are sometimes contradictory, but this does not matter because neoliberalism is a "secret" doctrine with a private face and a public face. While one thing can be admitted behind the MPS's closed doors, for example, another thing has to be presented to the rest of the world.

As a perspective of neoliberalism, this approach provides a close reading of neoliberal principles and assumptions as well as an in-depth exploration of its intellectual history. It helps to show how neoliberal ideas changed over time, how they ended up influencing policies, politicians, and publics, and how neoliberals deal with the contradictions inherent in their thought collective. A particular useful illustration of the latter – which I return to in depth in Chapter 6 – is the treatment of corporate monopoly within the Chicagoan wing of the NTC – it changed significantly over time from a negative attitude before the 1950s to a positive attitude afterwards (van Horn 2009, 2011).

Institutional analysis

Having discussed two perspectives centred on ideas, I now want to turn to the institutional perspective of neoliberalism (e.g. Campbell and Pedersen 2001; Dowd and Dobbin 2001; Prasad 2006). Largely emerging from economic sociology, this institutionalist approach critiques the notion that economic ideas are unproblematically translated into social transformations. Instead, institutionalists argue that new ideas are mediated by existing social institutions (e.g. the state, the family, the corporation, the education system, etc.). As Campbell and Pedersen (2001: 1) argue, from an institutionalist perspective neoliberalism is understood as a "political project concerned with institutional changes on a scale not seen since the immediate aftermath of the Second World War". Such institutional transformations include the restructuring of the state, labour relations, markets, regulations, and so on.

It is important, however, to understand the different forms of institutional analysis here. For example, Campbell and Pedersen

(2001) differentiate between *historical institutionalism* and *organizational institutionalism*. The latter incorporates informal institutions like norms, culture, and discourse in its analysis of the world, while the former does not. Moreover, the former is framed by assumptions about the path dependence of institutional forms, while the latter is not. As such, it is more helpful to analyse neoliberalism from an organizational institutionalist perspective because it opens up room for conflict and contestation. As Dowd and Dobbin (2001) argue, neoliberalism cannot be considered as a pristine or path-dependent project and restructuring process. It does not emerge in a vacuum, in that neoliberalism changes existing institutions rather than creating wholly new ones, and the direction of institutional change is not a given or necessarily path dependent (as the differences between countries and geographies illustrate, see Birch and Mykhnenko 2009). As Prasad (2006: 23) agues, it is better to think of institutions as helping to "structure the incentives of actors" and "generate feedback effects". As such, there is no simple or even self-evident way to implement neoliberal principles or ideas, or reason to assume that this implementation will happen as expected or imagined. A particular strength of this perspective is that it enables researchers to examine how neoliberalism plays out in different places (e.g. countries) with different starting conditions (e.g. Fourcade-Gourinchas and Babb 2002; Prasad 2006).

State theory and Regulation School

State theory and the *Regulation* School represent another institutional perspective, although distinct from the institutionalism discussed earlier. This approach is most closely associated with the work of the sociologist Bob Jessop (1993, 2002, 2010, 2016). He has produced an enormous amount of work on the regulation of capitalism, including neoliberal forms. As noted, Jessop's work is positioned within the Regulation School, which is a predominantly French tradition in political economy associated with people like Alain Lipietz, Michel Aglietta, Robert Boyer, and Bruno Amable. These Regulationists seek to analyse the social arrangements that stabilize – or regulate – capitalism and enable the transformation of capitalism from one regime of accumulation to another. In particular, they have focused on the transformation from Fordism to post-Fordism (e.g. Jessop 2002). According to Jessop and Sum (2006: 134), for example, the social arrangements underpinning Fordism were based on Keynesian principles, while those of post-Fordism are based "on a reinvigorated neoliberal program aimed at creating the conditions for a new, more stable accumulation regime appropriate to the post-Fordist environment".

It would be difficult to summarize Jessop's approach to neoliberalism properly here, but it is useful to highlight a few elements. Like others, Jessop (2010, 2016) emphasizes the need to think about neoliberalism as a heterogeneous process, which includes at least four forms: system transformation, regime shift, structural adjustment, and policy adjustment. Neoliberalism, according to Jessop, arises from crisis tendencies in the previous Keynesian regime of accumulation and mode of regulation, and it has persisted after the global financial crisis as the result of path dependencies in policies, strategies, and structures. Throughout, Jessop stresses that capitalist logics inform both social relations and regulation but not in a unidirectional fashion. The state plays an important role, making this Regulation approach distinct from the institutional analyses discussed earlier, even though they may have a similar methodological focus (i.e. institutions). Jessop and his collaborators over the years place more emphasis on the social relations of the state and social regulation of capitalism, rather than on institutions as social entities. His work has proved to be highly influential across the social sciences, but especially so in political-economic geography – which I discuss next.

Neoliberalization, human geography, and the processual perspective

The final perspective of neoliberalism I want to consider in this book comes from human geography, although it draws on elements from other social sciences. As Peck (2010) shows, the concept of neoliberalism has taken off massively in human geography over the last decade or so (also see Springer 2010). It could be argued that these debates in human geography have also driven discussions of neoliberalism across the wider academy as well. As noted, some of the seminal work in human geography on neoliberalism has been strongly influenced by Jessop's work on state theory and the regulation of capitalism (e.g. Brenner and Theodore 2002; Peck and Tickell 2002), but other perspectives have also been influential too. Not least of which is the work of Marxists like David Harvey (2005) – himself a geographer – on a number of others (e.g. Peet 2007). Foucault's work on governmentality has also been influential (e.g. Larner 2000, 2003). More recently, the likes of Simon Springer (2012, 2016) has sought a rapprochement between these Marxist and Foucauldian perspectives in his work.

Finally, human geographers have also engaged with work in political ecology in order to theorize the emergence of "neoliberal natures" (Castree 2008).

The main contribution that geographers have made are as follows. First, they have developed a conceptual approach based on understanding neoliberalism as a process – or *neoliberalization* – rather than a project, outcome, idea, or strategy. This *processual* perspective was first developed by people like Jamie Peck and Adam Tickell (2002), and has been taken up across the discipline and beyond. They argue that neoliberalization can be defined as a process of restructuring characterized by specific socio-economic forces and actors, including privatization, commodification, and marketization (see Birch and Siemiatycki 2016). As such it represents the "*mobilization of state* power in the *contradictory extension* and reproduction of *market(-like) rule*" (Tickell and Peck 2003: 166). Second, human geographers have stressed the need to think about the evolution of the neoliberalization process, in order to understand how it changes over time. For example, Peck and Tickell (2002) distinguish between periods of "roll-back" and "roll-out" neoliberalism, representing different forms of restructuring. Roll-back neoliberalism is associated with Thatcher and Reagan in the 1980s, reflecting the anti-statist privatization of state assets and deregulation of the economy; roll-out neoliberalism is associated with the Third Way doctrines of the mid- to late-1990s in countries like the USA, UK, and Germany, reflecting new forms of state building and marketization of public services and assets (Tickell and Peck 2003). Since the global financial crisis there have been attempts to analyse how neoliberalism has change again. For example, Sidaway and Hendrikse (2016) have posited the notion of a "neoliberalism 3.0" to account for the changes that have happened, including rising state surveillance (e.g. think of the 2013 National Security Agency leaks), shifting geopolitical and geoeconomic power (e.g. from West to East), and so on. Finally, and building on the last two points, human geographers emphasize the necessarily varied, variegated, hybrid, or diverse nature of neoliberalism, especially in terms of its outcomes and effects. This variability results from the restructuring process being layered on top of existing institutions, which creates hybrid forms of localized and place-specific change (Brenner et al. 2010). As a result of this approach, it is easier to understand how different countries, regions, and even cities or communities end up experiencing different effects from the process of neoliberalization (Birch and Mykhnenko 2009, 2010).

Conclusion

My aim in this chapter was to introduce readers to the different analytical approaches to understanding neoliberalism as a concept; it was not to provide my own analytical definition of neoliberalism. Before outlining the various, and basically critical, perspectives, however, I wanted to show how influential neoliberalism has become as a concept for understanding the world. In showing its influence – primarily in the academic world, but also in public discourse – it is evident that neoliberalism has become an increasingly important concept over time, especially after the global financial crisis, but there are also signs that it has peaked in terms of usage. Whether the mid-2010s represent a moment of "peak neoliberalism" or not is a question we cannot answer today, and must be left for future writers. I used the rest of the chapter to outline seven different critical perspectives of neoliberalism: Foucauldian, Marxist, ideational, institutional, epistemic, state-theoretic, and processual.

I want to make a few, brief comments about the ambiguities with each of these seven perspectives here, leading up to a more detailed critique in the following chapter. First, the governmentality perspective, especially in Foucault's (2008) lectures, provides no real discussion of the evolution of neoliberalism. Second, the Marxist approach tends towards a circular assumption that inequality results from neoliberalism because neoliberalism leads to inequality. Third, ideational analysis does not account for why some ideas ended up being influential, whilst others did not. Fourth, institutional analysis tends to emphasize continuity over change and lacks a clear sense of what is the causative driver at play (e.g. ideas, policies, etc.). Fifth, the epistemic approach provides limited details about how epistemic communities – or thought collectives – actually go about creating change (e.g. does it involve more than ideas?). Sixth, the state-centric perspective associated with the Regulation School centres on state actors rather than private actors as key drivers of change. Finally, the processual approach associated with human geography ends up becoming incredibly conceptually fuzzy because almost anything can end up being defined as part of the neoliberalization process. Aside from these (very) brief comments, it is notable that a growing body of literature has started to question the use of neoliberalism as a concept to define the world. I turn to these debates in the next chapter.

Before that, it is worth noting a few things about the critical perspectives I discussed in this chapter. First, the distinctions I make between different analytical takes on neoliberalism are often blurred in discussions of neoliberalism; for example, some characterizations of neoliberalism straddle approaches, others may not fit neatly into any of the categories I use here. Second, one of the main similarities between perspectives is the conceptualization of neoliberalism as a "market-based" *something* (e.g. process, project, restructuring, ideology, epistemology, etc.). In some ways, this common conception of neoliberalism (as a market "something-or-other") is really the one thing that brings the critical perspectives together and enables anyone to talk about neoliberalism without talking at cross-purposes with one another. Finally, many critical scholars of neoliberalism emphasize that neoliberalism is an analytical term, meaning that it does not matter whether "neoliberals" actually self-describe themselves as such. Like many other analytical terms in use – e.g. racist, misogynist, totalitarian, patriarchal, capitalist, etc. – the concept, therefore, does not need to be accepted by the people it describes.

Bibliography

Birch, K. (2015a), *We Have Never Been Neoliberal: A Manifesto for a Doomed Youth*, Winchester, UK: Zero Books.

Birch, K. (2015b), "Neoliberalism: the whys and wherefores . . . and future directions", *Sociology Compass*, 9(7), 571–84.

Birch, K. (2016), "Market vs. contract? The implications of contractual theories of corporate governance to the analysis of neoliberalism", *ephemera: theory & politics in organization*, 16(1), 107–33.

Birch, K. and Mykhnenko, V. (2009), "Varieties of neoliberalism? Restructuring in large industrially-dependent regions across Western and Eastern Europe", *Journal of Economic Geography*, 9(3), 355–80.

Birch, K. and Mykhnenko, V. (eds) (2010), *The Rise and Fall of Neoliberalism: The Collapse of an Economic Order?*, London: Zed Books.

Birch, K. and Siemiatycki, M. (2016), "Neoliberalism and the geographies of marketization: the entangling of state and markets", *Progress in Human Geography*, 40(2), 177–98.

Blyth, M. (2002), *Great Transformations*, Cambridge: Cambridge University Press.

Blyth, M. (2013), *Austerity*, Oxford: Oxford University Press.

Boas, T. and Gans-Morse, J. (2009), "Neoliberalism: from new liberal philosophy to anti-liberal slogan", *Studies in Comparative International Development*, 44(2), 137–61.

Bourdieu, P. (1998), "The essence of neoliberalism", *Le Monde Diplomatique*, December, accessed 11 November 2016 at http://mondediplo.com/1998/12/08bourdieu.

Bowman, S. (2016), "Coming out as neoliberal", www.adamsmith.org/ blog, 12 October, accessed 24 October 2016 at http://www.adamsmith.org/blog/coming-out-as-neo liberals.

Brenner, N. and Theodore, N. (2002), "Cities and the geographies of 'actually existing neoliberalism'", *Antipode*, 34(3), 356–86.

Brenner, N., Peck, J. and Theodore, N. (2010), "Variegated neoliberalization: geographies, modalities, pathways", *Global Networks*, 10(2), 182–222.

Brennetot, A. (2014), "Geohistory of 'neoliberalism': rethinking the meanings of a malleable and shifting intellectual label", *Cybergeo: European Journal of Geography*, 677, accessed 24 October 2016 at http://cybergeo.revues.org/26324.

Brown, W. (2015), *Undoing the Demos*, New York, NY: Zone Books.

Cahill, D. (2014), *The End of Laissez-Faire*, Cheltenham, UK and Northampton, MA, USA: Edward Elgar Publishing.

Campbell, J. and Pedersen, O. (eds) (2001), *The Rise of Neoliberalism and Institutional Analysis*, Princeton, NJ: Princeton University Press.

Castree, N. (2008), "Neoliberalising nature: the logics of deregulation and reregulation", *Environment and Planning A*, 40, 131–52.

Cerny, P. (2008), "Embedding neoliberalism: the evolution of a hegemonic paradigm", *The Journal of International Trade and Diplomacy*, 2(1), 1–46.

Chiapello, E. (2017), "Critical accounting research and neoliberalism", *Critical Perspectives on Accounting*, 43, March, 47–64.

Clark, T. (2012), "What is neoliberalism?", anotherangryvoice.blogspot.ca blog, 23 September, accessed 24 October 2016 at http://anotherangryvoice.blogspot.ca/2012/09/what-is-neoliberalism-explained.html.

Dardot, P. and Laval, C. (2014), *The New Way of the World*, London: Verso.

Davies, W. (2010), "Economics and the "nonsense" of law: the case of the Chicago antitrust revolution", *Economy and Society*, 39(1), 64–83.

Dean, M. (2014), "Rethinking neoliberalism", *Journal of Sociology*, 50(2), 150–63.

Dowd, T. and Dobbin, F. (2001), "Origins of the myth of neoliberalism: regulation in the first century of US railroading", in L. Magnusson and J. Ottosson (eds), *The State, Regulation and the Economy: An Historical Perspective*, Cheltenham, UK and Northampton, MA, USA: Edward Elgar Publishing, pp. 61–88.

Duménil, G. and Lévy, D. (2004), *Capital Resurgent*, Cambridge, MA: Harvard University Press.

Duménil, G. and Lévy, D. (2011), *The Crisis of Neoliberalism*, Cambridge, MA: Harvard University Press.

Flew, T. (2014), "Six theories of neoliberalism", *Thesis Eleven*, 122(1), 49–71.

Foucault, M. (2008), *The Birth of Biopolitics*, New York, NY: Picador.

Fourcade-Gourinchas, M. and Babb, S. (2002), "The rebirth of the liberal creed: paths to neoliberalism in four countries", *American Journal of Sociology*, 108(3), 533–79.

Gamble, A. (1986), "The political economy of freedom", in R. Levitas (ed.), *The Ideology of the New Right*, Cambridge: Polity, pp. 25–54.

Hall, S. (2011), "The neo-liberal revolution", *Cultural Studies*, 25(6), 705–28.

Harvey, D. (2005), *A Brief History of Neoliberalism*, Oxford: Oxford University Press.

Harvey, D. (2006), "Neoliberalism as creative destruction", *The Annals of the American Academy of Political and Social Science*, 610, 22–44.

Hay, C. (2004), "The normalizing role of rationalist assumptions in the institutional embedding of neoliberalism", *Economy and Society*, 33(4), 500–527.

Jessop, B. (1993), "Towards a Schumpeterian workfare state? Preliminary remarks on post-Fordist political economy", *Studies in Political Economy*, 40, 7–39.

Jessop, B. (2002), *The Future of the Capitalist State*, Cambridge: Polity.

Jessop, B. (2010), "From hegemony to crisis? The continuing ecological dominance of neoliberalism", in K. Birch and V. Mykhnenko (eds), *The Rise and Fall of Neoliberalism: The Collapse of an Economic Order?*, London: Zed Books, pp. 171–87.

Jessop, B. (2016), "The heartland of neoliberalism and the rise of the austerity state", in S. Springer, K. Birch and J. McLeavy (eds), *The Handbook of Neoliberalism*, London: Routledge, pp. 410–21.

Jessop, B. and Sum, N.-L. (2006), *Beyond the Regulation Approach*, Cheltenham, UK and Northampton, MA, USA: Edward Elgar Publishing.

Klein, N. (2007), *The Shock Doctrine*, Toronto, ON: Vintage Canada.

Laclau, E. and Mouffe, E. (1985), *Hegemony and Social Strategy*, London: Verso.

Larner, W. (2000), "Neo-liberalism: policy, ideology, governmentality", *Studies in Political Economy*, 63, 5–25.

Larner, W. (2003), "Neoliberalism?", *Environment and Planning D*, 21, 509–12.

Lemke, T. (2001), "'The birth of bio-politics': Michel Foucault's lecture at the Collège de France on neo-liberal governmentality", *Economy and Society*, 30(2), 190–207.

Mason, P. (2015), *Postcapitalism*, London: Allen Lane.

Mirowski, P. (2013a), *Never Let a Serious Crisis Go to Waste*, London: Verso.

Mirowski, P. (2013b), "The thirteen commandments of neoliberalism", *The Utopian*, 19 June, accessed 11 November 2016 at http://www.the-utopian.org/post/53360513384/the-thirteen-commandments-of-neoliberalism.

Mirowski, P. and Plehwe, D. (eds) (2009), *The Road from Mont Pèlerin: The Making of the Neoliberal Thought Collective*, Cambridge, MA: Harvard University Press.

Monbiot, G. (2016), "Neoliberalism – the ideology at the root of all our problems", *The Guardian*, 15 April, accessed 24 October 2016 at https://www.theguardian.com/books/2016/apr/15/neoliberalism-ideology-problem-george-monbiot.

Nik-Khah, E. and van Horn, R. (2012), "Inland empire: economics imperialism as an imperative of Chicago neoliberalism", *Journal of Economic Methodology*, 19(3), 259–82.

Peck, J. (2010), *Constructions of Neoliberal Reason*, Oxford: Oxford University Press.

Peck, J. and Tickell, A. (2002), "Neoliberalizing space", *Antipode*, 34(3), 380–404.

Peet, R. (2007), *Geography of Power*, London: Zed Books.

Pirie, M. (2016), "Neoliberalism is a force for good in the world, no matter what the Corbynistas say", *The Daily Telegraph*, 12 October, accessed 24 October 2016 at http://www.telegraph.co.uk/news/2016/10/12/neoliberalism-is-a-force-for-good-in-the-world-no-matter-what-th/.

Polanyi, K. (1944 [2001]), *The Great Transformation*, New York, NY: Beacon Press.

Prasad, M. (2006), *The Politics of Free Markets*, Chicago, IL: University of Chicago Press.

Rose, N. (1993), "Government, authority and expertise in advanced liberalism", *Economy and Society*, 22(3), 283–99.

Rose, N. (1999), *Powers of Freedom*, Cambridge: Cambridge University Press.

Seymour, R. (2010), "Why neoliberalism persists", leninology.co.uk blog, 18 May, accessed 31 October 2016 at http://www.leninology.co.uk/2010/05/why-neoliberalism-persists.html.

Shand, A. and Shackle, G. (1980), *Subjectivist Economics*, Exeter, UK: Pica Press.

Sherman, J. (2016), "Student heaps abuse on professor in 'neoliberalism' row", *The Times*, 24 September, accessed 24 October 2016 at http://www.thetimes.co.uk/article/student-heaps-abuse-on-professor-in-row-over-neoliberalism-27pvhbfnp.

Sidaway, J. and Hendrikse, R. (2016) "Neoliberalism version 3.0", in S. Springer, K. Birch and J. McLeavy (eds), *The Handbook of Neoliberalism*, London: Routledge, pp. 574–82.

Springer, S. (2010), "Neoliberalism and geography: expansions, variegations, formations", *Geography Compass*, 4(8), 1025–38.

Springer, S. (2012), "Neoliberalism as discourse: between Foucauldian political economy and Marxian poststructuralism", *Critical Discourse Studies*, 9(2), 133–47.

Springer, S. (2016), *The Discourse of Neoliberalism: An Anatomy of a Powerful Idea*, Lanham, MD: Rowman & Littlefield.

Swarts, J. (2013), *Constructing Neoliberalism*, Toronto, ON: University of Toronto Press.

Talbot, C. (2016), "The myth of neoliberalism", colinrtalbot.wordpress.com blog, 31 August, accessed 24 October 2016 at https://colinrtalbot.wordpress.com/2016/08/31/the-myth-of-neoliberalism/.

Tickell, A. and Peck, J. (2003), "Making global rules: globalisation or neoliberalisation?", in J. Peck and H. Yeung (eds), *Remaking the Global Economy*, London: Sage, pp. 163–82.

van Apeldoorn, B. (2002), *Transnational Capitalism and the Struggle over European Integration*, London: Routledge.

van Apeldoorn, B. and Overbeek, H. (2012), "Introduction", in H. Overbeek and B. van Apeldoorn (eds), *Neoliberalism in Crisis*, Basingstoke, UK: Palgrave Macmillan, pp. 1–20.

van Horn, R. (2009), "Reinventing monopoly and corporations: the roots of Chicago law and economics", in P. Mirowski and D. Plehwe (eds), *The Road from Mont Pèlerin*, Cambridge, MA: Harvard University Press, pp. 204–37.

van Horn, R. (2011), "Chicago's shifting attitude toward concentrations of business power (1934–1962)", *Seattle University Law Review*, 34, 1527–44.

van Horn, R. and Mirowski, P. (2009), "The rise of the Chicago School of Economics and the birth of neoliberalism", in P. Mirowski and D. Plehwe (eds), *The Road from Mont Pèlerin*, Cambridge, MA: Harvard University Press, pp. 139–78.

5   Struggling with neoliberalism as a concept

Introduction

I use neoliberalism as a concept to analyse the world all the time, but yet I have an admission to make, which should not come as a surprise at this point in the book. I struggle, and increasingly so, with the use of neoliberalism as a concept for explaining the world, in my own work and others. I find myself reading eminent scholars on the subject through a super-critical lens, watching and waiting for every contradiction or fuzziness or analytical fudge in their writings. In part, this is a consequence of my own dissatisfaction with neoliberalism as an explanation – usually for anything and everything bad in the world – and as the "thing" we need to explain – in order to save ourselves. As an example, I read Wendy Brown's (2015) latest book, *Undoing the Demos*, with growing frustration at the way she analyses the world as seemingly always "neoliberal", whether she was discussing corporate law, higher education, welfare, politics, or what-have-you. On top of that, I found her book chock full of hyperbole, snarky comments, rose-tinted visions of alternatives to neoliberalism, and much else besides. At the same time, it was missing any substantive evidence to support her claims – for example, do all people think the same way? How do we know that? I could throw similar comments at other critical scholars, and, no doubt, others say the same about me (e.g. Christophers 2015; Birch 2015a).

Perhaps it is the very popularity and diversity of current debates on neoliberalism that has led me here. To me, it is becoming ever more difficult to reconcile these different approaches to understanding neoliberalism – its representations – with the manifestations of supposedly "neoliberal" policies, practices, subjectivities, identities, and so on (and on) (Birch 2015b). In saying these sorts of things, I do not intend to be mean-spirited or hostile towards other points of view, although it might come across that way. As should be evident by now, I have read and continue to read an enormous amount of literature on neoliberalism (e.g. Springer et al. 2016), as well as use it in my analysis (Birch 2016). Nevertheless, and as I wrote earlier, I struggle with neoliberalism as a concept and how I might usefully deploy it in the future. I struggle precisely because neoliberalism has become such a popular analytical tool across so many different disciplines and so many different schools of thought. My worry is really that the diversity and variety of critical voices raised against neoliberalism mean the concept has become – or is becoming – analytically useless. It is possible, of course, that we could salvage something from this analytical ambiguity and confusion.

In thinking about neoliberalism, I therefore end up returning to a range of questions I think we need to answer – but might not be able to. How should we characterize or define neoliberalism? Is it a free market ethic? Or form of free market fundamentalism? Or process of economization? How are we to understand the evolution of neoliberal ideas and policies? Do neoliberal ideas cause neoliberal policies? If not, then what are the mediating processes, practices, or institutions? How are we to theorize the relationship between these ideas and policies? In order to address these questions, although not necessarily answer them, my aim in this chapter is to consider how neoliberalism is used in academic debate. I then consider the theoretical and empirical ambiguities with prevailing critical perspectives on neoliberalism, which I identified in the last chapter. I then finish by discussing the growing literature calling for a rethink in the use of neoliberalism as a descriptor of or explanation for contemporary capitalism and society.

How is neoliberalism used in academia?

As anyone who has written about neoliberalism should know – and as Figure 4.1 in the last chapter confirms – there is an enormous literature out there that uses or engages with neoliberalism as a concept. It would be nigh on impossible for anyone to read all that literature, let alone be able to synthesize it in any way for easy digestion. Leaving aside the issue of quantity, it becomes evident pretty quickly that any attempt to dig down into the literature with a fine-toothed pen (or should that be "keyboard" nowadays?) will not reveal the myriad ways that neoliberalism is used in academic debate. My aim in this section is more modest than that, however. In what follows, I simply want to show – and partially at best – the extent to which neoliberalism has been applied to

Table 5.1 Academic topics and neoliberalism

Topic	Mentions
Democracy/politics/citizenship	9
Multiculturalism/racism	7
Social, health & education policies	6
States & world/global order	5
Environment/nature/conservation/food	4
Crime/punishment	4
Internal aspects (e.g. theories)	4
Biopolitics/population/demography	4
Finance/financial crisis/debt	4
Economic policies & business	3
Urbanization	3
Class/labour	3
International relations	2
Protest/NGOs/alternatives	2

Source: Search of Google Scholar using term "neoliberal" – top 50 results; some terms have been excluded and others combined with each other; search undertaken in November 2016.

different topics of research and adopted across academic disciplines. I will have to leave it to others to do anything more detailed.

As should be obvious from Tables 5.1 and 5.2, neoliberalism is deployed as a concept across a huge range of academic fields – from education through politics to communication studies – and is used to analyse a huge range of topics – from the environment through racism to urbanization. This is a point reinforced by Rajesh Venugopal (2015) in his recent article when he cites the earlier work of Clarke (2008: 138) who listed the numerous instances "neoliberal" is used as an adjective to refer to:

> states, spaces, logics, techniques, technologies, discourses, discursive framework, ideologies, ways of thinking, projects, agendas, programs, governmentality, measures, regimes, development, ethno-development, development imaginaries, global forms of control, social policies, multiculturalism, audit cultures, managerialism, restructuring, reform, privatization, regulatory frameworks, governance, good governance, NGOs, third sector, subjects,

subjectivities, individualization, professionalization, normalization, market logics, market forms of calculation, the destatalization of government and the degovernmentalization of the state.

To give the reader some basic numbers, a simple search for "neoliberal" on Google Scholar – itself a broader database than others like Web of Science – returns around 619,000 results; a search for "neoliberalism" returns fewer results at around 200,000. Limiting my search to the top 50 publications on Google Scholar, using the search term "neoliberal" returns a huge variety of topics, as illustrated by Table 5.1. Even here, though, I had to combine a number of topics with one another (e.g. "democracy" and "citizenship") in order to ensure that the table does not become too unwieldy. Consequently, it is important to remember that this is purely an illustrative exercise and in no way reflects a definitive or very accurate representation of the term's actual usage. What it does show, however, is the extent to which "neoliberal" and "neoliberalism" are used as concepts across a diversity of topics and research areas. It is not, in this sense, restricted to discussions of economics, markets, and suchlike – in fact, Table 5.1 perhaps illustrates the reverse of this.

Not only is neoliberalism a common term used to analyse a range of diverse topics, it is also a term that is deployed across a number of social science (and humanities) disciplines. This time, drawing on the Web of Science database, I collected some basic data on the use of neoliberalism in different – and selectively chosen – disciplines by searching for "neo-liberal*" and "subject area". As Table 5.2 shows, neoliberal is a common term across several disciplines, including Geography, Sociology, and Anthropology. Whether these data can accurately reflect the influence of a concept like neoliberalism is dubious, and so the data should be treated with caution. Again, however, as an illustrative exercise it helps me make a few points. First, neoliberalism is obviously an important concept in a number of different academic disciplines; second, it seems to be used more in disciplines like Geography, Government & Law, Sociology, Business & Economics, and Social Sciences; and, third, it would be interesting to try and relate these data to the critical perspectives I discussed in the last chapter, but it would be difficult to clearly align the numbers with the various approaches.

All things being equal, the data in Tables 5.1 and 5.2 can only provide a limited illustration of the popularity of neoliberalism as a concept. It would require a far more in-depth research project to do much more

Table 5.2 Academic disciplines and neoliberalism

Discipline	Count
Geography	2,002
Government & Law	1,741
Sociology	1,222
Business & Economics	1,085
Social Sciences	1,080
Education & Educational Research	850
Anthropology	810
International Relations	739
Urban Studies	589
Cultural Studies	344
Communication	312
Psychology	182
Criminology & Penology	106

Source: Search of Web of Science using "neoliberal*" as TOPIC term and SUBJECT AREA.

than hint at some of the influences of neoliberalism in debates about various research areas or in various disciplines. Next, I want to come back to the critical perspectives I discussed in the last chapter in order to analyse the ambiguities and fuzziness in their claims and underlying assumptions.

Problems with different conceptions of neoliberalism

In the last chapter I outlined the dominant critical approaches used to understand and analyse neoliberalism (Birch 2015c). Here, I want to consider the specific ambiguities in or problems with the theoretical and methodological assumptions of these perspectives. To do this, I am going to do two things in this section. First, I am going to go through each critical perspective and highlight one or two issues with them. This is not as an attempt to demonstrate their "falsehood" or "wrongness", but rather a way to show that any analysis of neoliberalism is, and necessarily so, always partial, always bounded by analytical and methodological limits, always missing something. Second, I am going to outline some of the more germane – and perhaps most obvious – contradictions between the critical representations of neo-liberalism and its supposed manifestation.

Conceptual ambiguities in critical perspectives

First, when it comes to the *governmentality* perspective (Foucault 2008), it is worth considering the lack of dynamism in Foucault's approach. Although he distinguished between two variants of neoliberalism, he really only did so at a particular point in time; he did not undertake an analysis of their evolution or how they changed. Consequently, it is difficult to understand how particular policies or policy frameworks come to form certain forms of governmentality. For example, Ordoliberalism ended up underpinning Germany's "social market economy", which is often seen as a competing form of coordinated capitalism to that of liberal market economies (e.g. Hall and Soskice 2001). Governmentality does not, in this case at least, provide the analytical tools to examine how such transformations happen or how our conduct changes over time; how is it that we are transformed into neoliberal subjects? What are the social practices, policies, discourses, etc. that actually lead to this change? It is not clear if political rationalities or technologies of power change first, or if they change together, or what relationship they have with one another. For example, governmentality cannot properly explain why and how there was a major change in attitudes to corporate monopoly in American neoliberalism in the 1950s (Birch 2015b). Even contemporary updatings of Foucault like Dardot and Laval (2014) entail similar issues; for example, Dardot and Laval argue that neoliberalism involves people thinking of themselves as business enterprises. However, does this mean like enterprises from the 1930s as neoliberalism emerged, or the 1970s as neoliberalism started its ascent to dominance, or in the 1990s when neoliberalism was thoroughly established? At each point in time, it is possible to argue that the business enterprise and associated managerial philosophy were significantly different from one another (Khurana 2007; Birch 2016). This is a point I come back to in the next chapter.

Second, there are also issues with the Marxist perspective (e.g. Harvey 2005). I have already pointed out that Harvey (2005), for example, claims that neoliberalism is simply a legitimating ideology that is jettisoned as soon as it conflicts with the assertion of elite class interests. This means that neoliberalism – in these terms – could be considered as empty rhetoric, rather than anything with causative power. As Barnett (2009) notes, from a Marxist perspective it almost seems as if neoliberalism has no "function" beyond being one legitimating ideology of potentially many. For example, there is no reason why the restoration of elite class power could not be legitimated by, for example, nationalism or neo-conservatism. In this sense, Marxist perspectives often ignore the role of ideas and discourses in laying the ground for neoliberal restructuring, rarely outlining a clear body of neoliberal ideas and theories which inform economic policies (Venugopal 2015). A secondary issue with the Marxist perspective is that there is no clear reason why inequality is necessarily a manifestation of neoliberalism, rather than something else entirely (e.g. corporate power). Instead, it appears as though the Marxist perspective of people like Harvey assumes, in a circular fashion, that neoliberalism is the cause of inequality because rising inequality is an effect of neoliberalism.

Third, ideational perspectives (e.g. Blyth 2002) represent a reverse perspective to the Marxist ones. Again, there are limitations to this perspective. The sociologist Monica Prasad (2006) argues that ideational analysis is problematic because it assumes that neoliberal ideas were influential during the 1970s and 1980s when, in fact, they were not widely supported. As such, it is difficult to see how ideas alone can explain the implementation of specific policies, especially if only a few individuals supported them. It is also evident, as I show elsewhere (Birch 2015b), that a number of neoliberal ideas and theories were simply wrong (e.g. monetarism) or not implemented at the height of neoliberalism (i.e. 1980s) as commonly thought (e.g. public spending cuts). This means it is unclear how and why some ideas have an effect, whilst others do not. As Prasad (2006: 21) notes, this might be explained by the fact that "even quite narrowly defined economic ideas may be polyvalent and even self-contradictory, so that the same idea may come to mean quite different things at different times or to different audiences." An example might be helpful here. Monetarism, specifically associated with Milton Friedman, is usually characterized as a powerful neoliberal idea that shaped neoliberal policies (e.g. Blyth 2002). However, it was never properly implemented in places like the USA, UK, and Canada, and when it was implemented it was abandoned pretty quickly afterwards (Greider 1987). Monetarism is based on the idea that market supply and demand dynamics should determine interest rates – or the cost of money – rather than government fiat. For example, Friedman (1962: 51) argued that money needs to be "free from irresponsible governmental tinkering" in order to "prevent monetary policy from being subject to the day-to-day whim of political authorities". However, monetarism essentially failed. In its place, governments adopted an *ideological* preference for low inflation and inflation-targeting that is dependent on government action (e.g. sale and purchase of government bonds) – they did not adopt an actual *market-based* system for determining the price of money (Mann 2010). As this example shows, the notion that neoliberal ideas are powerful need not necessarily be wrong, but *how* those ideas are powerful is the real issue at stake; that is, they may change the way people think about problems (e.g. inflation is bad), but without actually changing the way they address them (e.g. government fiat).

Fourth, another set of ambiguities rears its head when it comes to historical and philosophical accounts of neoliberalism (e.g. Mirowski 2013). In particular, Mirowski and Plehwe's (2009) argument that there is a "neoliberal thought collective" (NTC) – or similar epistemic community – does not really explain how the NTC instigates institutional change beyond assuming that one follows the other; that is, the NTC emerges and its ideas spread, influencing other people and thereby changing institutions. It is difficult to analyse why and how certain ideas take hold, and why others do not. A more critical issue is the assumption that there is a unidirectional flow of influence. As Mirowski (2013: 68–9) quite explicitly states, there is a "double truth" in this epistemic community in which neoliberals present one set of ideas to the public (outsiders) and keep another for themselves (insiders). However, why and how epistemic influences flow from insiders outwards to outsiders and not vice versa is not really explained. It is, for example, worth considering whether the shift in the (second) Chicago School's attitude to corporate monopoly that happened in the 1950s and afterwards is the result of neoliberals trying to appease their external funders (e.g. corporations, business foundations), rather than an epistemic epiphany. For example, according to Dean (2014: 152) "the Volker Fund refused to distribute his [Henry Simons'] *Economic Policy for a Free Society* because of its anti-monopoly positions". The historical research of Phillips-Fein (2009) is also interesting in this regard. In her book, *Invisible Hands*, she traces the concerted efforts of American business people after World War II to overturn the New Deal. The funding from these business people for academics like Hayek were central to the spread of neoliberal ideas, but they also inflected those ideas with anti-state and pro-business sentiment, equating "free markets" with big business. Consequently, there might be something to the idea that the funding from business received by neoliberal scholars like Hayek and Friedman influenced their ideas, as much as the reverse.

Fifth, institutional analysis is not without its difficulties either. Most obvious is the analytical diversity in how to conceptualize institutions themselves, which differs between institutionalist approaches. As Campbell and Pedersen (2001) argue, different forms of institutional analysis have their own intellectual histories, specific methodological approaches, and analytical limitations. For example, *historical institutionalism* has a tendency to emphasize continuity over change, especially in an emphasis on path dependence. More broadly, institutional analysis implies a gradual layering of new ideas, policies, etc. on top of existing institutions, making it difficult to identify causative forces. It is, in this sense, difficult to identify why change happens (i.e. what stimulates it) and how it happens (i.e. what are the new mechanisms and processes at play). Another general issue to be alert to is the need to be careful when it comes to the conceptual treatment of institutions – it is important that any analysis does not reify them as social agents rather than treating them as relations between social actors. A similar set of issues are pertinent when considering the state-centric approaches emerging from the Regulation School (e.g. Jessop 2002). Although this perspective provides a useful means to analyse conflict and the local or variegated manifestations and formations of neoliberalism, it also has some limits. Primarily, the focus on the state necessarily diverts attention from other social actors, like business. Consequently, state-centric institutionalist perspectives end up saying less about how and why business has been restructured and reorganized over the last few decades, and the influence of this on the state (Birch 2015b).

Finally, when it comes to the processual perspective, which largely emerged from human geography, there is a general issue with how to differentiate between neoliberal restructuring and *not*-neoliberal restructuring. Some authors, including those who use the concept, warn that neoliberalism has a tendency towards fuzziness, which is not helped by the language often used by its proponents to theorize neoliberalism (Peck 2013). For example, someone like Castree (2006: 1) argues that the emphasis on process means that "its [neoliberalism] embedding in real-world situations muddies the clean lines of its conceptual specification". In a similar vein, Barnett (2009: 276), in a more critical commentary, argues that the processual theorizing characteristic of geographical perspectives of neoliberalism "makes it almost impossible to gainsay the highly generalized claims about neoliberalism as an ideology and neoliberalization as a state-led project". As a result, it is possible to identify almost anything as part of neoliberal restructuring, which perhaps explains why it is such a popular concept in geographical thought. For example, when it comes to something like ecosystem services or conservation (Collard et al. 2016), it is possible to argue that all the actors involved, from environmental NGOs all the way to corporate executives, contribute to the neoliberalization of nature. It therefore becomes difficult from this perspective to really identify the social actors promoting and supporting neoliberalism without having to include almost everyone (Birch 2015b).

Empirical ambiguities in critical perspectives

Having gone through the various critical perspectives of neoliberalism that I outlined in the last chapter and discussed some of the problems with each approach, it is worth unpacking some of the empirical ambiguities with these approaches as well. I now want to turn to the manifestations of neoliberal theories, ideas, and concepts in policies, regimes, and processes. I could look at all sorts of manifestations of neoliberalism here. For example, in a review of my book *We Have Never Been Neoliberal*, Brett Christophers (2015: 6) argues that I ignore "examples of *neoliberal policies* embodying and enacting *neoliberal ideas*", including "Independent central banks, anyone? Deunionization? Dismantling of capital controls? Welfare state retrenchment? Entrepreneurial urbanism? Workfare? Deregulation of financial markets? Structural adjustment programs? Privatization?" Although I do not want to address all these issues here, I did respond (Birch 2015a) to these claims by noting the following:

- Some central banks were established as independent of government before the ascendance of neoliberalism, meaning that this is not a specifically neoliberal policy;
- Deunionization can be linked to deindustrialization which started in the 1960s in countries like the USA and UK; it is not, in that sense, simply or even primarily a result of neoliberalism.
- Countries like China have capital controls, yet it is defined as a neoliberal economy by people like Harvey (2005).
- Social, welfare, and education spending actually increased under neoliberal regimes like Thatcher's government in the UK – which I return to later;
- There is a lot of debate about whether deregulation has been overstated, or is more complex than claimed, or did not happen in certain markets – another issue I return to later; and
- Privatization, public sector outsourcing, public-private partnerships, and suchlike, can be characterized as the granting of

"natural" (or constructed) monopolies rather than instituting competitive markets (see Birch and Siemiatycki 2016).

It is not a simple matter to assign causative power to neoliberalism, nor is it credible to ignore the ambiguities endemic to claims about the manifestation of neoliberal ideas. Even the claim that neoliberalism as a process produces hybrid outcomes and effects does not satisfy me anymore, analytically speaking. Manifestations of neoliberalism are frequently characterized as highly varied, and they are far less well-defined than the theoretical perspectives I criticized earlier imply. Most of these manifestations do not fit neatly into one or another of the critical perspectives, nor do they simply reflect one or another of the neoliberal schools of thought (see Chapter 2). However, I cannot cover everything here. Instead, I am only going to discuss a small range of policies or processes that are generally defined as the (empirical) manifestation of neoliberalism. These include financialization, deregulation, and public spending austerity.

The first empirical ambiguity concerns the relation between neoliberalism and the 2007–2008 global financial crisis. Many critics of neoliberalism sought to link the dominance of finance with the rise of neoliberalism, thereby claiming that neoliberalism was responsible for the global financial crisis. A more popular example of this claim is represented by Monbiot (2016) in *The Guardian* newspaper, and there are also a number of academic examples that directly equate neoliberalism with the global financial crisis in one way or another (e.g. Crouch 2011; Mirowski 2013; Dardot and Laval 2014). Much of this latter literature is premised on explaining *why* neoliberalism did not disappear after it was thoroughly bankrupted as a theoretical, moral, and political approach to governing the world. It is not surprising that neoliberalism and the financial crisis are often equated because a number of earlier writers, like Duménil and Lévy (2004) and Harvey (2005), had explicitly argued that finance and financialization – by which they mean the growing influence of the financial sector and financial logics in the wider economy and society – are key neoliberal processes. The major issue here is that the causation is off. By this I mean that the re-emergence and ascendance of finance – or financialization – began *before* neoliberalism started to replace Keynesianism in the 1970s, and resulted from the particularities of Keynesian political economy rather than neoliberal variant. First, I argue in my book *We Have Never Been Neoliberal* that financialization can be traced back to the emergence of the EuroMarkets in the 1950s and 1960s (Birch 2015b). Second, these EuroMarkets were (and still are) a response to Keynesian-forms of national financial regulation because they enable financial and other businesses to avoid capital controls, taxation of profits, etc. Moreover, the deregulation of financial markets – often associated with neoliberalism – which happened in places like the USA, UK, and Canada occurred before the rise of either Thatcher or Reagan (Panitch and Konings 2009). Consequently, it would be necessary to either stretch back the influence of neoliberals on financial regulation to the 1950s and 1960s, or conclude that neoliberalism first emerges as a policy regime with the Ford and Carter administrations in the USA and Wilson/Callaghan government in the UK.

The second empirical ambiguity concerns the idea that neoliberalism involves deregulation. Many scholars now argue that neoliberalism does not entail deregulation per se (e.g. Mirowski 2013), but it has often been presented as one of the defining features of neoliberalism in the past (e.g. Bourdieu 1998; Harvey 2005) – or at least for certain earlier stages of neoliberalism (e.g. Peck and Tickell 2002). Moreover, "neoliberal" thinkers themselves still seem to characterize their agenda in these terms – see Ostry et al. (2016) for example. Although there were definitely some significant regulatory changes in many economies during the 1970s and 1980s – like the ending of price, wage, and capital controls – this has to be weighed against the creation of new regulations. On the one hand, several countries (e.g. USA) introduced quite significant environmental regulation in the 1970s (Prasad 2006). On the other hand, the extension of markets necessarily entails the extension of regulations because markets are not "natural" but political-economic constructions. A number of scholars have made very specific arguments in this regard. First, Steven Vogel (1996) argues in *Freer Markets, More Rules* that market deregulation during the 1970s and 1980s was generally accompanied by the introduction of new regulation, such that it is better to think of the process as *reregulation*. This is even the case when it comes to the privatization of state assets (e.g. state-owned enterprises), which was often accompanied by the creation of new government or quasi-government regulatory agencies (Birch and Siemiatycki 2016; see Table 5.3 for details of these in the UK during the 1980s and 1990s). Second, even when it came to financial regulation, it is not the case that global finance was deregulated as the result of regulatory arbitrage – that is, businesses looking for the least regulated market – but rather that global financial rules were rewritten through global governance institutions like the Organisation for Economic Co-operation and Development (OECD) (Abdelal 2007). Finally, some scholars like John Braithewaite (2005)

Table 5.3 New regulatory agencies, UK

Agency	Established
Civil Aviation Authority	1971
Office of Telecommunications	1984
Office of Gas Supply	1986
Building Societies Commission	1986
Securities and Investments Board	1986
HM Inspectors of Pollution	1987
National Rivers Authority	1989
Office of Water Services	1989
Broadcasting Standards Council	1990
Office of Electricity Regulation	1990
Independent Television Commission	1991
Radio Authority	1991
Office of Rail Regulator	1993

Source: Vogel (1996: 132).

argue that contemporary capitalism is better characterized as "regulatory capitalism" rather than "neoliberalism" because many countries, like the USA, have seen an increase in regulatory staffing levels, regulatory agencies, regulatory codes and standards, and so on. As part of his argument, Braithewaite explicitly relates the extension of regulatory capitalism with the rise of big business, arguing that regulations help big business to stop the entry of new competitors. As noted previously, critics of neoliberalism now generally agree that neoliberalism involves forms of reregulation, as opposed to simple deregulation, which is often contrary to the anti-state rhetoric espoused by "neoliberal" thinkers, politicians, and commentators about free markets.

The last empirical ambiguity relates to the idea that neoliberalism is characterized by public spending cuts and austerity. As Blyth (2013) and others have shown more recently, since the global financial crisis many governments and other authorities (e.g. European Central Bank) have promoted and enforced forms of austerity. However, it is important to note that even here austerity is always *specific* rather than *general* in that overall public spending and public debt have not declined – in fact, they have risen quite dramatically in some cases (e.g. USA, UK, Greece, etc.). In this case it is perhaps better to look

Table 5.4 Government spending (% GDP)

Country	1970	1980	1990	2004
Canada	33.8	39.1	46	37.2
United Kingdom	36.7	43	41.9	39.7
United States	29.6	31.3	33.6	31.3

Source: Jackson (2009).

at levels of public spending before the crisis. However, there is pretty clear evidence that public or government spending has not declined significantly – or even at all – since the early 1980s (when neoliberal policies were first adopted). People like Cockett (1995: 316) point out that even supposedly neoliberal regimes like the UK's Thatcher government failed to reduce public spending in a range of government departments; in fact, between 1979 and 1991 spending increased in real terms (i.e. when adjusted for inflation) in Health (37 percent increase), Social Security (35 percent), and Education and Science (16 percent). More generally, government spending as a percent of GDP did not necessarily fall significantly during the 1980s in paradigmatic neoliberal countries like Canada, UK, and USA (see Table 5.4). In these cases, spending only fell as a percentage of GDP in the 2000s. Others have pointed to similar trends across a range of countries. For example, Flew (2014: 54) highlights the levels of public spending across 13 OECD countries between 1980 and 2009, illustrating the extent to which across these nations aggregate public spending has hovered around 45 percent of GDP during this period.

Struggling with neoliberalism as a concept

Having discussed some of the ambiguities with critical perspectives of neoliberalism, I now want to turn to the emerging critiques of neoliberalism as a concept. Other writers, far more capable than me, have started to question the usefulness of neoliberalism as a concept already. For example, Mitchell Dean (2014: 150) – an academic who works within the Foucauldian tradition – has argued recently that neoliberalism "is a rather overblown notion" that is used:

> to characterize everything from a particular brand of free-market philosophy and a wide variety of innovations in public management to patterns and

processes found in and across diverse political spaces and territories around the globe.

Others make similar claims, including prolific users of neoliberalism in their work; for example Peck (2010, 2013) has described it as a "fuzzy" or "rascal" concept. In many cases, these thinkers are not making these claims in order to jettison the concept; rather, they are criticizing other people's arguments in order to assert their own conceptions. My intention in this section is to introduce some of the more critical voices in this debate, people who have criticized the concept of neoliberalism and its usefulness for understanding contemporary capitalism. I am therefore not going to provide much of a synthesis of these critiques, although I will raise a few issues that seem to crop up across them.

One of the earliest critics, and someone whom I have already mentioned, is John Braithewaite (2005). His criticism centres, in particular, on the idea that contemporary capitalism is founded on free markets freed from regulation. In conclusion, he argues that "Those who believe we are in an era of neoliberalism – where this means hollowing out of the state, privatisation and deregulation – are mistaken" (p.34). Braithewaite focuses on the claims of people like Pierre Bourdieu (1998) who argued that neoliberalism reflected an attack on collective decision-making. As already noted, Braithewaite instead argues that contemporary capitalism is really better thought of as an increasingly and highly regulated economic system in which big business is dominant because larger firms find they can control markets through (public and private) regulation, rather than through market competition. In this sense, contemporary capitalism is not a "market"-like system; it is far more corporatist in structure and governance.

In the late 2000s, Boas and Gans-Morse (2009) and Barnett (2009) provide two different types of criticism of the concept of neoliberalism. First, Boas and Gans-Morse (2009) focus on its use in development studies, arguing that it has become an "anti-liberal" slogan associated "with multiple underlying concepts, including a set of policies, a development model, an ideology, and an academic program" (p.140). Neoliberalism had originally been used – at least up until the 1960s or 1970s – as a descriptor for moderate forms of liberalism represented by Ordoliberalism, and after that period it was linked with violent forms of oppression in Latin America, especially the Pinochet *coup d'état* in Chile, and the Chicago School of Economics. As a result, neoliberalism was increasingly used more by its critics than by its adherents. Second,

Barnett (2009) argues that neoliberalism has become a "strawman" concept, at least partially because there are so many conceptualizations of it that it has become difficult to define. Barnett is particularly critical of the Marxist and processual perspectives in geography because of their assumption that capital relations configure state action, government policy, and individual agency. On the one hand, he notes that neoliberalism is largely irrelevant because it is merely one ideological façade among many; for example, in the Marxist perspective it does not really matter if free markets or nationalism or racism are the driving ideology behind the restoration of elite power. On the other hand, Barnett is critical of the way processual perspectives reduce human agency to an issue of market relations and ignore other forms of agency.

By the early- to mid-2010s a number of scholars were engaging with the concept of neoliberalism from a more critical standpoint. Some, like Garland and Harper (2012), argue that the concept obscures a more vital focus on capitalism itself, with "capitalism" being replaced by "neoliberalism" in critical analyses. Although a simple test of Google's NGram Viewer illustrates how untenable their claims are in this regard, Garland and Harper do make the important point that the proliferation of critical terms can have significant political ramifications (e.g. loss of focus). Others, like Phelan (2014), Flew (2014), and Hardin (2014) focus their critical comments on the ubiquity of neoliberalism. For his part, Phelan (2014: 33) echoes Barnett in arguing that neoliberalism is often constructed as a static term, a "master signifier of a whole epoch". As such, Phelan thinks it is important to avoid leaving "too much analytic work" to neoliberalism; rather, it is necessary to avoid treating neoliberalism as a concept that explains everything and a phenomenon that steamrollers everything else in its path (also Eriksen et al. 2015). For his part, Flew (2014) makes a number of similar points, noting especially that as the concept of neoliberalism has been increasingly adopted to define and analyse the changes over the last few decades, it has increasingly lost much of its meaning. Flew is especially critical of the way the use of neoliberalism as a concept "presumes that political form does not matter" (p.52) and "downplays the significance of political institutions" (p.53). It is notable that Flew makes these charges against critics of neoliberalism because they reflect similar assumptions made by proponents of "neoliberal" ideas and policies. There are obviously exceptions to this, such as Davies (2014), but it raises the important question of how to study neoliberalism as market exceptionalism alongside the political – and just as important the legal – specificities that underpin social change. The final critical take of Hardin (2014) raises similar issues about the ubiquity of the concept – for example, "overuse and underspecify" (p.199) – but she also argues that neoliberalism is so flexible that it can always be adapted to whatever context its users want, meaning that it is not very useful analytically. Hardin goes on to argue that the "newness" of neoliberalism is its reconfiguration of "society as an economic system of corporations" (p.215). It is important to note that both Flew and Phelan still see some worth in the concept, and so they do not reject it outright, whilst Hardin seeks to re-imagine it as the basis of corporatism – echoing Klein's (2007) claims.

A number of far more critical takes on the concept of neoliberalism have appeared in the last few years. I would include my own critique in this literature (e.g. Birch 2015b), but do not want to do more than note it here because much of this book builds on those ideas – hence, it seems unnecessary. Instead, I am going to focus on the work of Weller and O'Neill (2014), Venugopal (2015), and Storper (2016). As their starting point, Weller and O'Neill (2014) argue their case study of Australia contradicts claims that Australia can be considered as an example of neoliberalism. They note that neoliberalism is often treated as "a motivating cause, a change agent and an effect of change", but prefer to frame it as an "overarching imaginary that promotes market-orientated logics" (p.110). From this perspective, they contend that Australia's political economy has not been subsumed under a market logic; instead, the (federal) state has retained its directing functions even when contracting out public services, reregulating financial and labour markets, provision of public services, etc. Their main point is that using neoliberalism as a concept makes it difficult to "identify processes that are not neo-liberal" (p.125). Although they have been criticized (e.g. Springer 2014), their general point reiterates the arguments of others about the omission of thinking through other (e.g. political) reasons that might explain social change. In perhaps the most trenchant take on the concept so far, Venugopal (2015: 183) argues that:

> neoliberalism serves as a rhetorical tool and moral device for critical social scientists outside of economics to conceive of academic economics and a range of economic phenomena that are otherwise beyond their cognitive horizons and which they cannot otherwise grasp or evaluate.

Just as I sought to do in Chapter 2, Venugopal stresses the fact that neoliberalism has changed over time, although in his case he notes that it has shifted from a term only used by economists (pre-1980) to one only used by non-economists (post-1980). My discussion of the various critical perspectives in the last chapter is perhaps indicative of Venugopal's comment that different approaches to neoliberalism end up coming to widely disparate conclusions. As an example, he turns to development debates in which the critique of "neoliberalism is judged as technically inadequate and also over-technocratic, de-politicized and deeply political, obsessed by economic growth and responsible for the lack thereof" (p.178).

A final critical take on neoliberalism is that of Michael Storper (2016), the well-known economic geographer. He makes a number of claims critical of the concept of neoliberalism, including that the critical literature "is indiscriminate in labelling many of these changes neo-liberal" and "misuses the label 'neo-liberal'" (p.243). Since he focuses on cities as his main object of study, Storper tends to use urban issues as examples to dispute claims about neoliberalization. For example, he argues that there has been no hollowing out of land-use regulation over the last few decades, but rather an entrenching of ownership rights and their protection from external threats to their value. In the end, Storper and others (e.g. Le Gales 2016) argue that neoliberalism is a concept that is often used with little care or precision.

Conclusion

As I stated in the Introduction to this book, I increasingly struggle with the concept of neoliberalism – hence why I am writing a book like this. The point of this chapter was to provide some sense of why I am struggling with it. Consequently, I started by outlining the popularity of the term in academia and how it is used at present. That then set up a discussion of the ambiguities and problematic assumptions that I think underpin the critical perspectives of neoliberalism I discussed in the previous chapter. I also discussed some of the empirical ambiguities, notably the extent to which neoliberalism can be characterized as a process of financialization, deregulation, and public sector austerity. Finally, I provided a brief introduction to the burgeoning literature that is critical of prevailing understandings of neoliberalism – a critique of critique, if you will.

Although I might struggle with the concept of neoliberalism, it is important to note that "neoliberal" policy regimes, especially those promoted by international financial institutions, are also being questioned by the very promoters of those policies. For example, a 2016 report by three IMF economists called "Neoliberalism: Oversold?" explicitly questioned the impacts of free movement of capital and government austerity policies. The economists Ostry, Loungani, and Furveri (2016: 38), claim that "There is much to cheer in the neoliberal agenda", although they temper this claim by noting that "there are aspects of the neoliberal agenda that have not delivered as expected". Rather than a full-blown renunciation of neoliberal-like policies, this article can be seen as an attempt to rehabilitate the "good" aspects of neoliberalism by disclaiming any responsibility for the "bad" aspects. In this sense, it is as much about finding another way to define and conceptualize the advice of the past few decades in order to defend at least some parts of those claims and decisions.

You might ask a simple question at this juncture, why does all of this matter? My answer would be that it is vital that anyone deploying the concept of neoliberalism does so with a clear sense of how they understand it, how that differs from other approaches, and what that means in terms of what you can say and what you cannot say about neoliberalism. Perhaps a truism, but it is worth remembering that imprecision is the enemy of clarity. Throwing a term like "neoliberal" around in your writing does nothing to explicate the intricacies and complexities of social life and social change. However, it increasingly seems like scholars, commentators, politicians, journalists, and others are doing precisely that.

Bibliography

Abdelal, R. (2007), *Capital Rules: The Construction of Global Finance*, Cambridge, MA: Harvard University Press.

Barnett, C. (2009), "Publics and markets: what's wrong with neoliberalism?", in S. Smith, R. Pain, S. Marston and J.-P. Jons III (eds), *The Sage Handbook of Social Geography*, London: Sage, pp. 269–96.

Birch, K. (2015a), "Critical dialogue – Kean Birch responds to Brett Christophers' 'Monopolizing Neoliberalism Away'", antipodefoundation.org, 7 April, accessed 11 November 2016 at https://antipodefoundation.org/2015/04/07/critical-dialogue-birch-christophers/.

Birch, K. (2015b), *We Have Never Been Neoliberal: A Manifesto for a Doomed Youth*, Winchester, UK: Zero Books.

Birch, K. (2015c), "Neoliberalism: the whys and wherefores . . . and future directions", *Sociology Compass*, 9(7), 571–84.

Birch, K. (2016), "Market vs. contract? The implications of contractual theories of corporate governance to the analysis of neoliberalism", *ephemera: theory & politics in organization*, 16(1), 107–33.

Birch, K. and Siemiatycki, M. (2016), "Neoliberalism and the geographies of marketization: the entangling of state and markets", *Progress in Human Geography*, 40(2), 177–98.

Blyth, M. (2002), *Great Transformations*, Cambridge: Cambridge University Press.

Blyth, M. (2013), *Austerity*, Oxford: Oxford University Press.

Boas, T. and Gans-Morse, J. (2009), "Neoliberalism: from new liberal philosophy to anti-liberal slogan", *Studies in Comparative International Development*, 44(2), 137–61.

Bourdieu, P. (1998), "The essence of neoliberalism", *Le Monde Diplomatique*, December, accessed 11 November 2016 at http://mondediplo.com/1998/12/08bourdieu.

Braithwaite, J. (2005), "Neoliberalism or regulatory capitalism", ANU: RegNet, Occasional Paper No. 5.

Brown, W. (2015), *Undoing the Demos*, New York, NY: Zone Books.

Campbell, J. and Pedersen, O. (eds) (2001), *The Rise of Neoliberalism and Institutional Analysis*, Princeton, NJ: Princeton University Press.

Castree, N. (2006), "From neoliberalism to neoliberalisation: consolations, confusions, and necessary illusions", *Environment and Planning A*, 38(1), 1–6.

Christophers, B. (2015), "Book review – Monopolizing Neoliberalism Away", antipo-defoundation.org, 30 March, accessed 11 November at https://antipodefoundation.org/2015/03/30/we-have-never-been-neoliberal/.

Clarke, J. (2008), "Living with/in and without Neo-liberalism", *Focaal*, 51, 135–47.

Cockett, R. (1995), *Thinking the Unthinkable: Think-Tanks and the Economic Counter-Revolution, 1931–1983*, London: Harper Collins Publishers.

Collard, R.-C., Dempsey, J. and Rowe, J. (2016), "Re-regulating socioecologies under neoliberalism", in S. Springer, K. Birch and MacLeavy, J. (eds), *The Handbook of Neoliberalism*, New York, NY: Routledge, pp. 455–65.

Crouch, C. (2011), *The Strange Non-Death of Neoliberalism*, Cambridge: Polity Press.

Dardot, P. and Laval, C. (2014), *The New Way of the World*, London: Verso.

Davies, W. (2014), *The Limits of Neoliberalism*, London: Sage.

Dean, M. (2014), "Rethinking neoliberalism", *Journal of Sociology*, 50(2), 150–63.

Duménil, G. and Lévy, D. (2004), *Capital Resurgent*, Cambridge, MA: Harvard University Press.

Duménil, G. and Lévy, D. (2011), *The Crisis of Neoliberalism*, Cambridge, MA: Harvard University Press.

Eriksen, T., Laidlaw, J., Mair, J., Martin, K. and Venkatesan, S. (2015), "Debate: 'The concept of neoliberalism has become an obstacle to the anthropological understanding of the twenty-first century'", *Journal of the Royal Anthropological Institute*, 21, 911–23.

Flew, T. (2014), "Six theories of neoliberalism", *Thesis Eleven*, 122(1), 49–71.

Foucault, M. (2008), *The Birth of Biopolitics*, New York, NY: Picador.

Friedman, M. (1962), *Capitalism and Freedom*, Chicago, IL: University of Chicago Press.

Garland, C. and Harper, S. (2012), "Did somebody say neoliberalism? On the uses and limitations of a critical concept in media and communication studies", *tripleC*, 10(2), 413–24.

Greider, W. (1987), *Secrets of the Temple*, New York, NY: Simon & Schuster.

Hall, P. and Soskice, D. (eds) (2001), *Varieties of Capitalism: The Institutional Foundations of Comparative Advantage*, Oxford: Oxford University Press.

Hardin, C. (2014), "Finding the 'neo' in neoliberalism", *Cultural Studies*, 28(2), 199–22.

Harvey, D. (2005), *A Brief History of Neoliberalism*, Oxford: Oxford University Press.

Jackson, P. (2009), "The size and scope of the public sector: an international comparison", in T. Bovaird and E. Loffler (eds), *Public Sector Management*, London: Routledge, pp. 27–40.

Jessop, B. (2002), *The Future of the Capitalist State*, Cambridge: Polity.

Khurana, R. (2007), *From Higher Aims to Hired Hands*, Princeton, NJ: Princeton University Press.

Klein, N. (2007), *The Shock Doctrine*, Toronto, ON: Vintage Canada.

Le Gales, P. (2016), "Neoliberalism and urban change: stretching a good idea too far?", *Territory, Politics, Governance*, 4(2), 154–72.

Mann, G. (2010), "Hobbes' redoubt: toward a geography of monetary policy", *Progress in Human Geography*, 34(5), 601–25.

Mirowski, P. (2013), *Never Let a Serious Crisis Go to Waste*, London: Verso.

Mirowski, P. and Plehwe, D. (eds) (2009), *The Road from Mont Pèlerin: The Making of the Neoliberal Thought Collective*, Cambridge, MA: Harvard University Press.

Monbiot, G. (2016), "Neoliberalism – the ideology at the root of all our problems", *The Guardian*, 15 April, accessed 24 October 2016 at https://www.theguardian.com/books/2016/apr/15/neoliberalism-ideology-problem-george-monbiot.

Ostry, J., Loungani, P. and Furceri, D. (2016), "Neoliberalism: oversold?", *Finance & Development*, June 2016, 38–41.

Panitch, L. and Konings, M. (2009), "Myths of neoliberal deregulation", *New Left Review*, 57, 67–83.

Peck, J. (2010), *Constructions of Neoliberal Reason*, Oxford: Oxford University Press.

Peck, J. (2013), "Explaining (with) neoliberalism", *Territory, Politics, Governance*, 1(2), 132–57.

Peck, J. and Tickell, A. (2002), "Neoliberalizing space", *Antipode*, 34(3), 380–404.

Phelan, S. (2014), "Critiquing 'neoliberalism': three interrogations and a defense", in L. Lievrouw (ed.), *Challenging Communication Research*, New York, NY: Peter Lang, pp. 27–42.

Phillips-Fein, K. (2009), *Invisible Hands*, New York, NY: W.W. Norton & Company.

Prasad, M. (2006), *The Politics of Free Markets*, Chicago, IL: University of Chicago Press.

Springer, S. (2014), "Neoliberalism in denial", *Dialogues in Human Geography*, 4(2), 154–60.

Springer, S., Birch, K. and MacLeavy, J. (eds) (2016), *The Handbook of Neoliberalism*, London: Routledge.

Storper, M. (2016), "The neo-liberal city as idea and reality", *Territory, Politics, Governance*, 4(2), 241–63.

Venugopal, R. (2015), "Neoliberalism as concept", *Economy and Society*, 44(2), 165–87.

Vogel, S. (1996), *Freer Markets, More Rules*, Ithaca, NY: Cornell University Press.

Weller, S. and O'Neill, P. (2014), "An argument with neoliberalism: Australia's place in a global imaginary", *Dialogues in Human Geography*, 4(2), 105–30.

Part III

A new research agenda for neoliberalism

6 Neoliberalism and the problem of the corporation

Introduction

I have now got to the point in the book where I am going to outline how I understand neoliberalism. As noted in the book's Introduction, this means addressing three major contradictions that are evident in both critical accounts of neoliberalism and the claims of supposed neoliberals. Over the next three chapters I address the following topics: (1) the relationship between the corporate entity and corporate monopoly in an era supposedly dominated by markets; (2) the increasing propensity towards rentiership over entrepreneurship in the economy; and (3) the importance of contract and contract law, rather than markets, in the organization of capitalism. I start in this chapter by looking at the first contradiction, which relates to the idea that neoliberalism entails the extension of market competition throughout society versus the expansion of corporate monopoly as a mode of political-economic regulation. It is important to stress that I am not the first person to notice this by any means, nor is this sort of argument limited to critical academic circles. For example, in late 2016 the generally right-leaning and mainstream economics magazine *The Economist* (2016a) argued that the business world is in hock to a range of "dead ideas", including the idea that contemporary capitalism is "more competitive than ever" and "that we live in an age of entrepreneurialism". Consequently, it is a pertinent time to consider these contradictions, as I see them, when even a magazine like *The Economist* is raising them.

The starting point for this chapter is the seeming contradiction between neoliberalism – as an analytical category used by its critics, or a political-economic project pursued by its adherents, or an epistemic community of like-minded thinkers – and the dominance of corporations and corporate monopolies in contemporary capitalist economies and societies. Considering the emphasis that both neoliberals and their critics place on (free) markets and market principles as the defining characteristics of neoliberalism, it seems incongruous that neoliberalism and corporate monopoly can sit so comfortably along-side one another. It was certainly anathema at one time for neoliberals to sanction monopoly, in whatever form, although the attitude towards corporate monopoly changed radically in the 1950s and 1960s inside certain schools of neoliberal thought, notably those based in the USA. This contradiction is a critical issue to address in debates about neo-liberalism because, as Mitchell Dean (2014: 156) argues, "the tension within neoliberalism over the question of monopoly lies at the centre of the crisis of 2008 and after". And, I might add, much else besides (Birch 2015).

The tensions that Dean – and myself – identify here are a consequence of the incompatibility between (free) markets and the corporation. It raises the question: how much economic activity actually takes place in markets nowadays? A seemingly simple question like this leads to a complex answer. According to a number of heterodox economists, including Gardiner Means (1983), Herbert Simons (1991), and Geoffrey Hodgson (2005), a significant proportion of all economic activity has been and still is undertaken within organizational entities, rather than within markets. For example, in Anglo-American countries like the USA, UK, and Canada, large business enterprises alone – those with over 500 employees – represent a significant proportion – between 35 and 50 percent – of total employment and total value added, although they represent less than 1 percent of total business enter-prises (Deakins and Freel 2012: 36–7) – and those figures reflect *large* enterprises only. As people like Hodgson (2005) argue, it seems over half of all economic activity and output occurs within organiza-tional entities rather than through some form of market competition. According to more orthodox economists, like Ronald Coase (1937) and Jensen and Meckling (1976), the existence of business (or any) organization is merely an issue of efficiency, in that such organizations only exist where economic activity is more efficiently organized col-lectively within business organizations than through market exchange. However, it is perhaps worthwhile remembering, in the context of these debates, that the "corporate" form emerged in the medieval era before capitalism (Barkan 2013). It is, therefore, also worth considering whether it is the business organization that underpins capitalism and not markets, rather than reflecting a *failure* of (free) markets (Birch et al. 2016).

Many critical accounts of neoliberalism refer to corporate power and seek to analyse it (e.g. Klein 2007; Mirowski 2013), while many other accounts simply equate business activities with market exchange or economistic thinking (e.g. Brown 2015). However, rarely does this literature do more than nod towards some of the complexities involved in understanding the interaction between business entities and markets – in relation to neoliberalism or otherwise. I want to unpack these complexities in this chapter in order to examine how the "corporation" – or really the "firm" – represents a problem for neoliberalism and for understandings of neoliberalism. In order to do this, I start by outlining the extent of corporate monopoly in contemporary societies. I then outline some of the contradictions between markets and business entities that are found in neoliberal ideas and policies. Afterwards, I provide a summary of the evolution of corporate form and governance over the last century-and-half in order to differentiate between types of business entity and its governance – an issue which will come up in the next chapter. Finally, I consider how neoliberalism actually legitimates corporate monopoly and how neoliberalism is reproduced through business schools and business education.

The problem of corporate monopoly?

In order for me to achieve my objectives in this chapter, it is necessary to provide some indication of the current extent of corporate monopoly. Corporate monopoly is not a simple thing either to examine or to analyse. Despite its seeming importance to ongoing debates in society about the role and power of markets (e.g. allocative efficiency) or big business (e.g. impacts of large retailers on small business), there is limited data on the forms and extent of monopoly (Birch 2015). Definitionally, Barry Lynn (2010) argues that monopoly should not be thought of as *one* person or organization controlling 100 percent of whatever activity is under consideration; rather, it is more helpful to use Friedman's (1962: 102) definition:

> Monopoly exists when a specific individual or enterprise has sufficient control over a particular product or service to determine significantly the terms on which other individuals shall have access to it.

As such, monopoly is about the ability of a person or organization to either ignore and/or set market prices, and this can arise for various reasons. In order to unpack corporate monopoly here, I specifically focus on the USA because it is the country at the centre of the neoliberal rehabilitation of corporate monopoly. That being said, I also consider some of the global implications too. As a starting point to the debate, however, it is important to understand the different layers of corporate monopoly that now exist in our societies.

In his work, Lynn (2010) provides a useful outline of the expansion of corporate monopoly over the last few decades. He identifies two layers to corporate monopoly. The first layer comprises brand name companies like Coca-Cola, Amazon, Google, Nike, and Apple, which dominate specific product, retail, or service markets. In this layer, monopoly can be derived from brand power (e.g. Coca-Cola's products), or infrastructure/network dominance (e.g. Google's search engine), or "enclave" economies (e.g. Apple's network complementarities between products and services), or intellectual property (e.g. pharmaceutical firms) (Lynn 2010; Keen 2015; Sayer 2015). Below these brand name companies sits a second layer of corporate monopoly comprising (largely) unknown suppliers who make or assemble the products or provide the services sold by brand name companies; an example here would be FoxConn which manufactures Apple products. Lynn (2010) points out that many of these supplier companies are monopolies themselves, manufacturing products or providing services for a number of different and supposedly "competing" brand name companies. In my view, there is another layer that sits on top of these two layers. This third layer comprises the financial institutions that invest in the other two layers (and themselves) (Davis 2008, 2009). It includes huge institutional investors, like the mutual funds Fidelity and Vanguard, which now own a large proportion of the overall corporate debt and equity of other companies. I come back to the implications of this third layer later.

It is possible to make claims about the monopoly power of individual companies; it is also necessary to consider how prevalent monopoly is in the US economy. Such arguments are not new by any means, and stretch back over a century to the days of the Robber Barons in late-19th century America. At that time, the US government introduced anti-monopoly regulations like the 1890 Sherman Antitrust Act in order to enforce competition between companies. As I discuss later, corporate monopoly was condemned by early neoliberals from the 1920s until the 1940s. It was also condemned by progressive and leftist thinkers in the 1950s and 1960s. For example, economists like John Kenneth Galbraith (1952) argued that American capitalism was defined by its oligopolistic character, whilst Marxists like Paul Baran and Paul Sweezy (1966) argued that American capitalism was characterized by a shift to "monopoly capital" based on large corporations. More recently, business scholars like Gerald Davis (2009) argue that large corporate monopolies have waned as financial markets have driven management decision-making. However, this claim only rings true if corporate monopoly has actually declined and, more importantly, if financial companies are discounted as potential monopolists. Issues I turn to next.

In light of Davis's (2009) claim, it is pertinent to ask to what extent corporate monopoly has waxed or waned over the last few decades. Again, the data on these changes exists but it does not seem to be a popular academic concern. Here, I draw on work in the Marxist journal *Monthly Review* and the orthodox economics magazine *The Economist* – writers in both argue that monopoly has increased since the mid-20th century and especially at the start of the 21st century. Starting with Bellamy Foster et al. (2011) in *Monthly Review*, they demonstrate a trend towards rising corporate monopoly in the USA:

- The percentage of manufacturing sectors dominated by the top four companies – defined as those four firms representing 50 percent of "shipment value" – declined from 30 percent in 1947 to 25 percent in 1987, but then rose to 40 percent in 2007.
- The revenues of the top 200 corporations rose from 21 percent in 1950 to around 30 percent in 2008.
- The gross profits of these top 200 corporations also rose from around 13 percent to nearly 30 percent in 2008.

As these data illustrate, the American economy is increasingly concentrated in the hands of large corporations. This is a global trend as well, as Bellamy Foster et al. (2011) illustrate:

- The total revenues of the top 500 global corporations as a percent of global GDP rose from 19 percent in 1960 to 32 percent in 2008.

Others have also analysed this global trend towards corporate monopoly, like the physicists Vitali, Glattfelder, and Battiston (2011). In their research, they show that 737 multinational corporations (MNC) control around 80 percent of the total value of global MNCs, while only 147 control around 40 percent.

It is interesting that *The Economist* – from the other end of the political-economic spectrum, as it were – provides a similar analysis of rising corporate monopoly. A recent report (*The Economist* 2016b) shows that two-thirds of 893 US industrial sectors were more concentrated in 2012 than 1997, by which they meant the share of total revenues accruing to the top four firms had increased. In particular, sectors like (a) IT, Telecoms and Media, (b) Manufacturing, (c) Transportations and Logistics, (d) Retail Trade, and (e) Finance and Insurance had all seen above-average consolidation and concentration (ibid.). The last of these is particularly interesting because it brings me back to Davis's (2009) claims mentioned previously. In some of his other work, Davis (2008) illustrates the extent to which the financial sector now dominates and shapes the US economy. For example, institutional investors (e.g. pension, mutual and insurance funds) owned 72 percent of the US Fortune 1000 in 2005, up from 35 percent in 1980; during the same period, the amount these financial organizations managed rose in absolute terms from US$134 billion to US$10 trillion; and only three institutional investors control around a third of these funds (Davis 2008, pp.15–16). Such concentration of financial assets belies the idea that there are no longer any large corporate monopolies and raises the question of how two companies with the same investor investing in them can or do compete with one another.

Neoliberalism, markets, and corporate monopoly

Having discussed the extent of corporate monopoly, I now want to turn to why this is a conceptual problem for neoliberals and their market-based principles, and how neoliberals have responded to corporate monopoly over time.

Neoliberals and markets

So far in this book I have argued that neoliberalism is a fuzzy concept that is hard to pin down. Its meaning has changed over time, as has its use. It was once used as a self-descriptor, although not consistently or necessarily by or for every branch of neoliberal thought (e.g. Friedrich 1955; Brennetot 2014). Nowadays it has ended up as a largely pejorative term whose meaning has become so broad that it covers an enormous range of topics (Venugopal 2015) – it is used, for example, to describe both the rise of free markets and the expansion of corporate power. Although there might be some examples of people trying to rehabilitate "neoliberal" as a term (see Chapter 4), it is generally used by critics of (free) markets rather than their proponents. In fact, the one area where critics and the object of their ire agree – the common denominator if you like – is the emphasis that these antagonists place on the importance and role of markets as the defining feature of either "neoliberal" understandings of the world (see Chapter 3) or critical understandings of "neoliberalism" (see Chapter 4). On the one side, neoliberals like Hayek (1944 [2001]) and Friedman (1962) argued that free markets – by which they mean competitive ones – are the most efficient *and* therefore moral institutions for organizing society and ensuring social order. On the other side, critics like Bourdieu (1998) and Harvey (2005) argued that neoliberalism is a political project to erase collective action and replace it with (utopian) markets.

Up to now, my approach has been to focus on understanding how others understand neoliberalism, rather than theorize how I understand it. Before I come to the latter, I intend to continue with the former in this section. In this regard, it is important to note that the critical perspectives of neoliberalism generally agree that neoliberalism is some sort of *market-based* or *-centred* "something". Alongside the idea that neoliberalism involves a market-based something (e.g. epistemology, project, process, etc.), critics of neoliberalism now generally agree that it does not entail the erosion or eradication of the state. Instead, critics argue, the state's functions are reconfigured to institute, maintain, and enforce markets and market competition, thereby distinguishing neoliberalism from blunt forms of *laissez-faire*. As such, neoliberals do not see markets as natural, but rather as social constructs (Mirowski 2013). However, neoliberals do naturalize markets as constructions of liberal rights, especially around freedom of contract (see Chapter 8), as well as non-coercive creators of social order, thereby legitimating their extension throughout society.

There are at least two contradictions here worth noting. First, the neoliberal conception of a market-based social order necessitates the thorough and complete spread of markets and market-like thinking into all areas of our lives. As Crouch (2011: 31) argues, markets can only work as imagined by neoliberals if everything is priced so that each person's self-interested choices can lead to an efficient allocation and distribution of resources across society; however, this requires a "common unit of measurement" (i.e. price) in order to coordinate choices through markets. This means no one can choose *not* to participate in markets, reflecting a rather illiberal sentiment. Second, and more pertinent for this chapter, market-based conceptions of social order necessitate that everyone is a *price taker* (i.e. competitor) and not a *price maker* (i.e. monopolist) because the ability to influence market prices obviously distorts the workings of markets and competition. As a result, monopolies are deeply problematic because they enable certain social groups – such as trade unions or large corporations – to distort market signals (i.e. prices) and disrupt market efficiency (p.29). The former contradiction problematizes the normative claims made by neoliberals, but the latter contradiction raises serious questions about the analytical conception of neoliberalism as a market-based "something" in respect to its rehabilitation of corporate monopoly, an issue which I come to next.

Neoliberals and corporate monopoly

Neoliberalism has a fascinating history when it comes to attitudes to business monopoly (Birch 2016a, 2016b). Almost all neoliberals – of whatever school or tradition – were opposed to any form of monopoly – business or otherwise – until the 1950s and 1960s (see Table 6.1 for some examples of these attitudes). Early neoliberals across the board had negative views of corporate monopoly, from Ordoliberals like Alexander Rustow and Wilhelm Ropke through Austrians like Friedrich Hayek to later Chicagoans like Milton Friedman (Peck 2010; Burgin 2012). At that point in time, neoliberals of all stripes thought monopolies – corporate or otherwise – distorted markets and competition, on which their epistemologies and moral claims were based.

This attitude began to change in the 1950s and 1960s as the position of the second Chicago School neoliberals radically shifted. According to the historical research of Rob van Horn (2009, 2011) and van Horn and Mirowski (2009), the reversal of Chicago School attitudes to corporate monopoly resulted from two major research projects undertaken at the University of Chicago in the 1940s and 1950s – the Free Market Study (1946–1952) and Anti-Trust Project (1953–1957), both funded by the Volker Fund. These research projects were not confined to the economics department, but included and were run by academics from the law school (e.g. Aaron Director) and business school (e.g. George Stigler). According to Caldwell (2011), the two projects were meant to examine the legal, regulatory, and institutional conditions necessary to ensure market competition. Their findings, however, suggested that corporate monopoly was less of a problem than initially thought and that market competition would limit its impacts. Subsequently, Chicago School neoliberals came to accept corporate monopoly as "a transitory phenomenon, which will ultimately be eroded by market

Table 6.1 Neoliberal perspectives of corporate monopoly, 1920s–1950s

Person	Quote
Wilhelm Ropke (1923)	Liberals must fight "for the idea of the state and against the lack of freedom in which private economic monopolies – supported by government leading a shadow existence – keep the economy captive"
Jacob Viner (1931)	"Nothing in the history of American business justified undue confidence on the part of the American public that it can trust big business to take care of the community without supervision, regulation or eternal vigilance"
Henry Simons (1934)	"The great enemy of democracy is monopoly, in all its forms: gigantic corporations, trade associations and other agencies for price control, trade unions"
Lionel Robbins (1934)	"The cartelisation of industry, the growth of the strength of trade unions, the multiplication of State controls, have created an economic structure which, whatever its ethical or aesthetic superiority, is certainly much less capable of rapid adaption than was the older more competitive system"
Friedrich Hayek (1944)	"This conclusion is strongly supported by the historical order in which the decline of competition and the growth of monopoly manifested themselves in different countries" (p.52); "the impetus of the movement toward totalitarianism comes mainly from the two great vested interests: organized capital and organized labor"
Milton Friedman (1951)	"It [laissez faire] underestimated the danger that private individuals could through agreement and combination usurp power and effectively limit the freedom of other individuals"

Source: Birch (2015: 36–8).

forces", while Ordoliberals stuck to the position that it is problematic (Siems and Schnyder 2014: 383; also, Gerber 1994).

Apart from denying claims that corporate monopoly was increasing, what these studies in the 1950s led to were numerous attempts to reconcile markets and monopoly – this is especially evident in the law and economics movement originating in the law school at the University of Chicago. According to Davies (2010), of particular importance to this project of reconciliation was the adoption of Ronald Coase's (1937) theory of transaction costs, which enabled a wholesale redefinition of the relationship between the firm and market, as well as reconsideration of the distorting impacts of monopoly on competition. In his theory, for example, Coase characterized markets and firms as part of the same continuum, meaning that the firm and the market can be treated analytically as part of the same process or system – this proved highly influential in the way financial economics defined the firm as a nexus of contracts (see later). Moreover, it meant that monopoly could be redefined as only temporary and subject to being competed away through market competition, and therefore an unimportant issue (Crouch 2011).

It is worth stressing at this point that there is no single historically consistent, analytically precise, or politically enacted conceptualization of markets, competition, or monopoly – as previous chapters illustrate, different players in these debates theorize them very differently (see Chapter 3 for example). Why is this important? Well, a key argument put forward by many critics of neoliberalism is that political-economic ideas – in this case, those primarily concerned with the extension and installation of markets across society – influence political-economic policies and practices. For example, many countries created anti-trust policies precisely because of technical concerns about the impact of monopolies on markets and competition. It was seen as a problem by politicians, commentators, and policymakers, theoretically and practically, and anti-trust regulations were created in order to deal with it. Over the last 30 to 40 years, neoliberal thinkers and politicians – by which I primarily mean people within or influenced by second Chicago and Virginia school traditions – have sought to legitimate and rehabilitate corporate monopoly *specifically* (Davies 2010; Eisinger and Elliott 2016), even though this is at odds with more orthodox assumptions about perfect competition, perfect information, and suchlike in market exchange (see Crouch 2011). My contention is that this Chicagoan version of neoliberalism became popular precisely because it turned to legitimating corporate monopoly, rather than limiting itself to more orthodox conceptions of the market and criticism of monopoly, but it could only do so through a reconceptualization of the corporation, its form, and its governance. It is important, therefore, to understand how the corporation has evolved as an organization and how understandings of its governance have changed as well.

The evolution of corporate form and governance

"Corporate" entities have existed for centuries and the "business corporation" has changed quite significantly over the last 200 years. It is helpful, therefore, to examine the corporation from an historical perspective in order to avoid treating it anachronistically as the same throughout history – something that critical perspectives seem to do quite often (see Chapter 7). However, it is not possible to do this in real depth in this book without veering off into another whole area of research entirely, and so what I write here is, necessarily so, a rather broad-brush analysis. As I argue elsewhere (Birch 2016a, 2016b), the history of the corporation over the last 200 years can be broken into three main eras – see Table 6.2.

First, and as Karl Polanyi (1944 [2001]) argued, the 19th century can be characterized as a form of *proprietary* capitalism dominated by British *laissez-faire*. Certain forms of business enterprise dominated the British economy during this period, namely small- and medium-sized owner-managed firms and partnerships or unincorporated joint stock trusts which acted like partnerships (Gillman and Eade 1995; Guinnane et al. 2007; Cheffins 2008). These firms did not entail a separation of ownership and control, and were part of a highly competitive, mainly familial business tradition; for example, they formed what Arrighi and Silver (1999: 127) call "an ensemble of highly specialized medium-sized firms held together by a complex web of commercial transactions". This era was underpinned by the notion that markets are "self-regulating", although this was more fiction than reality. In this context, a firm's success and failure depended on price competition, which reflected ideas about the market rewarding or punishing managerial decisions (Ireland 2010). As a social order, *laissez-faire* involved a rethinking of the market and economy that was distinct from mercantilism and co-produced with new forms of corporate organization and governance. To put it simplistically, *laissez-faire* was centred on epistemic claims that individual, self-interested action would create social benefits through market interaction (Barkan 2013: 44, 58). These ideas legitimated the argument that large-scale corporate organizations – whether state or quasi-state entities like joint-stock companies – distort markets through collusion and monopoly

Table 6.2   Three eras of corporate capitalism

	Proprietary (pre-1900)	Managerial (1900–1970s)	Neoliberal (1970s onwards)
CORPORATE GOVERNANCE (epistemology)	Market as self-regulating	Market as transaction costs	Market as (nexus of) contracts
	Corporation as fiction, concession	Corporation as real entity	Corporation as aggregation of contracting parties
	Transactions based on market price	Transactions based on historic cost accounting	Transactions based on contracts
CORPORATE FORM (practice)	Key businesses are small- or medium-size partnerships	Key businesses are large, oligopolistic corporations	Key businesses are large, mono-polistic corporations and others
	Businesses controlled through private property	Businesses controlled by securities law	Businesses controlled by contract law
	Business governance based on ownership	Business governance based on separation of management and ownership	Business governance based on shareholder primacy

Source: Birch (2016b).

(see Hessen 1983; Arrighi 1994 [2010]: 21, 252). Consequently, market competition and prices were naturalized as objective forces according to Bratton (1989: 1471), while large-scale organizations were characterized as disrupting this *natural* order.

Second, at the end of the 19th century, British hegemony began its steady decline as the UK was eclipsed by the USA as the result of the so-called "corporate revolution" (Fligstein 1990; Roy 1997). The era that followed has been described as *managerial capitalism* by people like Chandler (1977) and Whitley (1999), and lasted at least until the 1970s. It was characterized by the rise and expansion of large corporate enterprises and a rapprochement between organized labour and business after World War II. Corporations were treated as "real entities" – in contrast to the aggregate/contract view at the end of the 19th century (Bratton 1989; Harris 2006; Gindis 2009).[1] Corporate governance was shifted to securities law as stock markets became the mechanism through which "owners" (i.e. shareholders) and "managers" interacted (Hessen 1983). As a result of their scale and integration, a firm's success or failure ended up driven by new forms of cost accounting and cost-based planning, rather than price competition (Means 1983; Bratton 1989; Miller 1998). New understandings of markets and corporate organization and governance were entangled with the rise and dominance of the large corporation. In part, these ideas legitimated the role and responsibility of corporate managers to society (Khurana 2007), thereby reconciling the concentration of corporate power with the demands of liberal democracy (Bowman 1996). In the American context, this meant promoting rising standards of living through mass production, rising wages linked to rising productivity, and secure employment – although primarily on the basis of gendered household composition (i.e. men work for a wage, women work for free in the home) (Locke and Spender 2011). As a result, *laissez-faire* markets became a thing of the past. These new understandings of capitalism are evident in the work of people like Berle and Means (1932) who analysed the separation of ownership and control characteristic of large corporations. It was also evident in the emergence and expansion of dedicated business schools focused on specific forms of general management (Khurana 2007).

Finally, the 1970s and 1980s witnessed the upheaval of managerial capitalism and its replacement with what I call *neoliberal capitalism* – but what could as easily be defined as *financial capitalism* (Davis 2009). Shareholders, especially large institutional investors, took an increasingly central role in determining corporate form and governance through their decisions in share and capital markets (Lazonick and O'Sullivan 2000). It is an era dominated by the corporation and characterized by an expansion of corporate monopoly, as outlined earlier, legitimated by the "contractual theory" of the firm (Weinstein 2012). Unlike *laissez-faire*, the neoliberal era is underpinned by the idea that markets are constructs of the "presumption of freedom to contract" (Bowman 1996: 171), buttressed and protected by law and regulation from all and sundry (including the state). It is this emphasis on contract and contractual relations – which I come back to in Chapter 8 – that sets the neoliberal era apart from the 19th century. The market is conceived of as a series of contracts – and not price interactions or cost calculations – meaning anything can be re-imagined as part of the market because everything can be configured as a contract (e.g. city garbage collection, emissions reductions, etc.). This helps explain how the corporation can be reframed as merely one end of the spectrum of market(-like) relations. In particular, corporate form and governance were conceptualized as a series of contracts, exemplified by the "nexus of contracts" theory of the firm (Bratton 1989; Weinstein 2012).

Building on the work of Coase (1937), this contractual theory of the firm defines transaction costs as the costs of contracting (e.g. negotiation, enforcement, etc.) which helps to explain the decision either to internalize (in a firm) or to externalize (in a market) economic activity (Eisenberg 1999). Most closely associated with financial economists like Jensen and Meckling (1976) and Fama (1970, 1980), this theory has come to legitimate the corporation as nothing more than a nexus of contracting parties (e.g. investors, managers, workers, suppliers, etc.). Obviously, this involves a number of assumptions: "Contractual relations are the essence of firms" (Jensen and Meckling 1976: 310); the separation of ownership and control entails an "agency problem" because managers need incentives to run corporations for the benefit of shareholders (Fama 1980; Shleifer and Vishny 1997); public stock markets are efficient information processors (Fama 1970); and stock markets represent a "market for control" that enables shareholders to punish managers (Jensen and Meckling 1976). There are conceptual problems with this understanding, not least of which is the different conceptions of "contract" in economic theories – i.e. "reciprocal arrangement" – and in law – i.e. "legally enforceable promise" (Eisenberg 1999: 822–3; see also Chapter 8). As a way of understanding the corporation, however, these ideas helped to legitimate a particular imaginary, legal form, and governance of the corporation that was distinct from managerial and proprietary capitalism before it, and which began to dominate in the 1980s. It jettisoned the last remaining reservations about the problems with the economic concentration of power represented by large, oligopolistic or monopolistic business entities.

Finance, financial economics, and the neoliber, corporation

I now want to examine financial economics as a form that legitimates and reconciles the contradictions between corporate monopoly and conceptions of (free) markets in neoliberal capitalism. Financial economics emerged during the 1960s and 1970s with the work of neoclassical economists on the firm. However, these economists were largely based in business schools rather than economics departments. The epistemological basis of financial economics is the pricing of investment assets (e.g. share values) and corporate financing (e.g. a firm's sources of capital); its normative basis is the assumption that capital owners (i.e. investors) are the best people to determine the allocation of capital (i.e. investment), and not corporate managers (Styhre 2014). As such, financial economics is focused on increasing share values for investors through shaping the actions of managers. The normative assumption is somewhat tautological in that it assumes the market is the best mechanism for allocating capital because capital owners are the best allocators – leaving aside the question for now about who actually "owns" the capital (e.g. institutions or savers). Financial economics dominates corporate governance today, at least in Anglo-American economies, and legitimates a particular form of corporate governance in which "shareholder value" maximization is the (only) end goal (Lazonick and O'Sullivan 2000; Engelen 2002). That does not mean there are no alternatives, in form or legitimation (see Stout 2012).

Two elements of financial economics underpin this legitimisation of shareholder value. First, in his work Eugene Fama (1970: 383) argued that (public share) markets are inherently efficient in that "prices provide accurate signals for resource allocation" to investors – not to firms, it is important to highlight. This "efficient market hypothesis" (EMH) underpins the later theoretical contributions of people like Jensen and Meckling. EMH implies that markets prices are, by definition and nature, accurate reflections of underlying value; that is, share prices reflect all the information that investors know about a firm, which is a reflection of its real value (or earnings potential). However, Whitley (1986: 176) points out that "No empirical 'finding' about investor behaviour could demonstrate the truth or falsity of the EMH because it does not state what 'all relevant information' consists of". Second, the work of Jensen and Meckling (1976) on the theory of the firm has been influential in legitimating a particular form of corporate governance (see Shleifer and Vishny 1997 for review). In their work, Jensen and Meckling emphasized the "principal-agent problem" – leading to *agency theory* being used to refer to their perspective – by which they meant that managers need to have their interests aligned with "owners" (i.e. shareholders) (Dobbin and Jung 2010). From this agency perspective, the only goal for managers is to increase share value because it is difficult to balance more than one goal.

Agency theory was a response to the separation of ownership and control characteristic of large corporations. People like Fama (1980), for example, argued that corporate form and governance involved significant "agency costs"; that is, managers can exploit their insider knowledge to their benefit and the detriment of the owners. Agency theory was meant to correct that problem, although it made certain assumptions. First, it assumes that the firm is merely and only a nexus of contracting parties, building on Coase's (1937) earlier work on the theory of the firm. This meant that Jensen and Meckling (1976: 311) could define the firm as a market in another form: "In this sense the 'behavior' of the firm is like the behavior of the market; i.e., the outcome of a complex equilibrium process". Second, following on from the last point, it assumes that the firm does not really exist because it is a "legal fiction" and, therefore, it has no responsibilities. Third, the focus on investors and investor returns means that Jensen and Meckling can argue that "the existence of monopoly will not increase agency costs" and competition "will not eliminate the agency costs" (1976: 330) because it is investors that really determine the most efficient allocation of capital. Finally, in this way, they theorize away the problem of corporate monopoly; rather, agency costs are defined as the real problem because they stop investors (i.e. capital owners) reallocating their money more efficiently (i.e. from lower value investment to higher value ones).

The valuation of investments and assets is central to financial economics, meaning that it is bound up with accounting principles and practices. As Styhre (2014: 63) notes, all sorts of political-economic actors require training in finance in order for these assumptions to legitimate corporate monopoly. For example, managers, investors, analysts, brokers, etc. all need to share a similar understanding of value as market price and similar evaluation practices to assess tangible and intangible assets. It is interesting to note, therefore, that financial economics and especially the EMH "says remarkably little about market valuation processes" according to Whitley (1986: 175–6; also, see Power 2010).

Following up this point, Whitley argues that the threat of legal action – based on agency theory – against managers by investors led many managers to seek new forms of valuation in order to legitimate their own decisions, leading to a massive expansion of new valuation models (e.g. fair value accounting – Ronen 2008). Although these new models may claim to be "market-based", this does not mean they are based on a market transaction or market price. Rather, according to Power (2010), the idea of market-based valuation that underpins these new models (e.g. fair value accounting) does not entail a market valuation per se (i.e. sale). Instead it involves an expert judgement of value, thereby "shifting the focus from transactions to economic valuation methods", which helps to "embed further the principle of fair value accounting as the '*mirror*' of the market" (my emphasis) (p.201, 205). As Bignon et al. (2009: 11) argue, this means that fair value "is based more on the estimates of certified experts than on the current market price" and that "Values do not passively reflect the 'objectivity' of the market, but are the product of a measurement technology that, by demarcating and measuring resources, assists in the construction of the marketability of assets" (Napier and Power 1992: 87). This therefore explains how these ideas can legitimate corporate monopoly – since it is no longer necessary to derive value from market transactions (i.e. sale), value and valuation can be done via expert and *as if* calculations of "market" value that side-step any need to worry about the distorting power of corporate monopoly. As such, these neoliberal ideas underpinning corporate form and governance do away with the very need for market exchange at all.

Reproducing neoliberalism through the business school

The reason that the legitimation of corporate monopoly in financial economics is important is that it should move our focus away from the discipline of economics and towards business schools because this is where managers, investors, analysts, traders, market experts, and others (i.e. experts) receive their training – or indoctrination. My contention is that neoliberalism – if we want to use such a term at all – is reproduced in business schools through the acquisition of these legitimating knowledges and practices, which embed a particular set of assumptions about how to understand the firm (i.e. as a market) in con-tradiction with practices about how to value the firm (i.e. as "mirror" of a market). Although it is possible to see the (re-)orientation of business schools around financial economics as a neutral project based on new forms of economic knowledge, the resulting focus on pushing both free markets and corporate interests was not done in political isolation. For example, the now (in)famous 1971 Lewis Powell Memo to the US Chamber of Commerce, titled *Attack on American Free Enterprise System*, specifically suggested that the "Chamber should enjoy a particular rapport with the increasingly influential graduate schools of business" in order to support "Corporate America". Although this enrolment of business schools in support of corporate power is not the focus of this chapter, it does highlight the need to examine the role of the business school as a site of knowledge production in the reproduction of neoliberalism (see Khurana 2007; Dunne et al. 2008; Harney 2009; Henisz 2011; Locke and Spender 2011; Nik-Khah 2011; Styhre 2014; Birch 2016b).

Business schools first emerged in countries like the USA at the end of the 19th century, as the corporate revolution transformed the economy. According to Khurana (2007: 4), business schools played an important role in legitimating the role and activities of large corporations through the creation of a "managerial class that would run America's large corporations in a way that served the broader interests of society rather the narrowly defined ones of capital and labor". Thus, business schools helped legitimate the shift from proprietary to managerial capitalism (Whitley 1999). This led to what Locke and Spender (2011: x–xi) – and others – have called *managerialism*, or the emergence of a professional group (i.e. managers) who seek and acquire systematic control over (corporate) decision-making to the exclusion of others (e.g. shareholders, workers). Managerialism differs from *laissez-faire* because it is not centred on cut-throat market competition, but rather on cost and resource efficiencies in the pursuit of productivity, all based on supposedly technocratic and scientific decision-making (p.6). Up until the mid-20th century, business school curricula and pedagogy was dominated by these practical goals and was taught more by practitioners (i.e. business people) rather than academics (Fourcade and Khurana 2011). Towards the end of the 1950s, the managerial perspective started to lose its place in business education. At this point, there was a concerted effort to transform business and management into more technical and academic disciplines, especially through the incorporation of statistical modelling and quantitative methodologies. This change resulted from the demands of government planning, especially the development of operations research during World War II and the alliance of the state and business in response to the Cold War (Locke and Spender 2011), as well as the actions of philanthropic foundations like the Ford and Carnegie Fou These foundations sought to "professionalize" and "scienu.. ness school education through funding specific research and teaching programmes (Khurana 2007; Henisz 2011). These demands led to the incorporation and integration of a particular form of (financial) economics into business school curricula, which has had several important consequences.

One of the most important business schools at the centre of the reproduction of neoliberalism was and is Chicago. Usually, people focus on economics, like Chicago's famous economics department (e.g. Peck 2010), but Chicago's Graduate School of Business is just as important (Fourcade and Khurana 2011; Nik-Khah 2011). Business schools like Chicago's became increasingly dominated by financial economics, which reproduced certain epistemological and normative assumptions about business and business practices. According to Henisz (2011: 302), for example, "agency theory and models of asset pricing" that underpin financial economics have isolated other social scientific approaches in business schools. Moreover, business schools have "reinforced and diffused the belief system [in efficient markets, shareholder value, etc.] to traders, fund managers, analysts and managers" around the world (p.304). This process started with the integration of neoclassical economics into business schools in the 1950s, but gained a real hold in the 1970s with the emergence of financial economics and its influence on corporate governance. Henisz (2011) argues that this work ultimately embedded a "culture of selfishness" in business schools.

It is also important to remember that business schools do more than reproduce knowledge claims. They also train students in business ideas and practices, thereby disseminating the assumptions that underpin fields like financial economics. Business schools train and release an increasingly large number of undergraduate and graduate students every year. The huge increase in number of students taking business degrees is reflected in the growing *proportion* of all students who study business and management courses at university. For example, Harney (2009: 318) claims that "one in eight university undergraduates in Britain [are] studying business and management". By 2014 this was one in seven students, as data in Figure 6.1 illustrates. This graph also shows the rising popularity of business degrees, which is the most popular degree program in the UK. In the US context, Khurana (2007: 338) provides data on the number of American MBA programmes, which rose from 138 in 1955–1956 to 955 in 2003–2004. As Khurana

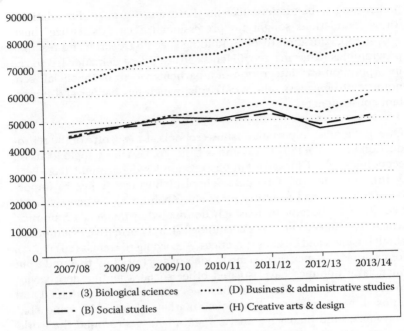

Source: HESA, https://www.hesa.ac.uk/news/12-02-2015/biology-business-and-maths-degrees, accessed 24 April 2017.

Figure 6.1   Four most popular undergraduate degrees in UK, 2007–2014

notes, the range in quality of these programmes is often significant, as are the benefits to students in their careers. In terms of total student numbers in the USA, those graduating with a business degree reached 266,000 undergraduates in 2001 and 120,000 MBAs in 2006, according to Fourcade and Khurana (2011).

Consequently, the influence of business schools is increasingly felt in the wider economy and society as more and more people enter the workforce after being exposed to a set of assumptions that promote specific business ideas and practices; for example, beliefs about agency costs, shareholder value, about incentives, about opportunity costs, and so on (Dobbin and Jung 2010). The careers that business students go into has diversified as well since the 1960s, meaning that these ideas and practices spread beyond the confines of corporate entities. For example, by the 1980s over 50 percent of students graduating from Harvard Business School went into consulting and finance rather than general management (Khurana 2007: 328). These employment growth areas – e.g. consulting, finance, investment banking, etc. – reflected broader political-economic trends like the growth of institutional investment (Whitley 1986), leading to an expansion of *finance*-minded employees across the economy. As Dobbin and Jung (2010) note, people trained in financial economics at business schools now work both inside *and* outside of businesses enterprises, especially in the financial intermediation sector which analyses, values, and assesses the performance of non-financial businesses. As a result, the focus on shareholder value that is embedded in financial economics has ended up providing managers, investors, analysts, government, and others with a single, simple indicator to work with, rather than more complex objectives like social responsibility, employment creation, quality of life, community sustainability, and such like.

Conclusion

My aim in this chapter was to raise the contradiction within neoliberalism itself and within critical analyses of neoliberalism around the notion that it is a market-based *something* – era, project, governmentality, epistemology, process, etc. – especially as this contrasts with the dominance of the corporation and corporate monopoly in our economies. There is a *problem* of the corporation in our understandings of neoliberalism that is not easily theorized away, even though that is exactly what (certain) neoliberals themselves sought to do in their legitimation of corporate monopoly.

I started by exploring the extent and importance of corporate monopoly in contemporary society, focusing on the USA. It is evident that the US economy is increasingly dominated by fewer and fewer large corporate entities, not simply in particular market sectors (e.g. dishwashers, cellphones, dog food, etc.), but across several layers of the economy (i.e. brand name retailers, unknown suppliers, and financial investors). There are practical implications from this concentration, not least of which is rising consumer prices (Eisinger and Elliott 2016), which we need to bear in mind. Neoliberals *should* see such monopolies as a threat to market competition, and they all did at one point in time (i.e. pre-1950s). However, the American schools of neoliberalism reversed their position on corporate monopoly during the 1950s and 1960s, ending up supporting it as a boon for consumer welfare (Crouch 2011), seeing it as an unnecessary concern since markets would erode it

), and re-imagining and reframing the firm as a market ' – i.e. a nexus of contracts (Birch 2016a, 2016b). The ation here is the need for critics of neoliberalism to of business knowledge, education, and practice that are often obscured in prevailing notions of neoliberalism as a market-based *something*. As I showed, business schools and business education play an important role in legitimating and reproducing corporate monopoly, in the name of markets.

My general argument in this chapter, and elsewhere (Birch 2015), is that neoliberals, through their theories and models, followed wider political-economic trends in society, rather than driving them as many critics argue. In particular, neoliberal theories have accommodated the rise of finance, the dominance of big business, the dismantling of anti-trust regulation, and such like, not because neoliberals were and are epistemically supportive of such things; rather, neoliberals saw and see the tactical (and personal) benefits of adapting themselves and their ideas to these wider trends. Neoliberalism, if we want to stick with such a term, is a parasitic epistemic and normative order, hitching itself to dominant social forces and institutions, providing them with a legitimating discourse, rather than coherent and consistent approach to installing markets across society.

Note

1 This evolution is too complex to really discuss here, so I can only point out a few aspects of this process as outlined by Harris (2006). First, the aggregate/contract view was specific to the US because of the emphasis on *contractual* relations (p.1468); this is something I discuss later in relation to neoliberalism. Second, the aggregate/contract view "could not be squared with the limited liability attribute of business corporations" because if corporations are mere aggregates of their shareholders then there is no reason why those same shareholders should receive liability protection (p.1470). This meant it did not survive very long before being replaced by real entity theory. Finally, real entity theory, which was partially derived from German legal concepts, enabled managers to claim control over corporate activities to the exclusion of shareholders (p.1474).

Bibliography

Arrighi, G. (1994 [2010]), *The Long Twentieth Century*, London: Verso.
Arrighi, G. and Silver, B. (1999), *Chaos and Governance in the Modern World System*, Minneapolis, MN: University of Minnesota Press.
Baran, P. and Sweezy, P. (1966), *Monopoly Capital*, New York, NY: Monthly Review Press.

Barkan, J. (2013), *Corporate Sovereignty*, Minneapolis, MN: University of Minnesota Press.

Bellamy Foster, J., McChesney, R. and Jonna, R. (2011), "Monopoly and competition in twenty-first century capitalism", *Monthly Review*, 62(11), accessed 19 November 2016 at http://monthlyreview.org/2011/04/01/monopoly-and-competition-in-twenty-first-cen tury-capitalism.

Berle, A. and Means, G. (1932), *The Modern Corporation and Private Property*, New York, NY: Macmillan.

Bignon, V., Biondi, Y. and Ragot, X. (2009), *An Economic Analysis of Fair Value*, Cournot Centre for Economic Studies: Prisme no.15.

Birch, K. (2015), *We Have Never Been Neoliberal: A Manifesto for a Doomed Youth*, Winchester, UK: Zero Books.

Birch, K. (2016a), "Market vs. contract? The implications of contractual theories of corporate governance to the analysis of neoliberalism", *ephemera: theory & politics in organization*, 16(1), 107–33.

Birch, K. (2016b), "Financial economics and business schools: legitimating corporate monopoly, reproducing neoliberalism?", in S. Springer, K. Birch and J. MacLeavy (eds), *The Handbook of Neoliberalism*, London: Routledge, pp. 320–30.

Birch, K., Peacock, M., Wellen, R., Hossein, C., Scott, S. and Salazar, A. (2016), *Business and Society: A Critical Introduction*, London: Zed Books.

Bourdieu, P. (1998), "The Essence of Neoliberalism", *Le Monde Diplomatique*, December, accessed 16 November 2016 at http://mondediplo.com/1998/12/08bourdieu.

Bowman, S. (1996), *The Modern Corporation and American Political Thought*, University Park, PA: Pennsylvania State University Press.

Bratton, W. (1989), "The new economic theory of the firm: critical perspectives from history", *Stanford Law Review*, 41, 1471–527.

Brennetot, A. (2014), "Geohistory of 'neoliberalism': rethinking the meanings of a malleable and shifting intellectual label", *Cybergeo: European Journal of Geography*, article 677, accessed 1 October 2016 at http://cybergeo.revues.org/26324.

Brown, W. (2015), *Undoing the Demos*, New York, NY: Zone Books.

Burgin, A. (2012), *The Great Persuasion*, Cambridge, MA: Harvard University Press.

Caldwell, B. (2011), "Hayek, Chicago, and Neoliberalism", in R. van Horn, P. Mirowski and T. Stapleford (eds), *Building Chicago Economics*, Cambridge: Cambridge University Press, pp. 301–34.

Chandler, A. (1977), *The Visible Hand*, Cambridge, MA: Belknap Press.

Cheffins, B. (2008), *Corporate Ownership and Control*, Oxford: Oxford University Press.

Coase, R. (1937), "The nature of the firm", *Economica*, 4(16), 386–405.

Crouch, C. (2011), *The Strange Non-Death of Neoliberalism*, Cambridge: Polity Press.

Davies, W. (2010), "Economics and the 'nonsense' of law: the case of the Chicago antitrust revolution", *Economy and Society*, 39, 64–83.

Davis, G. (2008), "A new finance capitalism? Mutual funds and ownership re-concentration in the United States", *European Management Review*, 5, 11–21.

Davis, G. (2009), *Managed by the Markets*, Oxford: Oxford University Press.

Deakins, D. and Freel, M. (2012), *Entrepreneurship and Small Firms*, London: McGraw-Hill.

Dean, M. (2014), "Rethinking neoliberalism", *Journal of Sociology*, 50(2), 150–63.

Dobbin, F. and Jung, J. (2010), "The misapplication of Mr Michael Jensen: how agency theory brought down the economy and why it might again", in M. Lounsbury and P. Hirsch (eds), *Markets on Trial*, Bingley, UK: Emerald, pp. 29–64.

Dunne, S., Harney, S., Parker, M. and Tinker, T. (2008), "Discussing the role of the business school", *ephemera: theory & politics in organization*, 8, 271–93.

Engelen, E. (2002), "Corporate governance, property and democracy: a conceptual critique of shareholder ideology", *Economy and Society*, 31, 391–413.

Eisenberg, M. (1999), "The conception that the corporation is a nexus of contracts, and the dual nature of the firm", *Journal of Corporation Law*, 24, 819–36.

Eisinger, J. and Elliott, J. (2016), "These professors make more than a thousand bucks an hour peddling mega-mergers", propublicca.org, 16 November, accessed 19 November 2016 at https://www.propublica.org/article/these-professors-make-more-than-thousand-bucks-hour-peddling-mega-mergers.

Fama, E. (1970), "Efficient capital markets: a review of theory and empirical work", *Journal of Finance*, 25, 383–417.

Fama, E. (1980), "Agency problems and the theory of the firm", *Journal of Political Economy*, 88, 288–307.

Fligstein, N. (1990), *The Transformation of Corporate Control*, Cambridge: Harvard University Press.

Fourcade, M. and Khurana, R. (2011), *From Social Control to Financial Economics: The Linked Ecologies of Economics and Business in Twentieth Century America*, Harvard Business School: Working Paper 11–071.

Fourcade, M., Ollion, E. and Algan, Y. (2014), *The Superiority of Economists*, Paris: MaxPo Discussion Paper No.14/3.

Friedman, M. (1962), *Capitalism and Freedom*, Chicago, IL: University of Chicago Press.

Friedrich, C. (1955), "The political thought of neo-liberalism", *The American Political Science Review*, 49(2), 509–25.

Galbraith, J.K. (1952), *American Capitalism: The Concept of Countervailing Power*, Boston, MA: Houghton Mifflin.

Gerber, D. (1994), "Constitutionalizing the economy: German neoliberalism, competition law and the 'new' Europe", *The American Journal of Comparative Law*, 42, 25–84.

Gillman, M. and Eade, T. (1995), "The development of the corporation in England, with emphasis on limited liability", *International Journal of Social Economics*, 22(4), 20–32.

Gindis, D. (2009), "From fictions and aggregates to real entities in the theory of the firm", *Journal of Institutional Economics*, 5(1), 25–46.

Guinnane, T., Harris, R., Lamoreaux, N. and Rosenthal, J.-L. (2007), "Putting the corporation in its place", *Enterprise and Society*, 8(3), 687–729.

Harney, S. (2009), "Extreme neo-liberalism: an introduction", *ephemera: theory & politics in organization*, 9, 318–29.

Harris, R. (2006), "The transplantation of the legal discourse on corporate personality theories: from German codification to British political pluralism to American big business", *Washington and Lee Law Review*, 63(4), 1421–78.

Harvey, D. (2005), *A Brief History of Neoliberalism*, Oxford: Oxford University Press.

Hayek, F. (1944 [2001]), *The Road to Serfdom*, London: Routledge.

Henisz, W. (2011), "Leveraging the financial crisis to fulfill the promise of progressive management", *Academy of Management Learning and Education*, 10, 298–321.

Hessen, R. (1983), "The modern corporation and private property: a reappraisal", *Journal of Law and Economics*, 26, 273–89.

Hodgson, G. (2005), "Knowledge at work: some neoliberal anachronisms", *Review of Social Economy*, 63(4), 547–65.

Ireland, P. (2010), "Limited liability, shareholder rights and the problem of corporate irresponsibility", *Cambridge Journal of Economics*, 34, 837–56.

Jensen, M. and Meckling, W. (1976), "Theory of the firm: managerial behavior, agency costs and ownership structure", *Journal of Financial Economics*, 3, 305–60.

Keen, A. (2015), *The Internet Is Not the Answer*, New York, NY: Atlantic Monthly Press.

Khurana, R. (2007), *From Higher Sims to Hired Hands*, Princeton, NJ: Princeton University Press.

Klein, N. (2007), *Shock Doctrine*, Toronto, ON: Vintage Canada.

Lazonick, W. and O'Sullivan, M. (2000), "Maximizing shareholder value: a new ideology for corporate governance", *Economy and Society*, 29, 13–35.

Locke, R. and Spender, J.-C. (2011), *Confronting Managerialism*, London: Zed Books.

Lynn, B.C. (2010), *Cornered*, New York, NJ: John Wiley & Sons.

Means, G. (1983), "Power in the marketplace", *Journal of Law and Economics*, 26(2), 467–85.

Miller, P. (1998), "The margins of accounting", in M. Callon (ed.), *The Laws of the Markets*, Cambridge: Basil Blackwell, pp. 174–93.

Mirowski, P. (2013), *Never Let a Serious Crisis Go to Waste*, London: Verso.

Napier, C. and Power, M. (1992), "Professional research, lobbying and intangibles: a review essay", *Accounting and Business Research*, 23, 85–95.

Nik-Khah, E. (2011), "George Stigler, the Graduate School of Business, and the pillars of the Chicago School", in R. van Horn, P. Mirowski and T. Stapleford (eds), *Building Chicago Economics: New Perspectives on the History of America's Most Powerful Economics Program*, New York, NY: Cambridge University Press, pp. 116–47.

Peck, J. (2010), *Constructions of Neoliberal Reason*, Oxford: Oxford University Press.

Polanyi, K. (1944 [2001]), *The Great Transformation*, Boston, MA: Beacon Press.

Power, M. (2010), "Fair value accounting, financial economics and the transformation of reliability", *Accounting and Business Research*, 40, 197–210.

Ronen, J. (2008), "To fair value or not to fair value: a broader perspective", *Abacus*, 44, 181–208.

Roy, W. (1997), *Socializing Capital*, Princeton, NJ: Princeton University Press.

Sayer, A. (2015), *Why We Can't Afford the Rich*, Bristol: Policy Press.

Shleifer, A. and Vishny, R. (1997), "A survey of corporate governance", *Journal of Finance*, 52, 737–83.

Siems, M. and Schnyder, G. (2014), "Ordoliberal lessons for economic stability: different kinds of regulation, not more regulation", *Governance*, 27(3), 377–96.

Simons, H. (1991), "Organizations and markets", *Journal of Economic Perspectives*, 5, 25–44.

Stout, L. (2012), *The Shareholder Value Myth*, San Francisco, CA: Berrett-Koehler Publishers.

Styhre, A. (2014), *Management and Neoliberalism*, London: Routledge.

The Economist (2016a), "Management theory is becoming a compendium of dead ideas", 17 December, accessed 20 December 2016 at http://www.economist.com/news/business/21711909-what-martin-luther-did-catholic-church-needs-be-done-business-gurus-management?fsrc=scn/fb/te/bl/ed/managementtheoryisbecomingacompendiumofdeadideas.

The Economist (2016b), "Too much of a good thing", 26 May, accessed 16 November 2016 at http://www.economist.com/news/briefing/21695385-profits-are-too-high-america-needs-giant-dose-competition-too-much-good-thing.

van Horn, R. (2009), "Reinventing monopoly and corporations: the roots of Chicago law and economics", in P. Mirowski and D. Plehwe (eds), *The Road from Mont Pèlerin: The Making of the Neoliberal Thought Collective*, Cambridge MA: Harvard University Press, pp. 204–37.

van Horn, R. (2011), "Chicago's shifting attitude toward concentrations of business power (1934–1962)", *Seattle University Law Review*, 34, 1527–44.

van Horn, R. and Mirowski, P. (2009), "The rise of the Chicago School of Economics and the birth of neoliberalism", in P. Mirowski and D. Plehwe (eds), *The Road from Mont Pèlerin: The Making of the Neoliberal Thought Collective*, Cambridge MA: Harvard University Press, pp. 139–78.

Venugopal, R. (2015), "Neoliberalism as concept", *Economy and Society*, 44(2), 165–87.

Vitali, S., Glattfelder, J. and Battiston, S. (2011), "The network of global corporate control", *PLoS ONE*, 6(1), e25995.

Weinstein, O. (2012), "Firm, property and governance: from Berle and Means to the agency theory, and beyond", *Accounting, Economics, and Law*, 2(2), 1–55.

Whitley, R. (1986), "The transformation of business finance into financial economics: the role of academic expansion and changes in US capital markets", *Accounting, Organizations and Society*, 11, 171–92.

Whitley, R. (1999), *Divergent Capitalism*, Oxford: Oxford University Press.

7 From entrepreneurship to rentiership in neoliberalism

Introduction

As I argue in the last chapter, there is a contradiction in "neoliberalism" – as an epistemology, process, project, or otherwise – between the valorisation of competition as the most efficient and moral way to organize society *and* the political-economic dominance of the corporate form and corporate monopoly. Neoliberal – or pro-market – thinkers, especially economists working in business and law schools, legitimate this contradiction by arguing that the business organization (i.e. firm) merely reflects market competition in another guise (e.g. Coase 1937; Jensen and Meckling 1976; Fama 1980). As such, and as Geoffrey Hodgson (1999: 169, 175) notes, these thinkers have largely theorized away any distinction between market competition and business organization by placing an emphasis "on pure exchange rather than on production and its peculiarities" and by imagining "markets all around them, including within firms". The primary way these thinkers have done this is through an analytical-normative claim that capital owners – that is, "investors" – are the people best able to allocate capital efficiently because they, as the owners of capital, have greatest interest in receiving the highest return on its use (Styhre 2014). As long as there are investors, either market competition or business organization will produce the most efficient and moral outcomes as those investors search for the highest returns on their investment. As noted, all of this reflects the position of neoliberal thinkers, like Gary Becker and Richard Posner (who I discussed in Chapter 3), that everything is already a market.

It is noticeable, however, that many critical approaches to neoliberalism tend to ignore the implications of this theoretical sleight of hand, focusing instead on the supposed effects of (free) markets on social life – there are obvious exceptions (e.g. Crouch 2011; Dean 2011). Within critical approaches to neoliberalism, the clearest example of this ambivalence towards the firm is found in the conceptualization of neoliberalism as a subjectivity underpinned by entrepreneurship, especially the transformation of individuals into "entrepreneurs of the self" (e.g. Foucault 2008). A more recent take on this is the idea that individuals themselves are transformed – or transform themselves – into business enterprises (e.g. Dardot and Laval 2014; Brown 2015). Basing their analysis on Gary Becker's work on human capital, these critics argue that individuals are incentivized to think of and treat themselves as "investment" opportunities. For example, if you learn a new skill or gain a new educational qualification then these can be characterized as ways to increase your own human capital, which is conceived as a productive resource that you own, can use, and can sell for a wage. Whether or not human capital theory – or any other notion of "capital" outside of political economy, like social capital – is analytically and normatively unproblematic is another question, one that seems to be ignored in the critical literature. For example, Hodgson (2014) specifically argues that human capital cannot be treated like "monetary" capital (i.e. money) because it cannot be treated as collateral.

To me, it looks like this critical understanding of neoliberalism is built on the adoption of the analytical and normative claims of neoliberal thinkers themselves, in assuming that market competition has infiltrated our lives, identities, and subjectivities with little effective agency on our part to resist or subvert this process (cf. Barnett 2009). It would seem that this perspective is a consequence of drawing on Michel Foucault's analysis of neoliberalism, which some have argued is sympathetic, or at least ambivalent, towards neoliberal ideas (Becker et al. 2012). Or, at the very least, it could be because the critical literature seems often to be based on an acceptance of the claims of neoliberal – or orthodox – economic theory, especially the idea that everything is already a market and, therefore, directed and governed by market competition, rather than business organization. As such, it is unsurprising that there is such an emphasis on *entrepreneurship* – conceived as the creative and productive response to market signals and incentives – in this critical literature, especially "of the self" in the transformation of our beliefs and behaviours into subjects of market competition. In my view, this represents the second contradiction underlying the assumption that the world is already a market, and one which I want to problematize in this chapter.

Much like neoliberalism, the term "entrepreneurial" gets thrown around a lot in academic debate by scholars critical of (free) markets. The word pops up in relation to "states", "nations" and "countries", "strategies", "projects", and other social relations, places processes, and so on. For example, human geographers Harvey (2005) and Jamie Peck (2010) use the term to der ticular kind of place-based governance. Harvey (1989) uses the idea of "urban entrepreneurialism" to outline the transformation in urban governance since the 1970s, which Peck (2010) uses in his critique of Richard Florida's "creative cities" programme. This has led others, like Roger Keil (2016), to theorize the "neoliberal city". It is also used by Foucauldian scholars like Dardot and Laval (2014) and Brown (2015) to conceptualize a particular form of "entrepreneurial governmentality" that shapes our individual choices, actions, and behaviours; that is, our very "self", hence why they write about neoliberalism leading to people becoming "entrepreneurs of the self" (Foucault 2008). As such, entrepreneurialism and entrepreneurship have become very closely aligned with neoliberalism, and are frequently used in conjuncture with it. However, its popularity raises questions about its use and the meaning ascribed to it, especially in relation to the conceptualization of entrepreneurship by neoliberal thinkers. In this chapter, I want to problematize its use in describing and explaining the transformation of individual subjectivities as suggested by the likes of Dardot and Laval (2014), Brown (2015), and other Foucauldians.

My contention is that neither our economies nor our subjectivities have been transformed by neoliberalism into sites or centres of entrepreneurship or entrepreneurialism. Rather, neoliberalism – which I still use for want of a better term – is underpinned by forms of *rentiership*, or the (unproductive) appropriation of value through fiat (e.g. laws, regulations, standards), monopoly rights (e.g. intellectual property rights), and organizational configurations (e.g. network externalities, business models). I start the chapter by discussing the way entrepreneurship is theorized in "neoliberal" thought, before seeing how critical approaches deploy the concept. Then I discuss the problems with theorizing neoliberalism as entrepreneurship (of the self or otherwise) and highlight the role of the rentier in contemporary capitalism. I conclude with some of the implications of my analysis.

Entrepreneurship in neoliberal thought

Entrepreneurship is a tricky concept to pin down. According to Deakins and Freel (2012), which I draw on in the rest of this paragraph, there are a number of ways to conceptualize entrepreneurship, including: (1) economics approaches, (2) psychological approaches, and (3) social-behavioural approaches. First, early economics thinkers, like the French *physiocrats* for example, considered entrepreneurs to be people who found new ways to organize the factors of production (land, labour, money) and thereby act as key agents of economic change and development. Later economics theorists of entrepreneurship included people like Frank Knight, Joseph Schumpeter, Friedrich Hayek, and Israel Kirzner, who I consider in more detail later because of their association with various neoliberal traditions. Second, psychological approaches tend to emphasize personality traits like risk-taking, confidence, autonomy, and creativity, primarily because certain kinds of people are associated with certain kinds of activity (e.g. starting up a firm, making new markets, etc.). Third, social-behavioural approaches tend to stress things like social and cultural context; for example, particular cultures (e.g. USA) might provide more incentive to pursue entrepreneurial activities than other cultures (e.g. UK) because they are more tolerant of failure.

For the rest of this section I am going to focus on "neoliberal" conceptions of entrepreneurship (Eagleton-Pierce 2016). If the first Chicago School is considered as a neoliberal tradition, then one of the earliest thinkers on the subject was Frank Knight (1921 [2006]) in his book *Risk, Uncertainty and Profit*. In Knight's view, the entrepreneur is someone whose "role is to improve knowledge, especially foresight, and bear the incidence of its limitations [i.e. risk]" (p.xii). In his treatment of uncertainty, Knight identified it "as the central obstacle to rational economic behavior" and that it could be "reduced by grouping like instances" (Kreitner 2007: 149). In this way, entrepreneurs are people who deal with uncertainty by combining the preferences of individual consumers and thereby "foresee the wants of a multitude with more ease and accuracy" (Knight 1921 [2006]: 241). A Knightian entrepreneur is a risk-taker, whether they are establishing a new firm, or making a new market, or introducing a new production process, etc. They perform an important economic role by increasing knowledge and, thereby, foresight of future demand or opportunities. Another early thinker was Ronald Coase, who joined Chicago University's law school in 1964. He was and is known for his work on the theory of the firm. According to Coase (1937), the firm represents the replacement of market transactions with an "entrepreneur-co-ordinator, who directs production" (p.388), meaning that entrepreneurship involves an alternative process for the coordination of production than markets and market competition.

Entrepreneurship is most closely associated with the Austrian School of economics, although not always with its neoliberal wing. On the non-neoliberal side sit people like Joseph Schumpeter (1942 [2008]), who has been enormously influential in shaping modern conceptions of innovation and entrepreneurship. According to Schumpeter:

> the function of entrepreneurs is to reform or revolutionize the pattern of production by exploiting an invention or, more generally, an untried technological possibility for producing a new commodity or producing an old one in a new way, by opening up a new source of supply of materials or a new outlet for products, by reorganizing an industry and so on. (p.132)

As Eagleton-Pierce (2016) notes, Schumpeter's theory of entrepreneurship is based on a "heroic" model in which individual people – in Schumpeter's early work – or individual firms – in Schumpeter's later work – provide the dynamic impetus behind the periodic "gales of creative destruction" which transform capitalism and ensure that it does not stagnate or collapse. As such, entrepreneurship is a creative process, as much through its destruction of prevailing processes or incumbent sectors and firms, as through its introduction of new technologies, processes, sectors, and firms. Despite this, Eagleton-Pierce argues that Schumpeter was far more pessimistic about the ability of entrepreneurship to save capitalism than were other Austrian thinkers like von Mises and Hayek (and their adherents).

Turning to the neoliberal wing of the Austrian School, it is useful to consider the work of Ludwig von Mises and Friedrich Hayek and their alternative conception of entrepreneurship from more mainstream economics traditions and even other Austrian's like Schumpeter (Dardot and Laval 2014). According to Hayek (1944 [2001]: 56), for example, markets are mechanisms for discovering information about the world:

> This is precisely what the price system does under competition, and which no other system even promises to accomplish. It enables entrepreneurs by watching the movement of comparatively few prices, as an engineer watches the hands of a few dials, to adjust their activities to those of their fellows.

Here, entrepreneurship becomes an almost passive process, especially as Hayek stressed that "the individual producer has to adapt himself [sic] to price changes and cannot control them" (ibid.). However, it is also a radical position because Hayek – as with von Mises – emphasized that entrepreneurship is a distributed characteristic of *all* economic activity that humans engage in. For example, in *Human Action* von Mises (1949 [1998]: 253) argued that "In any real and living economy every actor is always an entrepreneur *and speculator*" (emphasis added). The reason I highlight the last part of this quote will become evident in the following discussion. Perhaps the clearest expression of this conception of entrepreneurship is in the work of Israel Kirzner, a student of von Mises. Contrary to more neoclassical schools of economic thought, Kirzner (1973) critiqued ideas like perfect competition, arguing instead that imperfect knowledge can be exploited by people who can take advantage of their superior knowledge by positioning themselves as intermediaries in exchange or can identify profitable opportunities in the market. Again, an important point to stress about Kirzner is that anyone can be an entrepreneur, leading critical thinkers like Dardot and Laval (2014: 111) to argue that entrepreneurship has become a ubiquitous form of subjectivity and self-government.

Making neoliberal subjectivities: "entrepreneurs of the self"

It is necessary to go back to Foucault in this section in order to see where so many critical scholars picked up their analytical lens regarding the transformation of ourselves into entrepreneurial subjects. In his 1978–79 lectures at the College of France, Foucault (2008) outlined "the birth of biopolitics". What this means can sometimes seem opaque because the term "biopolitics" is used in many different ways – much like "neoliberalism". In his course summary, Foucault defined biopolitics as:

> the attempt, starting from the eighteenth century, to rationalize the problems posed to governmental practice by phenomena characteristic of a set of living beings forming a population: health, hygiene, birthrate, life expectancy rate . . . (p.317)

He continued by asking:

> How can the phenomena of "population," with its specific effects and problems, be taken into account in a system [i.e. liberalism] concerned about respect for legal subjects and individual free enterprise? (ibid.)

The lectures provided an answer to this question as it related to 20th century liberalism, with Foucault distinguishing between two forms, namely German neoliberalism (i.e. Ordoliberals) and American neoliberalism (i.e. Chicagoans).

One of the key points taken up by later Foucauldian critics of neoliberalism is the idea that neoliberalism involves an adoption of an entrepreneurial or enterprise-like attitude and subjectivity. In his discussion of German Ordoliberalism, Foucault argued that the:

> society regulated by reference to the market that the [German] neo-liberals are thinking about is a society in which the regulatory principle should not be so much the exchange of commodities as the mechanism of competition. (p.147)

In follow-up, Foucault argued German Ordoliberalism is premised on certain principles, including "the basic units [of the social fabric] would have the form of the enterprise" (p.148); "this multiplication of the 'enterprise' form within the social body is what is at stake in neo-liberal policy" (p.148); and "obtaining a society that is not orientated towards the commodity and the uniformity of the commodity, but towards the multiplicity and differentiation of enterprises" (p.149). As such, neoliberalism is not about exchange or consumption, but rather "enterprise and production"; it is an "enterprise society" (p.147).

Similarly, American neoliberalism, according to Foucault (2008: 224), was about the transformation of humans into enterprises, although through a different rationality. Here Foucault focused on dissecting human capital theory, noting that it centred on a reframing of wages paid for labour power as an income derived from human abilities (i.e. human capital). In this sense, American neoliberalism is built on the idea that "the worker himself appears as a sort of enterprise for himself [sic]" (p.225). It is not, therefore, the individual who matters, "but enterprises" (ibid.). By this, Foucault means that the liberal individual – or *homo economicus* – "is an entrepreneur, an entrepreneur of the self" (p.226). American neoliberalism was more radical than the German version because it extended economic analysis to non-economic aspects of life (e.g. crime, marriage, discrimination). Here, according to Foucault, there is an interesting corollary between the enterprise form and the household in that they both involve a long-term contract, meaning they can "avoid constantly renegotiating at every moment the innumerable contracts which would have to be made in order for domestic life to function" (p.245). I come back to this issue in the next chapter, although mainly as it relates to political-economic activity.

One thing is worth noting about Foucault's analysis before moving on to more contemporary applications: Foucault was analysing the conceptual claims made by neoliberals and was not providing a rigorous empirical analysis of their deployment or implementation in his lectures. This is important because, as I highlight in the last chapter, the firm (i.e. enterprise form) has changed over time, including around the time that Foucault is analysing neoliberalism (i.e. 1960s and 1970s).

It is now useful to look at the contemporary deployment of Foucault's ideas. My aim is not to provide an exhaustive outline of the burgeoning literature on changing "neoliberal" subjectivities (e.g. Gill 2008; Langley 2008; Barnett 2009; Mirowski 2013; Joseph 2014; McRobbie 2015), but rather to examine two recent books in some detail. First, *The New Way of the World* by the French sociologists Pierre Dardot and Christian Laval (2014); and second, *Undoing the Demos* by political theorist Wendy Brown (2015). The reason I focus on these two books is that they have proven in a very short space of time to be very influential developments of Foucault's ideas for the 21st century. Like other works, they argue that neoliberalism has infiltrated our lives, finagling its way into our attitudes, behaviours, choices, and subjectivities. As such, they are essentially arguing that each and every individual now embodies a set of entrepreneurial principles built on the notion that markets are everywhere.

First, Dardot and Laval (2014: 3) argue that neoliberalism is "*productive* of certain kinds of social relations, certain ways of living, certain subjectivities", specifically those based on "generalized competition" in which the individual is "now called on to conceive and conduct him- or herself as an enterprise". Although it is not always clear and obvious who is doing what and how in their argument, Dardot and Laval do provide a detailed intellectual history of neoliberal thought on these topics. They also provide a useful analysis of how neoliberalism incorporates the firm into its rationality, unlike classical liberalism in their view (p.23). In particular, Dardot and Laval argue that entrepreneurship "is constructed in general competition, which is the potentially universal principle of conduct most essential to the capitalist order" (p.102). They go on to discuss Hayek, von Mises, and Kirzner as the theoretical basis for this claim, stressing that self-government – of and for everyone – is characterized by entrepreneurship. This means that individuals become "profit centres" competing with each other, leading to the "contractualization of social relations" as all social relations are subsumed into a market-based notion of social life (e.g. education is human capital) (p.177). Although they provide some support for their claims in later chapters, Dardot and Laval also tend to generalize their arguments with little empirical support for them. First, in their final substantive chapter, called "Manufacturing the neo-liberal subject", they contend, for example, that "Voluntary contracts between free persons – contracts certainly always underwritten by the sovereign body – thus replaced institutional forms of alliance and filiation and, more generally old forms of symbolic reciprocity" (p.257). I come back to this sort of discussion in the next chapter. Second, they argue that "individuals must no longer regard themselves as workers, but as enterprises that sell a service in the market" (p.266), ignoring the extent of and changes in self-employment over the last few years (see later). All in all, a lot of claims are wrapped together in the assumption that neoliberal ideas have been adopted largely unchanged and that everyone now thinks of themselves as an entrepreneur/enterprise, but without showing how that happened or whether it is actually an accurate reflection of the world.

Second, Wendy Brown (2015) has written another key contemporary updating of Foucault. She claims that neoliberalism is "a peculiar form of reason that configures all aspects of existence in economic terms" (p.17), thereby threatening the basis of democracy. She stresses that neoliberalism is about the "economization" of political life. It is important, in reading Brown, to remember that she is a political theorist rather than an empirical researcher and her book is peppered with often unsubstantiated yet generalist claims about the world (e.g. "The conduct of government and the conduct of firms are now fundamentally identical", p.27). As an updating of Foucault, she is concerned with how people's subjectivities and behaviours are transformed by a neoliberal rationality so that "persons and states are constructed on the model of the contemporary firm", which involves "entrepreneurialism, self-investment, and/or attracting investors" (p.22). Her focus frequently turns to higher education, where she bemoans the fact that so many students now want some sort of "return" on their education. It is not always clear how Brown conceives of "economic" or "market" in her theorizing because she conflates the two; for example, she writes about economization on one page and then immediately writes on the next page "the point is that neoliberal rationality disseminates the *model of the market* to all domains and activities" (p.31). One area where Brown is spot on, in my opinion, is in her emphasis on examining the investor figure in any discussion of neoliberalism (p.34), although she then seems to conflate investors with entrepreneurs (p.36). Overall, Wendy

Brown, like Dardot and Laval, is too focused on how neoliberal rationality is implicated in "remaking citizenship and the subject" (p.40).

As should be obvious in these brief outlines, I think there are several problems with these sorts of updating of Foucault. First, both Dardot and Laval (2014) and Brown (2015) follow a similar logic in their argument, namely they identify a set of "neoliberal" ideas and then relate them to social phenomena, while assuming that the former necessarily leads to the latter. This is perhaps explained by the fact that these authors do not present clear empirical support for their arguments, relying instead on anecdotal claims or stories. This tendency is perhaps worse in Brown, where her final chapter, which is supposed to be about human capital but fails to discuss it in any detail, is nothing more than a series of complaints about how the university has fallen apart as a social institution (in her eyes). In contrast, it would have been helpful to see some evidence of whether people think of their education as "human capital", as training for citizenship, as a broadening of the mind, as just something that is expected of them, or as something else entirely. Second, and problematically, people from diverse social groups are treated as the same; for example, these critical scholars tend to assume that the subjectivities of *all* people are transformed by neoliberal rationality in the same way (i.e. turning them into enterprises). Instead, and as Jodi Dean (2011) notes, it makes more sense to analyse how neoliberal ideas transform *certain* people's attitudes and identities, especially those in higher income brackets, but not others – akin to the *dominant ideology* thesis of yore. This is an issue I come back to in the conclusion and next chapter, so will leave for now. Third, it is almost as if Dardot and Laval (2014) and Brown (2015) – and maybe Foucault – actually end up reproducing and reinforcing the claims made by the neoliberal thinkers they are critiquing through the idea that neoliberal rationality has infiltrated all aspects of our lives. Finally, there is limited understanding in the two books about how and in what ways the firm has changed over time, which I went over in the last chapter *and* the reason why I went over it. For example, Dardot and Laval argue that neoliberalism is distinct from classical liberalism because it incorporates the firm into its rationality; however, this totally misses the point that the firm today bears no resemblance to the firm in the 19th century, meaning that it is not possible to compare the two eras that way. A similar point could be made about the firm in the 1970s and today. As a result, the discussion of neoliberalism as the transformation of individuals into "entrepreneurs of the self" ends up missing what is so distinct about contemporary, technoscientific capitalism, which I discuss after examining the extent of entrepreneurship in Anglo-American countries.

Are we all entrepreneurs now?

As should be evident from the previous discussion, I think it is important to unpack the claim that we are now all entrepreneurs of the self or otherwise as a direct or indirect result of neoliberalism. For me, it raises a very basic question: what is the evidence to support this claim? This raises a second basic question: what is entrepreneurship? According to neoliberals, it is the ubiquitous and even innate human ability to identify market opportunities by responding to market prices (e.g. von Mises, Hayek, and Kirzner). It is, in this sense, very much associated with the production of goods and services in response to consumer demands, which is how it tends to be framed in more mainstream entrepreneurship literatures (Deakins and Freel 2012). From a critical perspective (e.g. Dardot and Laval 2014; Brown 2015), this involves a highly problematic shift in the decision-making process from a range of possible social drivers (e.g. beauty, democracy, family, etc.) to only one (i.e. "price" signals). Everything is basically subsumed under market prices, including everyone's behaviour, decision-making, and self-understanding – that is, our subjectivity.

In order to demonstrate empirically that this general claim about the transformation of our subjectivities into *market monsters* is accurate would require in-depth interviews with a large number of people from various backgrounds and walks-of-life, in order to understand how they make decisions and what drives those decisions. As such, it is difficult to assess empirically the idea that we *all* act like entrepreneurs now as the result of neoliberalism. A more everyday way to understand entrepreneurship, and one which national governments (e.g. USA) and international organizations (e.g. Organisation for Economic Co-operation and Development, OECD) tend to use and collect data on, is through indicators like *self-employment rates* and *new firm start-ups* (and exits). These are supposed to reflect things like individual desire for work autonomy; individual profit drive; individual economic dynamism; and suchlike. Since I have not done (and cannot do) an in-depth survey of people's attitudes to their lives and subjectivities – and bear in mind that neither have the Foucauldians I mention – I want to look at quantitative data on the two indicators I mentioned. I do this in order to examine two things: (1) how they have changed over time; and (2) whether they are different in different countries. The first issue might help to illustrate whether (or not) neoliberalism has led to the wholesale transformation of our souls over time; for example, we might expect that as we become entrepreneurs of the self, we are more inclined to work for ourselves rather than others, leading to rising levels of firm start-ups (and self-employment). The second issue might help illustrate whether (or not) neoliberalism has spread through certain countries more than others; for example, we might expect that countries like the USA – the epicentre of neoliberalism for many – would have higher rates of self-employment.

In order to consider the first issue, I collated secondary data on new firm start-ups and firm exits in the USA – see Figure 7.1. As this graph shows, there was a slight increase in the absolute number of new firm entries between 1977 (or pre-neoliberalism) and 2008 (or pre- "post"-neoliberalism); however, this is not a dramatic increase and could be accounted for by (significant) population growth in the USA during the same time period. More generally, the new firm start-up numbers have hovered around 700,000 per year this whole time, rising during

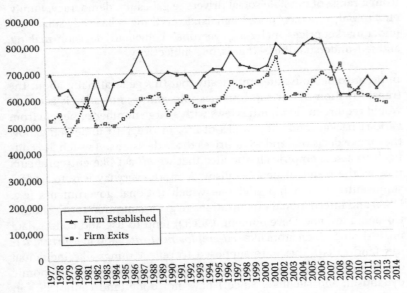

Source: US Census Bureau, Business Dynamics Statistics, http://www.census.gov/ces/dataproducts/bds/data_estab.html, accessed 24 April 2017.

Figure 7.1   Firm entry and exit rates – USA (1977–2014)

economic booms (e.g. late 1980s, late 1990s, early-to-mid 2000s). What this data does not show is a surge in entrepreneurial activity by individuals over time, reflecting a more entrepreneurial outlook on their part as neoliberalism becomes more embedded across society. One reason for this is that whether someone becomes an entrepreneur or not (using this sort of indicator) is really driven by one thing, namely their access to capital (Blanchflower and Oswald 1998). It has nothing to do with personality (or even subjectivity), but rather depends on personal wealth whether that is housing equity, inheritance, or gifts. Wealth is a way to mitigate risk, implying that a majority of people cannot suddenly be transformed into entrepreneurs (of the self or otherwise), nor should they be considered as some sort of enterprise. This has significant implications for how we understand the effects of neoliberalism, which I will come back to in the conclusion. For now, it is worth stressing that people likely do not become "entrepreneurs of the self" when they have no resources (i.e. personal wealth) because the risk is too great. As such, paying for more education or training – that is, upgrading "human capital" – in order to get a better job is likely to be beyond the reach of most people.

In order to consider the second issue, I collated secondary data on self-employment rates across three quintessentially "neoliberal" countries: USA, UK, and Canada (see Figure 7.2 for an outline of these findings). As is evident from this data, the self-employment rate – indexed to 2007 – is quite different over time across these different countries. For example, the rate in the USA has fallen by about 10 percent since 2007, which represents a fairly significant drop over an eight-year period. Obviously, this trend is probably explained by the fact it follows the 2007–2008 global financial crisis, although the self-employment rate in the UK and Canada – that is, other Anglo-American economies with, presumably, similar "neoliberal" regimes – have increased since 2007. I cannot really explain this trend in the USA from this data alone. However, it is interesting to note that a significant proportion of the American population are not self-employed and, therefore, operating (literally) as an enterprise. For example, data from the Pew Center (2015) show that only 10 percent of Americans were self-employed in 2014, down from 11.4 percent in 1990. Moreover, this downward trend in self-employment has been relatively constant between 1990 and 2014. It is safe to say that this time period has not been characterized by a rise in entrepreneurialism, if we assume that entrepreneurship is reflected in self-employment figures. Again, this data does not support the idea that people in the USA are now *more* entrepreneurial;

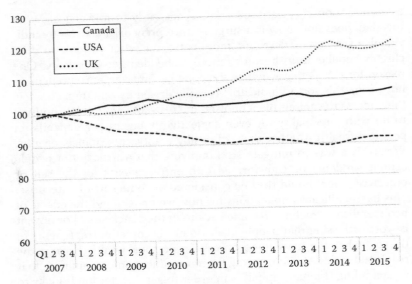

Source: OECD, Entrepreneurship at a Glance 2016, accessed 24 April 2017.

Figure 7.2 Self-employment rates (2007=100) – USA, UK, and Canada (2007–2015)

however, it is more ambivalent about whether people are forced to become entrepreneurs of the self (Dardot and Laval 2014; Brown 2015).

In the context of this data, is it worth considering whether people are doing something else entirely that might represent a form of "entrepreneurship of the self", such as spending more on higher education (i.e. investing in their human capital). More data on the USA from the Pew Center (2014) shows that household student loan debt is increasing at a faster rate than other kinds of debt, having reached US$1.08 trillion at the end of 2014. It might be possible to argue that this kind of spending reflects an investment in the "self", if we take the theory of human capital at face value. However, it is important to consider that student loan debt did not seem to increase significantly until the mid-2000s (Quinterno and Orozco 2012), meaning that it would not provide evidence of spread of neoliberalism in the 1980s or 1990s and its embedding in our subjectivities. Moreover, overall household debt is still dominated by mortgage debt, at US$8.05 trillion in 2014 (Pew Center 2014), while spending on things like home renovations topped US$300 billion in 2016 alone (Wall Street Journal 2016). In the

USA, and I would contend the UK and Canada as well, p
to "invest" far more in housing than on anything that m
human capital (e.g. education), even though housing is not a prou
tive resource per se.

Neoliberalism and rentiership

If neoliberalism is not characterized or even dominated by entrepreneurship, it is therefore necessary to consider whether there is a more
apt concept to describe the construction of the self in contemporary
capitalism. My contention is that neoliberalism is actually characterized by a *non*-entrepreneurial rationality, which, for 60 to 70 percent
of people in Anglo-American societies at least, concerns the pursuit
of housing ownership, housing renovation, and housing speculation,
or what Crouch (2011) calls "privatized Keynesianism". For me, this is
better conceptualized as a form of *rentiership* because it involves the
appropriation of value through government fiat (e.g. laws, regulations,
standards), monopoly rights (e.g. location), and organizational reconfiguration (e.g. mortgage securitization). It is not, in this sense, about the
production or creative generation of value or wealth; rather, it reflects a
reliance on unearned income and speculative wealth (Sayer 2015). For
example, buying a house largely involves buying something that already
exists with a state-sanctioned property title, while its value is largely a
consequence of changing public and private locational investment and
circumstance (e.g. transport links, school quality, facility investment,
etc.), rather than the owner's actions. Renovation could be considered
as a form of "creative" investment, but even here any added value might
be better thought of as a response to what Veblen (1908) described as
"habits of life", represented by social tastes in fashion, interior design,
and suchlike (i.e. doing something out of the ordinary will likely reduce
the value of a property). All in all, *ownership* of a house is really the only
necessary action to appropriate value from a range of social investments; that is, there is limited need for risk-taking, creative destruction,
or even responding to price signals and incentives. As Andrew Sayer
(2015: 50) argues, "A person who derives unearned income from ownership of existing assets or resources is known in political economy as
a *rentier*". It is interesting to note that even Foucauldians like Wendy
Brown (2015: 66) go so far as to state that finance capitalism embedded
in neoliberalism is "rooted in productivity by economic rents", although
she does not extend this line of thinking much further.

Investors and rentiership under neoliberalism

The idea that contemporary capitalism is rife with rent-seeking and rentiership represents another contradiction to prevailing understandings of the world as already a market (see Chapter 3), both in neoliberal thought itself and in the literature critical of neoliberalism. Entrepreneurship may still be an important process in society, but it is increasingly being eclipsed by rentiership as ownership rights come to trump creative production. In order to understand this rise of rentiership it is necessary to analyse the construction of individuals as *speculative investors*, or speculators, and *not* entrepreneurs. First, it involves the social, political, economic, and legal reconfiguring of physical assets as immaterial and financial assets; for example, the conversion of bricks and mortar (e.g. a house) into pieces of paper (e.g. mortgage debt, deeds to a house). Second, it involves a new way of thinking about the world and ourselves premised on a particular kind of financial logic arising from point one, especially as it relates to the elevation of speculative investors as societal judge, jury, and executioner of political-economic efficiency (see Chapter 6).

On the first point, the conversion of physical resources and assets – like land – into a paper claim helps to transform a "thing" into a legal title to the earnings from that thing, thereby disguising the origins of the income and the thing itself (Mineau 2016). For example, "real property" (e.g. land) is increasingly transformed into a paper claim on property (e.g. mortgage debt), meaning that the latter – an immaterial and financial asset – becomes as valuable as the underlying asset itself (Kozolchyk 1991). At the same time, it is easier to trade and can therefore generate a liquid secondary market in all sorts of physical assets (e.g. infrastructure, housing, reputation, etc.), which speculators can invest in. Consequently, as Bezemer and Hudson (2016) argue, this collapses the distinction between land and capital, as well as rent and income, thereby leading to the wholesale reorientation of political-economic knowledges, practices, and processes:

> That is what makes the seemingly empirical accounting format used in most economic analysis an expression of creditor-oriented pro-*rentier* ideology. Households do not receive incomes from the houses they live in. The value of the "services" their homes provide does not increase simply because house prices rise, as the national accounts fiction has it. The financial sector does not produce goods or even "real" wealth. And to the extent that it

produces services, much of this serves to redirect revenues to rentiers, not to generate wages and profits. (p.749)

Since the 1970s, intangible assets (e.g. intellectual property, brands and reputation, software and databases, goodwill, etc.) have generally come to constitute more and more of the value of businesses, governments, and individuals. As I have written elsewhere (Birch 2015, 2017a, 2017b), this identification of intangible assets has required a reworking of accounting and corporate governance practices and standards, so that the value of something like an image (i.e. brand logo) can be calculated and capitalized as future earnings (Muniesa 2014). As a result of this restructuring, more and more "things" are turned into assets, or resources with few if any substitutes (i.e. monopoly) and where ownership rights (i.e. government fiat) determine control and, therefore, the resulting rent stream (e.g. there is only one copyright to the music of *Metallica*). As a result, more and more things in our lives can be converted into intangible assets from which owners can accrue rent.

On the second point, in the last chapter I discussed the way that capital owners – that is, speculative investors – have been put upon a pedestal in financial economics. It is noticeable, however, that this elevation of the speculative investor as the source of all political-economic wisdom, does not necessarily percolate down through the rest of the social body (cf. Chiapello 2007, 2015). So, and unlike some critics of neoliberalism I mentioned earlier, I do not want to suggest that this financial logic shapes and transforms *all* of our subjectivities (see also Chapter 8). Rather, it changes the decision-making of certain, often key, individuals in the economy, which obviously has a rippling, but ambiguous, effect on the rest of us. In particular, this logic comes to dominate financing decisions because the imaginary of "the investor" is used to legitimate financial decision-making in venture capital firms, pension and mutual funds, investment banks, etc. (Ortiz 2013, 2014), largely on the basis of opportunity cost analyses (i.e. judgements about what investment will generate the highest returns). According to Coase (1990), the introduction of opportunity cost analysis was strongly influenced by his work at the London School of Economics (LSE) during the 1930s and reflected the influence of people like Frank Knight, Lionel Robbins, and Friedrich Hayek – all neoliberals of one sort or another. It is based on an assumption that prices are "a result of the operations of the market" – an analytical claim – and that resources "will be employed in such a way as to maximize the value in production" – a normative claim – if we assume "that the operation of the market is costless" (p.10). There is no underlying notion of value from this perspective, although there is also no reason why value maximization must follow, unless we assume that everyone is already a rational and competitive individual maximizer. The fact that the last assumption may not be true (see Chapter 8) means that the logic need not result in financial value reflecting anything like an underlying or foundational value. Rather, as Crouch (2011: 100) argues:

> even corporate accounting systems were changed, so that instead of estimating the values of the assets of a firm in terms of the value of its labour, capital, markets, etc., accounting looked at the stock market value of these assets, a value formed by traders' beliefs about other traders' beliefs, etc.

The speculative investor chases alternative investments on the basis of rising asset values – premised on appropriation of rents – that reflect the assumptions of other speculative investors, who are themselves chasing other investors, and so on. It is not hard, therefore, to understand how the global financial crisis occurred. An example of how this logic plays out in contemporary capitalism is in the world of high-tech financing where venture capitalists (i.e. financiers), management consultants, brokers, and others exhort high-tech managers to "think more like an investor" (Ernst & Young 2015) or task themselves to "take an investor first view of everything we do" (Human Proof of Concept n.d.). By this, however, they primarily mean that managers should think about how to increase financial value, rather than risk investment in production development. This is why biotech and pharmaceutical firms spend so much on stock buybacks, reflecting a strategy to "return value" to speculative investors rather than create new products (Lazonick and Mazzucato 2013).

Rentiership under neoliberalism

Rentiership is characterized by the social dominance of ownership in the economy, at least over production. This contrasts to notions of (creative) entrepreneurship – of the self or not – in taking a risk to bring together money, labour, and other resources in order to make new products and services for a market. Originally associated with the work of classical economists like David Ricardo in the 19th century, the concept of *economic rent* has had a complicated intellectual evolution since then (see Haila 2015). It is important to remember that "rent" does not equate to "lease"; instead, it is an analytical term to denote the payment made to a property or resource owner for the right to then use that property or resource – the more productive the resource, the higher the payment. Initially and usually it is associated with land, but it has been applied to a wider array of assets over time, including intellectual property (Zeller 2008; Birch 2017a, 2017b; Birch et al. forthcoming). There is a growing interest across the political spectrum with the threat that rentiership represents, including:

- Left-leaning scholars like Andrew Sayer (2015), Bezemer and Hudson (2016), Guy Standing (2016), amongst others;
- . . . or British and American left-leaning commentators like Paul Mason (2015) and Peter Frase (2016);
- Think tanker and Blair government advisor Geoff Mulgan (2013);
- American liberal professor and columnist for the *New York Times* Paul Krugman;
- American-based Internet entrepreneur and author Andrew Keen (2015);
- Canadian ex-CEO of the firm Blackberry Jim Balsillie (Castaldo 2016); and
- Academics at the University of Chicago business school, who have set up a website called *ProMarket* with a dedicated section on "rent-seeking".

It is difficult to provide a simple and concise definition of rent-seeking or rentiership, so I will only offer a brief synopsis of several viewpoints here, drawing on the people identified in the previous list. First up, it is useful to see how neoliberals understand rent-seeking. According to neoliberals like James Buchanan and Gordon Tullock – of the Virginia School (see Chapter 2) – rent-seeking is the result of government restrictions (e.g. regulations) or government-sanctioned interventions (e.g. trade unions) on the operations of the (free) market (see Krueger 1974). As such, and by definition, markets are incompatible with rent-seeking (i.e. economic rents cannot result from markets); instead, it is always and necessarily the result of government or other intervention. According to Le Gales (2016: 162), this leads neoliberals to "criticisms of politics and democracy, seen in terms of rentiers, corruption and clienteles". This is why neoliberalism entails support for strict laws and rules as the condition for the operation of markets and market competition – and, therefore, freedom, liberty, and all those good things – although without much consideration for what a rigid and strict rule of law means when it comes to ownership and property rights. However, as Storper (2016: 248) points out, neoliberalism contradictorily also provides "de facto support for rent-seeking

monopolies, cronyism, and elite corporatism" in some parts of the economy (also see Crouch 2011). As an example, Storper refers to the fact that
"Large corporations often unashamedly game legal systems" by doing
things like "developing obscure contracting procedures with consumers"
(p.252). I return to this issue in the next chapter.

Second, entrepreneurs themselves, especially in the tech-world,
have sought to conceptualize rentiership as well, in ways that reflect
broader concerns with the establishment of knowledge monopolies
and monopoly rents (see Tyfield 2008; Zeller 2008; Sayer 2015). It is
interesting to note the similarity in analysis between critics of intellectual property (IP) and tech entrepreneurs, not because they agree on
the societal implications – which they do not – but because they both
emphasize the fact that monopoly rights (e.g. patents, copyright) have
become an integral part of contemporary capitalism. As I have argued
elsewhere (e.g. Birch 2017a), knowledge is increasingly turned into IP
assets that can then be monetized because they end up as a state-
sanctioned monopoly (see also Romain Felli (2014) on "climate rents").
Taking a slightly less analytical approach, people like Jim Balsillie, the
ex-CEO of Blackberry, describes contemporary capitalism in terms of
this reliance on IP rights:

> Intellectual property works on a principle of restricted rights or constraints –
> essentially, government-granted monopolies. The government makes the
> market for ideas and intellectual property. It's the exact opposite of free
> trade and of the traditional economy. You only have a market if the govern-
> ment's there. And you only have a market that advances prosperity if CEOs
> and the policy community are talking. (Balsillie quoted in Castaldo 2016)

According to Balsillie, moreover, IP often entails a form of market control not generally considered in relation to IP ownership; this is the fact
that IP can become a market standard: "Now each standard embodies
IP. If your IP is picked as a standard, you have a lottery ticket. Your
competitors have to pay you" (quoted in Castaldo 2016). For example,
something like Microsoft Office has become the standard for word pro-
cessing, or Google for search engines. It is interesting to note Balsillie's
take on these forms of rentiership – i.e. IP monopolies – because he is
a business person; and yet his fears for the future reflect those of more
leftist thinkers like Mason (2015), Sayer (2015), and Frase (2106). For
example, both Balsillie and Mason argue that contemporary capitalism
is characterized by the establishment of monopoly ownership rights
and not by free markets.

Third, several writers who address rentiership directly, like Boutang (2011), Mulgan (2013), and Sayer (2015), seek to distinguish between entrepreneurship as productive activity and rentiership as nonproductive activity. In doing so, Mulgan (2013) argues that many information technology companies nowadays are simply platforms on which users generate value through their interactions, relations, etc. (Langley and Leyshon 2016). Other companies in supposedly dynamic high-tech sectors like pharmaceuticals and biotechnology are underpinned by other forms of rentiership (e.g. IP monopolies). Former tech entrepreneur Andrew Keen (2015) makes a number of similar points to Mulgan in his discussion of the rise of social media companies like Uber, Airbnb, Snapfish, Facebook, etc. Many are developed using a business model in which financial success depends on the total dominance of a particular market sector (e.g. taxi, room rental, photography, etc.), the subsequent eradication of well-paid work, and the exploitation of the "social factory" (Boutang 2011), as our own social relations, interactions, and emotions are mined as a resource for making money (e.g. personal data being sold to marketers). In effect, we become part of the "production function" (Keen 2015), a network of users who add value by simply using a website or service, or writing an online review or sharing a link, and so on. As many Autonomist Marxists have noted, we are doing all this work for free, and yet it is being appropriated and capitalized by private firms (e.g. Lazzarato 2015).

This brief foray into the intellectual world of rentiership illustrates some of the complexities of modern capitalism. The very ambiguity of economic rents and rent-seeking that this discussion raises leads me to conceptualize rentiership as consisting of several components, sometimes overlapping but sometimes distinct. First, rentiership involves forms of *fiat ownership* established by a variety of government legislation (e.g. property rights), legal process (e.g. contract law), and private regulation (e.g. standards) (Busch 2011). Second, rentiership involves forms of *monopoly*, including both monopoly through exclusion (e.g. IP rights) and through quality (e.g. locational advantages). For example, David Harvey (2005) discusses the rents accrued from cultural products like art, wine, etc. directly from monopoly control. Third, rentiership involves new *configurations* of business and market organization, especially through the construction of business models that enable the mining of the social factory. For example, autonomist Marxists like Boutang (2011), Lazzarato (2015), and others (e.g. Pike 2015) point out that things like brand value reflect a firm's reputation among a population, meaning that brands represent the mining of consumer preferences, tastes, and suchlike. The "work" underpinning brand value is done by consumers for free, while private firms appropriate that work to make money. Finally, and perhaps less obvious amongst the authors I discuss, is the fact that rentiership involves a series of *ongoing activities and operations*, it is more than ownership alone. For example, ownership of a physical or immaterial asset without an expectation of its use significantly affects its value; for example, a toll-road needs to be used for it to generate earnings. As such, use and unpaid work are directly implicated in the appropriation of value from an owned asset or resource.

Conclusion

The basis for this chapter is the second contradiction of neoliberalism I identified in the book's Introduction, namely the emphasis on entrepreneurship in neoliberal thought and critical perspectives of neoliberalism versus the increasing prevalence and dominance of rentiership as a political-economic process. As with the other contradictions I discuss in this book, this one derives from the assumption that markets are already everywhere (see Chapter 3), and that humans already think like entrepreneurs (or increasingly think like them). As I sought to show in this chapter, it is problematic to conceive of everyone in these terms. Critiques of neoliberalism are as prone to do this as are neoliberal thinkers themselves, which is evident in the work of Foucault (2008), Dardot and Laval (2014), and Brown (2015). In their attempts to theorize the neoliberal transformation of our subjectivities as the emergence of "entrepreneurs of the self", these authors tend to reinforce the claims of neoliberal thinkers rather than challenge them. Moreover, it is problematic that these critical authors provide limited empirical evidence to support their contentions, relying instead on personal stories or anecdotes or readings of policy statements. In order to examine these claims in more depth, I analysed some data on two indicators used as proxies for entrepreneurship: firm start-ups and self-employment. As the data show, these indicators do not reflect a surge in entrepreneurialism across Anglo-American countries like the USA, UK, and Canada. In fact, my argument is that these countries are now increasingly dependent on forms of rentiership, represented by things like housing ownership, intellectual property ownership, and suchlike.

Rentiership, or the appropriation of value through fiat, monopoly, or organizational and market reconfiguration, entails certain negative and problematic effects – and these effects are obscured by a focus on entrepreneurship. The main negative implication of rentiership that affects a majority of people in countries like the USA, UK, and Canada relates to housing, but is applicable to other assets. Specifically, rising asset-price inflation, resulting from increasing "investment" in rent-earning assets (e.g. titles of already existing houses) and driven by expectations of rising returns on that investment (e.g. capital gains), have meant that housing in certain parts of the USA, UK, and Canada has been transformed into an investment asset class that is simply beyond the reach of the average resident (Slater 2017). Mainstream media outlets are increasingly picking up on this issue with stories of empty houses or apartments, overseas owners, speculative builders, astronomical salary-to-house price ratios, and similar. Although this example reflects the particularities of housing, it is applicable to broader trends in a political economy dominated by rentiership.

It is important to think about the implications of rentiership because it problematizes the idea that everyone has become more entrepreneurial as the result of the rise and dominance of markets under neoliberalism. It is questionable whether most people are becoming entrepreneurs, either in the practical sense of setting up new firms or working for themselves or in the Foucauldian sense of transforming their subjectivities. Rather, most people are still very much attached and embedded in a wider mesh of social, political, and cultural beliefs, identities, and motivations that belie the economistic focus of both neoliberals and their critics. For me, this helps to explain the turn against prevailing political-economy in the last two or three years, exemplified by the British referendum vote to leave the European Union and the 2016 American election of Donald Trump. Both reflect the fact that for most people the supposed benefits of free markets never arrived and, moreover, were never really expected to emerge. Rather, as Blyth (2016) points out, decades of stagnant wages married to rising debt *and* deflation after the global financial crisis have led to a situation in which mainstream commentators praise our leaders for their steady hand on the tiller, while for a majority of people their standard of living simply gets worse and worse. We are not entrepreneurs in this sense, but have returned to the days of debt peonage.

Bibliography

Barnett, C. (2009), "Publics and markets: what's wrong with neoliberalism?", in S. Smith, R. Pain, S. Marston and J.-P. Jons III (eds), *The Sage Handbook of Social Geography*, London: Sage, pp. 269–96.

Becker, G., Ewald, F. and Harcourt, B. (2012), "Becker on Ewald on Foucault on Becker: American Neoliberalism and Michel Foucault's 1979 *Birth of Biopolitics* lectures", University of Chicago: Coase-Sandor Institute for Law & Economics Working Paper No. 614.

Bezemer, D. and Hudson, M. (2016), "Finance is not the economy: reviving the conceptual distinction", *Journal of Economic Issues*, 50(3), 745–68.

Birch, K. (2015), *We Have Never Been Neoliberal: A Manifesto for a Doomed Youth*, Winchester, UK: Zero Books.

Birch, K. (2017a), "Rethinking *value* in the bio-economy: finance, assetization and the management of value", *Science, Technology and Human Values*, 42(3), 460–90.

Birch, K. (2017b), "Financing technoscience: finance, assetization and rentiership", in D. Tyfield, R. Lave, S. Randalls and C. Thorpe (eds), *The Routledge Handbook of the Political Economy of Science*, London: Routledge, pp. 169–81.

Birch, K., Tyfield, D. and Chiapetta, M. (forthcoming), "From neoliberalizing research to researching neoliberalism: STS, *rentiership* and the emergence of commons 2.0", in D. Cahill, M. Konings and M. Cooper (eds), *The Sage Handbook of Neoliberalism*, London: Sage.

Blanchflower, D. and Oswald, A. (1998), "What makes an entrepreneur?", *Journal of Labor Economics*, 16(1), 26–60.

Blyth, M. (2016), "Global Trumpism", *Foreign Affairs*, 15 November 2016, accessed 23 November 2016 at https://www.foreignaffairs.com/articles/2016-11-15/global-trumpism

Boutang, Y.M. (2011), *Cognitive Capitalism*, Cambridge: Polity Press.

Brown, W. (2015), *Undoing the Demos*, New York, NY: Zone Books.

Busch, L. (2011), *Standards: Recipes for Reality*, Cambridge MA: MIT Press.

Castaldo, J. (2016), "Jim Balsillie on how Canada is doing innovation wrong – and how to fix it", *Canadian Business*, 7 October 2016, access 25 November 2016 at http://www.canadianbusiness.com/leadership/jim-balsillie-interview/.

Chiapello, E. (2007), "Accounting and the birth of the notion of capitalism", *Critical Perspectives on Accounting*, 18, 263–96.

Chiapello, E. (2015), "Financialisation of valuation", *Human Studies*, 38, 13–35.

Coase, R. (1937), "The nature of the firm", *Economica*, 4(16), 386–405.

Coase, R. (1938), "Business organization and the accountant", *The Accountant*, 13, 470–72.

Coase, R. (1990), "Accounting and the theory of the firm", *Journal of Accounting and Economics*, 12, 3–13.

Crouch, C. (2011), *The Strange Non-Death of Neoliberalism*, Cambridge: Polity Press.

Dardot, P. and Laval, C. (2014), *The New Way of the World*, London: Verso.

Deakins, D. and Freel, M. (2012), *Entrepreneurship and Small Firms*, London: McGraw-Hill.

Dean, J. (2011), "Three theses on neoliberalism", unpublished manuscript, accessed 22 November 2016 at https://www.academia.edu/1145526/Neoliberalism_and_its_contradictions.

Eagleton-Pierce, M. (2016) *Neoliberalism: The Key Concepts*, London: Routledge.

Ernst & Young (2015), *Biotechnology Industry Report 2015: Beyond Borders*, Boston, MA: Ernst & Young LLP.

Fama, E. (1980), "Agency problems and the theory of the firm", *Journal of Political Economy*, 88, 288–307.

Felli, R. (2014), "On climate rent", *Historical Materialism*, 22(3–4), 251–80.

Foucault, M. (2008), *The Birth of Biopolitics*, New York, NY: Picador.

Frase, P. (2016), *Four Futures: Life After Capitalism*, London: Verso.

Gill, R. (2008), "Culture and subjectivity in neoliberal and postfeminist times", *Subjectivity*, 25, 432–45.

Haila, A. (2015), *Urban Land Rent*, Chichester, UK: Wiley Blackwell.

Harvey, D. (1989), "From managerialism to entrepreneurialism: the transformation in urban governance in late capitalism", *Geografiska Annaler: Series B, Human Geography*, 71(1), 3–17.

Harvey, D. (2005), *A Brief History of Neoliberalism*, Oxford: Oxford University Press.

Hayek, F. (1944 [2001]), *The Road to Serfdom*, London: Routledge.

Hodgson, G. (1999), *Economics and Utopia*, London: Routledge.

Hodgson, G. (2014), "What is capital? Economists and sociologists have changed its meaning: should it be changed back?", *Cambridge Journal of Economics*, 38, 1063–86.

Human Proof of Concept (n.d.), *Brian Bloom: Hockey Sticks and Cheerleaders Do Not Go Together*, accessed 25 November 2016 at http://humanpoc.com/.

Jensen, M. and Meckling, W. (1976), "Theory of the firm: managerial behavior, agency costs and ownership structure", *Journal of Financial Economics*, 3, 305–60.

Joseph, M. (2014), *Debt to Society: Accounting for Life Under Capitalism*, Minneapolis, MN: University of Minnesota Press.

Keen, A. (2015), *The Internet Is Not the Answer*, New York, NY: Atlantic Monthly Press.

Keil, R. (2016), "Urban neoliberalism", in S. Springer, K. Birch and J. MacLeavy (eds), *The Handbook of Neoliberalism*, London: Routledge, pp. 385–97.

Knight, F. (1921 [2006]), *Risk, Uncertainty and Profit*, New York, NY: Dover Publications Inc.

Kozolchyk, B. (1991), "On the state of commercial law at the end of the 20th century", *Arizona Journal of International and Comparative Law*, 8, 1–32.

Kirzner, I. (1973), *Competition and Entrepreneurship*, Chicago, IL: University of Chicago Press.

Kreitner, R. (2007), *Calculating Promises: The Emergence of Modern American Contract Doctrine*, Stanford, CA: Stanford University Press.

Krueger, A. (1974), "The political economy of the rent-seeking society", *American Economic Review*, 64(3), 291–303.

Langley, P. (2008), *The Everyday Life of Global Finance: Saving and Borrowing in Anglo-America*, Oxford: Oxford University Press.

Langley, P. and Leyshon, A. (2016), "Platform capitalism: the intermediation and capitalisation of digital economic circulation", *Finance and Society*, early view.

Lazonick, W. and Mazzucato, M. (2013), "The risk–reward nexus in the innovation–inequality relationship: who takes the risks? Who gets the rewards?", *Industrial and Corporate Change*, 22(4), 1093–128.

Lazzarato, M. (2015), *Governing by Debt*, South Pasadena, CA: Semiotext(e).

Le Gales, P. (2016), "Neoliberalism and urban change: stretching a good idea too far?", *Territory, Politics, Governance*, 4(2), 154–72.

Mason, P. (2015), *Postcapitalism*, London: Penguin Books.

McRobbie, A. (2015), "Notes on the perfect: competitive femininity in neoliberal times", *Australian Feminist Studies*, 30, 3–20.

Mineau, D. (2016), "How economists duped us into attacking capitalism instead of parasitic rent-seeking", evonomics.com, 19 November, accessed 25 November 2016 at http://evonomics.com/economists-duped-attacking-capitalism/

Mirowski, P. (2013), *Never Let a Serious Crisis Go to Waste*, London: Verso.

Mulgan, G. (2013), *The Locust and the Bee: Predators and Creators in Capitalism's Future*, Princeton, NJ: Princeton University Press.

Muniesa, F. (2014), *The Provoked Economy*, London: Routledge.

Ortiz, H. (2013), "Financial value: economic, moral, political, global", *HAU: Journal of Ethnographic Theory*, 3(1), 64–79.

Ortiz, H. (2014), "The limits of financial imagination: free investors, efficient markets, and crisis", *American Anthropologist*, 116(1), 38–50.

Peck, J. (2010), *Constructions of Neoliberal Reason*, Oxford: Oxford University Press.

Pew Center (2014), "Fed report says household borrowing is rebounding from Great Recession", pewresearch.org, accessed 23 November 2016 at http://www.pewresearch.org/fact-tank/2014/02/19/fed-report-says-household-borrowing-is-rebounding-from-great-recession/.

Pew Center (2015), "The self-employment rate in the U.S., 1990 to 2014", pewsocialtrends.org, accessed 23 November 2016 at http://www.pewsocialtrends.org/2015/10/22/three-in-ten-u-s-jobs-are-held-by-the-self-employed-and-the-workers-they-hire/st_2015-10-22_self-employed-02/.

Pike, A. (2015), *Origination*, Chichester, UK: Wiley Blackwell.

Quinterno, J. and Orozco, V. (2012), *The Great Cost Shift*, New York, NY: Dēmos.

Sayer, A. (2015), *Why We Can't Afford the Rich*, Bristol, UK: Polity Press.

Schumpeter, J. (1942 [2008]), *Capitalism, Socialism and Democracy*, New York, NY: Harper Perennial.

Slater, T. (2017), "Planetary rent gaps", *Antipode*, 49(S1), 114–37.

Standing, G. (2016), "The five lies of rentier capitalism", socialeurope.eu, 27 October 2016, accessed 25 November 2016 at https://www.socialeurope.eu/2016/10/five-lies-rentier-capitalism/#.

Storper, M. (2016), "The neo-liberal city as idea and reality", *Territory, Politics, Governance*, 4(2), 241–63.

Styhre, A. (2014), *Management and Neoliberalism: Connecting Policies and Practices*, London: Routledge.

Tyfield, D. (2008), "Enabling TRIPs: The pharma-biotech-university patent coalition", *Review of International Political Economy*, 15(4), 535–66.

von Mises, L. (1949 [1998]), *Human Action*, Auburn, AL: The Ludwig von Mises Institute.

Veblen, T. (1908), "On the nature of capital: investment, intangible assets, and the pecuniary magnate", *Journal of Economics*, 23(1), 104–36.

Wall Street Journal (2016), "Spending on home improvement is set to pick up as building pace slows", *Wall Street Journal*, 21 August, accessed 23 November 2016 at http://www.wsj.com/articles/spending-on-home-improvement-is-set-to-pick-up-as-building-pace-slows-1471771801.

Zeller, C. (2008), "From the gene to the globe: extracting rents based on intellectual property monopolies", *Review of International Political Economy*, 15(1), 86–115.

8 Neoliberalism as a contract-based order

Introduction

The implications of my argument in the last chapter is that value in contemporary capitalism is increasingly conceived of and constituted by the future earnings of assets – which includes skills and training, intangibles like brands or intellectual property, and tangibles like buildings and machinery – and generally framed in terms of opportunity cost (i.e. societal efficiency is constituted by the highest potential future earnings). This has been theorized in terms of "capitalization", or the discounting of those future earnings in the present using various valuation formulae (e.g. discounted cash flow) to work out their value, discounting any costs (e.g. inflation, depreciation) (see Nitzan and Bichler 2009; Muniesa 2014; Birch 2017). As such, the appropriation and capture of value, which I associate with forms of rentiership (see Chapter 7), necessitates the ownership and control over those future earnings. However, in considering the importance of these capitalist relations and logics in contemporary capitalism (e.g. Roth 2016), it should be evident that future earnings are not *realized* through market transactions in the present, but rather result from contractual arrangements that secure those future earnings in the future (even though they may be accounted for in the present). It is important, in this sense, to differentiate between "transaction" and "contract" as political-economic terms; something which is often ignored in debates about markets and market competition (e.g. Coase 1937; Jensen and Meckling 1976).

Capitalism is often presented as an economic system underpinned by property rights and freedom of contract (e.g. Hayek 1944 [2001]; Friedman 1962; Bowman 1996; Hodgson 1999, 2015). My concern here is with contract because the former seems to have attracted more attention in academic and public circles critical of neoliberalism, even though the latter is as interesting (if not more so, in my opinion). We need to analyse the difference between market transaction and contract I pointed to earlier in order to understand properly this *thing* people call neoliberalism. Although it might seem like a merely semantic distinction, contract has a very different meaning in law than in (mainstream) economics, and this difference has some important implications for how people might want to theorize neoliberalism. First off, according to Eisenberg (1999: 822–3), "contract" can mean "agreement" in "ordinary language", "reciprocal arrangements" in economics (especially financial economics), and "legally enforceable promise" in contract law. Eisenberg also notes that "contract" is often conflated with "markets" as a result of its fuzzy treatment in economics. Second, and returning to the issue of future earnings, it is important to highlight that contracts comprise more than market transactions, not only in legal terms but also conceptually and practically. Contracts represent an alternative coordination mechanism to market prices and market competition beloved of neoliberals, especially as this relates to future earnings because they enable political-economic actors to determine the timing and time-period for transactions (e.g. employment contract), to establish prices outside market price dynamics (e.g. administered prices), to speculate on changing prices (e.g. hedging), and suchlike (Means 1983; Hodgson 1999; Birch 2016). Finally, as Bowman (1996: 45–6) and others point out, the origins of the modern corporation (see Chapter 6) can be traced back to legal rulings that establish business entities as distinct legal persons on the basis that they represent contractual arrangements between individuals (e.g. *Dartmouth College vs. Woodward* 1819, USA), and not "market" transactions.

My aim in this chapter is to examine the conceptual relevance of contract and contract law to our understandings of neoliberalism. I do so in order to problematize the notion, common in both critical and supportive literatures, that contemporary capitalism is dominated or configured by market (i.e. neoliberal) principles (see Chapters 2, 3, and 4). This focus on contract is important for at least three reasons. First, as noted in Chapter 6, most economic activity actually takes place within organizations (e.g. business entities) rather than markets, and these organizations are defined by contractual relations (e.g. employment). Second, as noted in Chapter 7, contemporary capitalism is underpinned by a value logic based on future earnings (see earlier), which necessitates an understanding of how future events and actions are transformed into present valuations through contractual arrangements and contract law. Finally, although a number of neoliberals, including Friedrich Hayek (1960) and members of the Ordoliberal School, were concerned with law and the legal framework necessary for market competition, law has not been a major concern with critics – there are exceptions, obviously (e.g. Davies, 2010; Nik-Khah and van Horn, 2012; Aksikas and Andrews, 2014; Grewal and Purdy 2014; Purdy 2014; Birch 2016; Brabazon 2016).

I start with a discussion of the evolution of contract law in order to illustrate how conceptions of contract and contract law have changed over time, just as other concepts (e.g. competition, monopoly, etc.) have evolved as well. In this discussion, I outline the emergence of classical (or "formalist") contract law in the early 19th century and its subsequent replacement by "realist" and then "neo-formalist" perspectives in the 20th century. After this, I examine the importance of contract and contract law in neoliberal thought, specifically in relation to the work of Friedrich Hayek (1960). My aim is to outline how assumptions about markets and market competition hinge upon contract law, especially on certain forms of *standard form* – or "boilerplate" – contracts. These standard contracts entail certain problematic limitations for contracting parties that contradict (liberal) notions of freedom, autonomy, and independence on which much neoliberal thinking is premised.

The evolution of contract law

What is contract law?

Freedom of contract is often used to distinguish capitalism from feudalism, or other economic systems. For example, in 1861 Henry Sumner Maine famously described "modern" societies as a "movement from status to contract" (quoted in Zumbansen 2007: 211, fn 121). Hayek (1944 [2001]: 87) also cited Maine in *The Road to Serfdom*. Similarly, Henry Sidgwick wrote some years later in 1879:

> In a summary view of the civil order of society, as constituted in accordance with the individualistic ideal, performance of contract presents itself as the chief *positive* element, protection of life and property being the chief *negative* element. (Quoted in Waddams 1999: 3)

Although the emergence of classical contract law in the late 18th and early 19th centuries, on which such statements are based, can be framed in these sorts of generic societal or political terms, it also reflects changes in political-economic activities and markets, including the rise of "futures" trading, insurance industry, and notions of risk (Horwitz 1974; Pratt 1988). As a result, classical contract law has to be understood in relation to the specific evolution and configuration of capitalism; the same can then be said of the subsequent changes to contract law in the 20th century. In this sense, contemporary contract law – defined as *neo-formalism* or *anti-antiformalism* – has to be understood in relation to neoliberalism – and vice versa. Before I get to this evolution of contract law, however, it is important to define "contract" in legal terms and the differences between this definition and the definition in neoclassical economics.

In neoclassical economics, as already mentioned, contract is often simply defined as some form of reciprocal arrangement between two (or more) parties (Eisenberg 1999), leading to a confusing conflation of contract with "exchange" or "transaction" (Hodgson 2015). An example would be Jensen and Meckling's (1976) discussion of contract in relation to their "agency theory" of the firm. Moreover, Hodgson (1999: 65) argues that there is a tendency in economics, especially those versions based on notions of rational individualism, to ignore the underlying social, political, and legal basis of "contract" (when using it in the economistic sense of the term). Examples of these underlying aspects include formal and informal institutions like the justice system, trust, etc. In contrast to the use of contract in economics, the term has a more specific definition and usage in law, especially commercial law. In particular, and as already mentioned, contract is used as a term to define "legally enforceable promises" (Eisenberg 1999). For example, legal scholars define contract law in terms of "mutual promises" (Horwitz 1974: 919); "the law was enforcing a promise" (Gordley 2000: 1847); "the art of enforcing promises" (Kreitner 2007: 1); and "ensuring that voluntary agreements between private parties are legally binding" (Hart 2011: 4). This difference between economics and law is important because it complicates various conceptions of markets and market competition that are put forward by neoliberals and are used in critical accounts of those neoliberal claims. For example, Horwitz (1974: 937) has specifically argued that "Contract then becomes an *instrument for protecting against changes in supply and price* in a market economy" (emphasis added). It is therefore helpful to think of contract not as the exchange or transfer of property "but as creating an expected return" through an exchange of promises (ibid.).

I would suggest that part of the confusion in usage of the term contract in neoclassical economics results from the fact that contract – and property rights for that matter – did not arise because of or emerge with capitalism; in fact, contract and contract law existed well before capitalism, although contract law has changed quite significantly over time (as has capitalism). In this sense, it is too simplistic to equate freedom to contract with capitalism or capitalist markets or market individualism or similar; rather, it is necessary to understand how contract law has changed and in what ways this is the result of emerging and also evolving capitalist pressures. Moreover, it is necessary to ask whether more recent contract law has changed as the result of neoliberal political-economic pressures and dynamics.

A brief history of contract law

In order to understand this evolution of Anglo-American contract law, I outline three phases in contract law since the early 19th century in this section. Legal scholars have broadly defined these phases as *formalism* (1860–1930s), *realism* (1930s–1990s), and *neo-formalism* (post-1990s) (see Hart 2011: 10). It is important to note that these sorts of easy classifications are problematic, not least in terms of how different perspectives appropriate different claims about the different eras to promote their agendas (Kreitner 2007). That being said, it is helpful to have some sense of how contract law has changed over time and so I adopt this chronology for simplicity's sake. Before I get into these eras, however, I have to start with a discussion of "pre-capitalist" notions of contract in order to set the stage. It is also important to note that much of what I discuss here is particular to common law regimes, especially those of England and the USA.

Before the formalist era, contract law was constrained by sovereign will, in that certain promises required a sovereign's seal of approval and certain rights were applied differently to the sovereign, aristocracy, and commoners – for example, the (fair) prices charged by a producer had to be "on a scale suitable to his [sic] station in life" (Kozolchyk 1991: 3). According to Horwitz (1974: 919), pre-capitalist "exchange" reflected the immediate transfer of property between owners, whereas "executory exchange" (i.e. promise) only developed in the 17th century. At this historical juncture and up until the late 18th century, contract and contract law were dominated by traditional forms of contracting, namely *covenant* and *assumpsit*; the former represented promises entered into "under seal" of the sovereign, while the latter represented promises that carried "consideration" (Gordley 2000: 1847). Consideration is a key concept in contract law and refers to the principle that only some promises are enforceable, namely those involving a mutual promise defined by a reason for making that promise (Waddams 1999). Before 19th century formalism, moreover, consideration had to represent something of "equivalent value to what he [sic] gave", meaning that contracts had to reflect an equitable arrangement between two parties which limited enforceability of contracts to equitable exchange (Gordley 2000: 1849). Consequently, this meant that market transactions at the time were limited to sovereign-enforced rules or to the exchange of things of equivalent value. Obviously this placed significant limits on the types of market activity that people could engage in, leading Kozolchyk (1991: 7) to argue that its replacement by classical contract law (or formalism) represented "the emancipation of the merchant class in Europe".

Generally speaking, classical contract law – or *formalism* – emerged at the start of the 19th century in England and then spread to the USA, and dominated legal debate and decisions until around the Great Depression in the 1930s (Hart 2011). It centres on a particular conception of "man" – which is a term I deliberately use to reflect the gendered nature of these legal ideas – through a reworking of key concepts like consideration. Classical legal theorists and judges sought to create a formal, essentialist, and universal notion of contract and its underlying constituent elements (e.g. consideration, individualism) as a way to circumvent the status-centred approach to contract that dominated political economies previously (see earlier discussion). In particular, as contract law was increasingly formalized, the definition of consideration was narrowed, according to Waddams (1999: 17), so that it meant a commercial reason (i.e. monetary value) for making a (mutual) promise – that is, where the promise entails value for *both* parties (i.e. a bargain). As such, contract excluded gifts or other gratuitous relations. According to Kreitner (2007: 17), this formulation of consideration entailed – and necessitated – the conception of man as an "economically rational agent" in order to legitimate the "withdrawal of state power from the sphere associated with economic rationality, in other words the market". As such, the classical conception of consideration is closely aligned with a "will theory" of contract in which individuals were deemed to be able to enter into contracts themselves because they were characterized as autonomous and able to calculate and consent to the benefits of said contracts without (paternalistic) interference from the state (or anyone else).

This change in contract law had significant implications on a number of political-economic levels. First, through the emphasis on a rules-based approach to contract, formalism engendered "certainty and predictability in the marketplace" according to Miller (2010: 498). In particular, classical contract law was driven by the idea that it was the performance rather than status of individual contracting parties that matters. Second, and as noted earlier, these changes were premised on the notion of people – really men – as individual, rational, and calculating political-economic actors (Kreitner 2007; Miller 2010). It opened up the ability of people to engage in almost unlimited contractual arrangements, entailing forms of supposedly "private" lawmaking through mutually constituted obligations (for example, see Purdy (2014) on the consequences of this in the so-called *Lochner* era in the USA (1905–37)). Third, it meant that value in consideration came to mean anything that people decided it to mean because they were seen as best able to judge the value of something to themselves (Gordley 2000). As a result, contractual parties were no longer limited to exchanging things of equivalent value. Finally, as Horwitz (1974: 918) notes, "will theory" and the function of contract law and contracts "shifted from that of simply transferring title to a specific item to that of ensuring an expected return". This opened up an array of political-economic activities that were previously (legally) unavailable (or at least uncertain), including futures contracts that were emerging around agricultural commodities and insurance (Pratt 1988).

At the start of the 20th century, formalism was increasingly criticized for its essentialist and inflexible approach, especially in an era that was dominated by large corporations that could perpetuate inequality through unequal bargaining in contractual relations (see Chapter 6). For example, Zumbansen (2007: 202) argues that Legal Realists in the late 19th and early 20th centuries saw formalism "as advantaging the already powerful over those who ideally should share the power in a modern, democratic society". As a result, thinking in contract law shifted to a *relational* or *realist* position by and after the 1930s (Miller 2010). In particular, Kreitner (2007: 188, 191) argues that realism was especially aligned with "a progressive socialization of contract law"; by this he meant that rather than reasoning from abstract first principles, realism was premised on the idea that the everyday views of business people should shape the law – basically, "norms" not first principles. It is this sort of "relational" reasoning that is embedded in things like the *Uniform Commercial Code* (est. 1952) and two *Restatements of Contract* (est. 1932 and 1979) that were developed in the USA (Gordley

2000). According to Miller (2010), moreover, realism acknowledges that markets are not perfect, information is not symmetrical, and that there can be significant bargaining disparities between contractual parties, for example between large corporations and individual citizens. As a result, the realist approach to contract law was seen as an "activist" position. For some this meant a negative interference in the private contractual relations between consenting parties, while for others it meant a positive interference in ameliorating the power differences between contracting parties (Kreitner 2007).

Like formalism, modern or realist contract law entailed a number of political-economic implications. First, and unlike formalism and its emphasis on essentialist principles, realism involves a concern with values- or status-based approach in which ideas of "fairness" and "good faith" in contractual relations are meant to ameliorate power differences between the parties (Gordley 2000). This was an especially important issue in the 20th century as large corporations came to dominate the US economy. Second, realism reflected new forms of contracting practices associated with the emergence of these large corporations at the end of the 19th century (Pratt 1988). In particular, the inflexibility of formalism was associated with simple, one-time transactions (e.g. exchange of property title), while realism was associated with more complex transactions (e.g. employment contract); for example, complex contracts required that contract law "take account of variations in the wills and consent of the parties over the duration of their long-term relationship" (Trakman 2010: 1065). Finally, realism acknowledges that contract law is not a "private" affair, involving only the individual contracting parties. As Miller (2010) points out, contract law necessarily entails the application of state power (i.e. public law) in the pursuit of private interests when the law intervenes (e.g. bailiffs, police, law courts, etc.). That is, contract law actually involves the enrolment of full state power in the assertion of one party's interests against the other.

As noted, realism was defined as a problematic interventionist approach in contract law by a number of legal thinkers, especially those in the Economics and Law movement that emerged from the Chicago University law school (see Chapter 3 on Richard Posner). These thinkers argued and continue to argue for a return to formalist principles in contract law on the basis that contract law is defined by "the parties' lawmaking power and minimizes the extent to which contract (necessarily) involves state impositions of obligations" (Kreitner 2007: 193).

According to Hart (2011), this *neo-formalism* – or, tongue-twistingly, "anti-antiformalism" – has come to dominate contract law since the 1990s. It is primarily concerned with reducing the role of the law in configuring economic activities, premised on the notion that contracts and contract law represent a form of transaction cost (see Coase 1937), which reduces the naturalized efficiency inherent in an idealized free market – in which there are no transaction costs – as imagined by people like Richard Posner (Harcourt 2012: 139). As Trakman (2010: 1069) argues, for example, "Such 'efficiency' is usually ascribed to neoliberal principles grounded in free market economics and rooted in utilitarian philosophy". Although neo-formalism is an attempt to resurrect certain aspects of classical contract law (e.g. essential principles), it also incorporates aspects of the realist approach. According to Hart (2011: 12), for example, neo-formalism is characterized by an attempt to "give effect to norms of fairness and cooperation as supplements to, but not replacements of, the classical norms of individual autonomy and liberty". It does not represent a wholesale reversion to 19th century notions of contract and contract law. In part, this perspective could be seen as building on the realist argument that business people are best placed to determine contractual relations, although Charny (1999) makes the point that this is based on the expansion of (formal) standards developed by trade associations. This then raises the question of whether these sorts of standards represent another form of rent-seeking as dominant business interests limit market access (ibid.; see Chapter 7).

Neoliberalism and the law of contract

Having discussed the history and evolution of contract law, it is now necessary to analyse whether (and how) the latest phase in contract law – *neo-formalism* – reflects neoliberal principles and pressures. Before doing that, though, I examine how neoliberals, specifically Friedrich Hayek, understood contract and contractual arrangements. As I have argued elsewhere (Birch 2016), it is important to note that contract law and contract are central planks in neoliberal thought, although far more attention has been paid to property rights, privatization, and the commons in the critical literature (e.g. Harvey 2005; Prasad 2006; Peck 2010; cf. Foucault 2008). In fact, a number of early "neo-liberals" – especially those in the Ordoliberal School – were lawyers or were interested in law, especially because it relates to the establishment of the framework conditions necessary for market competition (Gerber

1994). As this would imply, contract law – and other forms of commercial law – were seen as directly implicated in the construction of social order, especially one based on markets and competition. Aside from the mentions I made to neoliberalism in the legal discussion earlier, another key example of the relationship between neoliberalism and contract (and contract law) is contained in the later work of Friedrich Hayek. In particular, in his major treatise on law, *The Constitution of Liberty*, which he wrote whilst at the University of Chicago, in which Hayek (1960) discussed the relationship between contract, markets, and liberty.

Hayek (1960) argued that the reason "other people's property can be serviceable in the achievement of our aims is due mainly to the enforceability of contracts" meaning that "the whole network of rights created by contracts is as important a part of our own protected sphere, as much the basis of our plans, as any property of our own" (p.208). Hayek's main point here is that any form of market exchange – which he associated with "free" social interactions and spontaneous social order – is only possible and feasible when there are both private property rights and, just as importantly, rules of contract. It is the latter that enables property owners to exchange their property and, in his words, "competition [is only] made possible by the dispersion of property" (p.124). It is this dispersion of property which is dependent on contract law. Why? Well, without rules of contract there is no way to exchange property securely with one another. As a result, there can be no exchange; without exchange, there can be no prices generated by the market; without prices, there can be no way for individuals to determine what they should produce or buy; and hence society cannot benefit from forces of competition (e.g. reducing production costs, introduction of new products and services, etc.). From this perspective, there can be no social order without contract law, only chaos.

From Hayek's perspective, it is contract – and in the legal rather than economistic sense (see earlier) – that enables individual decision-making and social relations with one another, although this might also be necessarily framed by "the reign of general and equal laws" (1960: 222). Hayek had a clear preference for the common law in this regard (p.329) because he considered it as a form of law that avoided the "arbitrary" interference in social life – and by "arbitrary" he meant:

> It is the rule of Law, in the sense of rule of formal law, the absence of legal privileges of particular people designated by authority, which safeguards

that equality before the law which is the opposite of arbitrary government. (Hayek 1944 [2001]: 87)

Accordingly, Hayek (1960: 338) argued that there were certain minimum legal arrangements necessary for a market order, especially consistent with forms of market competition, which had to be enforced by the state. Generally, Hayek argued that markets and market competition are underpinned by contract law and individual contracting, which, in turn, are buttressed by a general set of laws all enforced by the state. In discussing Hayek's arguments here, my aim is to highlight the importance of contract law in the conceptualization of a neoliberal order, as imagined by the likes of Hayek. It is notable that this sort of analytical understanding of the relationship between contract, markets, and social order is necessarily built on a set of assumptions about human beings; that is, their capacities, their responses, their behaviours, and so on. As the earlier discussion of contract law should illustrate, however, these assumptions inform the configuration of contract law and notions of contract. In relation to this chapter, for example, they reflect the expectation for how social agents act and behave in markets, and the limits to their rationality.

Making and unmaking neoliberal actors through contract law

I deliberately left off the discussion of the political-economic implications of neo-formalism until now in order to develop this discussion in more depth in relation to neoliberalism. Neo-formalism, like classical and modern contract law, is based on a set of assumptions and expectations about how people make decisions, choose how to act, and understand the world in which they live. Briefly, and to repeat myself somewhat, classical contract law (or formalism) was based on the idea that emerging capitalist markets required the predictability and certainty offered by formal rules and principles (Miller 2010). In contrast, modern contract law (or realism) was based on the idea that there are significant power differentials between social actors – e.g. corporation and individual person – which need to be mitigated through norms of fairness and good faith (Gordley 2000). When it comes to neo-formalism, Hart (2011: 14–15) argues that it is premised on a series of problematic assumptions about markets, namely contracts are private, voluntary, and informed transactions, they involve arm's-length relations between rational actors in the market, and contract law represents the main form of market regulation with minimal state interference. As is evident, each of these approaches to contract law entailed a different perception of individual social agents (Kreitner 2007).

First, formalism witnessed a shift from an "equitable theory" of contract, in which contractual obligations were legally limited by fairness and "insulated from the purposes of commercial transactions" (Horwitz 1974: 927), to a "will theory" in which "contract law begins to separate itself from property [law]" on the basis of differentiating between transactions and expectations (p.937). With will theory, individual business-"men" – again, a specific use of gendered terms – were conceived as autonomous and rational, and therefore able to make their own decisions about the obligations they wished to enter into (even if they were or seemed inequitable) without the intervention of the state or courts in their affairs. Second, realism represented a shift from will theory to a concern with power differentials between contracting parties, especially in relation to complex and incomplete contracts (Gordley 2000). This concern is reflected in the development of norms of fairness and good faith bargaining in which performance, rather than formal or literal obligation, became the focus of legal attention, leading to the increasing involvement of courts in contractual relations (Pratt 1988). At the same time, courts sought to interpret contract law from the perspective of the average business person, rather than abstract principles. Finally, neo-formalism represents an uneasy union of sorts between formalism and realism in which there is an attempt to return to first principles and formal obligations, while accepting that different market actors have different capacities to act rationally, or in a "sophisticated" manner (Miller 2010). However, as Trakman (2010: 1073) notes, neo-formalism, as an "efficiency analysis", extends this approach "selectively to include some equity and fairness values while excluding others". As such, neo-formalism seeks both to frame some contracting parties as autonomous and rational, while framing others as unsophisticated and irrational.

In the rest of this section, I am interested in unpacking the neo-formalist conceptualization of individual agency because it represents the construction of a specifically "neoliberal" social actor (cf. subjectivity). Three issues are of particular importance in this regard: disclosure, sophistication, and consent. The first two can be seen as legal attempts to construct market actors as autonomous and rational, while acknowledging that there are legal limits to this framing of individual human action; the last one can be seen as a legal attempt to erase the issue altogether through a presumption of assumed – but not given – "rational" consent. I see them all as part of the legal construction of idealized market actors necessary to meet the principles underpinning neoliberal thought, but contradictorily leading to a wholesale erosion of individual, autonomous, and rational decision-making through the imposition of standard form contractual arrangements (which I discuss later).

First, disclosure rules in contract law necessarily highlight the fact that real-life markets are not *perfect* (see Crouch 2011) in the sense that not all market actors automatically (or naturally) have access to the same information, or have the same ability to collect information or process the information they can collect, or have the capacity to act on that information. There are considerable inequities in bargaining as a result. That being said, Hart (2011: 21) argues that even though "modern contract law assumes that unequal bargaining power exists" it does so "in an unproblematic way" through disclosure rules. The point of disclosure rules is to enable the market to "work" as it is naturalized to do, even though, analytically-speaking, the very fact of disclosure rules demonstrates that markets are social constructs and do not reflect some idealized natural mechanism (see Chapter 3). Disclosure rules are meant to enable market actors to make better "market" decisions by improving informed choices, even though they leave bargaining disparities very much intact (p.27–8). However, Hart argues that this framing of disclosure ends up presenting "informed choice" as a justification for holding contracting parties to account through the notion that disclosure rules are proof of mutual consent. Although it is not possible to argue that all – or even most – market actors are "sophisticated" (see later), disclosure rules provide a way to assume that they are because all parties have information and information means rational (i.e. better) choices are possible. For example, it assumes "A person acts rationally where she perfectly processes available information about alternative courses of action and then ranks the possible outcomes in the order of expected utility" (p.47).

Second, the issue of sophistication highlights how courts recognize the different abilities and capacities of market actors to contract with one another, even from a neo-formalist perspective. According to Miller (2010: 495), the concept of party sophistication is one way that neo-formalism has preserved in "the context of a transaction" while returning to notions of autonomy and the literal interpretation of contract obligations (on the basis that they represent the will of the contracting parties). Sophistication is a way to differentiate between market actors, primarily on a spectrum from sophisticated to unsophisticated contracting parties, which then "allows courts to avoid more difficult questions about the relative positions of the contracting parties" (p.496). This means courts, and contract law, do not need to address the trickier, political issue of unequal bargaining power between parties. Miller also notes that neo-formalism is influenced by the efficiency arguments of the Law and Economics movement, closely linked to Chicago University Law School. The concept of sophistication is premised on the idea that different market actors can and should be held to a "different set of rules, grounded in freedom of contract" (p.501). On the one hand, sophisticated parties are held to a set of rules, while on the other hand, unsophisticated parties are held to a set of norms. Who then counts as sophisticated? Primarily, according to Miller (2010: 509), it is "commercial entities" – that is, businesses – and government entities (i.e. organizations). Secondarily, however, it includes a range of individuals who engage in contractual relations, like business people, lawyers, and other professionals, or are represented by sophisticated parties (e.g. lawyer, accountant). It is possible to argue that it is only these "business-like" entities and individuals who, as sophisticated market actors, represent "actually existing" neoliberal agents, able *and* willing to act in a "rational" and utility maximizing manner. The reason why is quite simple – they are forced to act "rationally" by courts that treat them differently from other individuals without the position and status *of* "rationality" (which is associated with information asymmetries; Miller 2010). Contract law does not treat people (and even some entities) as individual, rational actors – as many neoliberal critics might imagine – but rather only treats certain people as such. It is therefore interesting to note that neo-formalism represents a return to pre-formalist approach in which status determines who, in principle, counts as having autonomy and rationality.

Finally, while disclosure and sophistication represent legal concepts that configure certain individuals (and entities) as autonomous and rational, namely those engaged in business activities, they leave the vast proportion of the population as ingénues. This presents a problem when it comes to the issue of consent in contractual relations. According to Sonja Amadae (2016), however, consent is framed by neoliberal legal thinkers like Richard Posner (see Chapter 3) in such a way as to erase autonomy, rationality, and consent altogether from political-economic activities. As a result, most people are erased as market actors, sidelined by a set of assumptions about who they are and how they act. For example, according to Amadae (2016: 10):

> Consent is rendered superfluous [as result of neoliberalism] because knowledge of an individual's preferences over all possible outcomes makes it possible to deduce what that individual would choose to do "in every situation which may conceivably arise".

Consent is erased as the result of, first, assuming that individuals are rational and autonomous maximizers such that they will *always* choose the "opportunity" (i.e. property) that results in the best outcome (i.e. opportunity cost thinking) (Amadae 2016: 209); and, second, assuming "that resources are socially best allocated when held by the highest bidder, who by definition puts them to their most efficient use" (p.211). On this basis, Amadae argues that the legal thinker and judge Richard Posner promotes the notion that "a reassignment of property rights can be as effective as an actual market exchange in realizing surplus value" (p.211), thereby mitigating any need for markets to exist. In this sense, all that is needed are "prosthetic markets" (Davies 2014) and "market-like" experts (Power 2010) which can act in the place of market exchange. At its base, this position assumes that consent is always given if an action leads to the most "rational" outcome: "Posnerian law and economics has the unsalutary effect of putting every resource up for sale for market prices determined independently of actual consent" (Amadae 2016: 218). Effectively, therefore, Amadae argues that there is no need for markets at all from this Posnerian perspective, thereby *unmaking* most individuals as autonomous and rational market actors, to be replaced by an automatic process of property (re-)allocation based on expert, technical judgements about value and who can "best" use property.

Making and unmaking markets through standard contracts

What does this all mean for understanding the relationship between contract law and neoliberalism? The discussion of contract in economics generally and neoliberalism specifically can often seem confusing or fuzzy because "contract" means different things to different people. If we follow Hayek, however, then contract and contract law are the underpinnings of "neoliberal" social order because they are the means to engender market competition through contractual relations. However, if we follow Posner, then contract and contract law are largely irrelevant because property can be legally re-assigned without consent, or even market transactions. Obviously, the former appears far preferable politically than the latter approach, but are there any problematic aspects to the Hayekian position as well? In this section I discuss the key problem with Hayek's approach to contract law, namely the dependence on "standard contracts" – also called "boilerplate" contracts.

Markets, neoliberalism, and standard contracts

A major issue with the notion of a social order based on contractual relations, as theorized by Hayek (1960), is that it assumes each individual person can and does construct their own contractual relations with one another. However, in this scenario social interaction would quickly bog down because a wide-array of social interactions would entail continual and ongoing contractual negotiations, monitoring, and enforcement. This is especially the case if the economistic concept of contract is used – that is, "contract" as "reciprocal arrangements" (Eisenberg 1999). For example, Weinstein (2012) argues that the contractual theory of the firm developed by the likes of Jensen and Meckling (1976) was meant to conceptualize the firm as the market. In Weinstein's (2012: 28 fn. 69) words:

> Let us say that there was a shift from a representation of the market order as a multilateral system of simultaneous, anonymous relations to a representation in terms of bilateral relations that are necessarily personal, and from coordination through prices (and equilibrium) to coordination through negotiation and contracts. This made it possible to reduce the opposition between market and firm, or even reduce the firm to a particular market.

However, market relations cannot be conceived of as only or even mainly discrete, one-time transactions. Ongoing, relational contracts – highlighted in the legal literature on contract law – are common in business and market exchange; however, such contractual relations are ignored in most neoliberal conceptions or deployment of contract and contract language (Trakman, 2010). The same could be said in relation to critical perspectives of neoliberalism. Importantly, when the market is conceived as a series of one-time "contractual" relations (i.e. transactions), any extension of the market necessarily increases transaction costs – because it increases the number of these "contractual" relations – and thereby reduces the efficiency of the market. This represents a key contradiction in neoliberalism and our analytical understandings of it.

If, as Paul Treanor (2005) claims, neoliberalism is characterized by the "desire to intensify and expand the market, by increasing the number, frequency, repeatability, and formalisation of transaction", then neoliberalism promotes the extension of (market) transactions, conceived as or equated with contracts to everything. This leads to an increase in the frequency of contractual negotiations, a decrease in their duration, and an intensification in forms of contractual audit. As such, and analytically speaking, neoliberalism is constituted by increasing the number, frequency, duration, and intensity of "contractual" relations. With neoliberalism, everything is turned into a contract and these contracts are meant to be (re-)negotiated constantly, reduced to the shortest possible timeframe to enable constant (re-)negotiation, and watched constantly – a starker utopia than the market-based order that critical scholars usually present. This neoliberal nightmare implies that as more activity – economic, social, political, etc. – becomes (supposedly) "market-based", it will significantly increase the aggregate cost of contracting because every social action – now covered by the "market" – will necessitate contractual negotiation, coordination, monitoring, and enforcement.

The resulting increase in transaction costs would be phenomenal if everything was swept up into contracting, and it would likely lead to the "market" grinding to a halt. In fact, it would seem that the only way to resolve this dilemma from a neoliberal perspective is to standardize contractual arrangements; that is, to construct *standard form contracts* that can cover a range of social interactions. For example, even though Hayek (1960: 339) argued that each individual should be able to construct their own contractual relations with each other, he also noted that the standard contract "often greatly facilitates [such] private dealings" (p.339). It is for this reason that any understanding of neoliberalism as a concept requires an examination of the conceptual and practical importance of these standard form contracts (from now on "standard contract"), a task which is often obscured by the emphasis on markets in critical perspectives of neoliberalism (Birch 2016). Standard contracts, however, raise more contradictions in our understanding of neoliberalism, both analytically and empirically, which I turn to next.

Standard contracts as the underbelly of neoliberalism

A standard contract – or boilerplate contract – is a contractual arrangement in which one party, usually buyer or consumer, has no or little input in determining the terms of the contractual agreement (e.g. Slawson, 1971; Bebchuk and Posner, 2006; Gilo and Porat, 2006; Trakman, 2010; Zamir, 2014). An everyday example would be an end user license agreement (EULA) between software provider (or similar) and customer – this is a generic contract many of us enter into on a daily basis through the purchase or download of software apps for smartphones. Standard contracts are no longer negotiated or even negotiable. It is hard, therefore, to consider them to be free and voluntary arrangements – as imagined in formalist and neo-formalist contract law – because one party has no power to enact their demands. However, as Hayek claimed, they are necessary for modern capitalism because without them every contract – which means every transaction to a neoliberal – would need to be individually negotiated, monitored, and enforced.

This would create an enormous cost for any society to bear, and explains why someone like Richard Posner might seek to do away with consent altogether in order to improve "efficiency" (Amadae 2016). It is hardly surprising, therefore, that standard contracts now represent "more than 99% of the contracts currently entered, whether consumer or commercial" (Zamir 2014: 2096). They are everywhere, and they are not limited to individual consumers – business, the state, and consumers use them on a daily basis. According to Zamir, it is not "coincidental" that US law has failed to address problems with standard contracts (e.g. asymmetric power) because such contracts reflect:

> the fundamentally individualistic ethos of American society, the entrenched suspiciousness of – and even hostility to – government regulation, and the great influence of right-wing, Chicago-style economic analysis of private and commercial law in the past decades. (p.2096)

Bearing all this in mind, standard contracts highlight at least three significant contradictions within neoliberalism and even with current critical perspectives of neoliberalism: (1) they engender anti-competitive practices; (2) they replace market transactions; and (3) they enable privately made law that is as arbitrary as autocratic privilege.

First, standard contracts are contradictory – in relation to neoliberal ideas of market competition – because they enable and legitimate various forms of anticompetitive practice as a result of their complexity and the fact that few people, if any, actually read standard contract terms (Gilo and Porat 2006). For example, cellphone operators can tacitly collude with one another through the creation of complex and incommensurate cellphone contracts (pp.1006–7). As standard contracts become increasingly complex and differentiated from one another it becomes almost impossible to compare suppliers and prices. This has meant that it is the "transaction costs [i.e. negotiating, monitoring, enforcing] imposed upon consumers, from which the supplier expects to gain" (p.986). It becomes difficult to see how market price competition is promoted, enabled, or facilitated as a result, suggesting that characterizing neoliberalism in analytical terms as only or mainly a market-based order misses a key issue – most markets are "administered" in one way or another (see Means, 1983). There are "neoliberal" responses to this claim, outlined by Zamir (2014) for example, that amount to the argument that an "informed minority" (i.e. those people who read standard contract terms) of sophisticated buyers ensures terms are "efficient". However, this is premised on the idea that informed consent or assent is basically unnecessary for the vast majority of "unsophisticated" buyers (Amadae 2016). Even where informed consent is protected, it is done so through disclosure rules that assume individuals are capable of reading and, moreover, understanding contractual terms, an assumption that is deeply problematic according to Hart (2011). For example, Hart highlights research showing that 90 million people in the USA have marginal or no real literacy skills; at best, Hart argues, only 3–4 percent of people can actually understand contract language.

Second, standard contracts are also contradictory because they replace market transactions with contractual arrangements, in the legal sense of the term (i.e. "legally enforced promises"). Butler (1989: 119) notes that the standard contract "reduces the transaction and negotiating costs of reaching and adhering to optimal contracts". In this sense, contract law provides the underpinnings of neoliberalism because it enables the extension of *market-like* relations – conceptualized as contracts – to all areas of society. Basically, contract law increases the "efficiency" of markets, at least according to neoliberal legal scholars (Zumbansen 2007). However, this leads to a catch-22 in that without standard contracts the extension of market-like relations would entail increasing transaction costs, which would militate against the extension of those market-like relations in the first place. It is therefore unclear how neoliberals justify and legitimate the idea that "the market" – conceived as market transacting – is the best or only mechanism for coordinating the economy, the firm, or society more generally. If the market was the best or only mechanism needed, then there would be little need for contract law. However, the latter is crucial for ensuring market-like relations can and do happen without too high a cost. More critically, the more that our social relations are converted into *market-like* interactions, the less efficient the market will be unless those interactions are reduced to standard and non-negotiable contracts; this is hardly the basis for liberty or choice. Nor is it the basis for a (free) market economy because contract is "an instrument for protecting against changes in supply and price" (Horwitz 1974: 937). Rather, and building on the arguments in the last chapter, standard contracts represent a form of "rent-seeking" in which formal rules "garner rents by reducing the volume of transactions in which rivals could engage" (Charny 1999: 856).

Finally, standard contracts represent a way for private individuals and especially organizations to establish their own private system of law and governance, which explains why "neoliberalism" can seemingly sit so comfortably with the rise and dominance of large, monopolistic businesses (Braithewaite, 2005). This point goes back to the 1970s when Slawson (1971: 530) argued that standard contracts, which he claimed had already "engulfed the law of contract" and "become a considerable portion of all the law to which we are subject", are a form of "privately made law". The lack of negotiations – or even capacity to negotiate on the part of some parties – in standard contracts reflect the *delegation* (or arrogation) of legal power and authority to private business, especially in the areas of incorporation, employment and association (p.536; also Miller 2010; Hart 2011). What this implies, and as Miller (1972: 63) pointed out long ago, is that government and the law are "used to permit economic power (the corporations) to prescribe the terms and conditions of most of those transactions called contracts". The stipulation of non-negotiable terms and conditions in standard contracts, based on asymmetries in power between business and customer, severely limits any sense of freedom of contract. As such, standard contracts reflect a form of arbitrary power as defined by Hayek (1944 [2001]: 87), namely "legal privileges of particular people designated by authority".

Conclusion

I started out this chapter by noting that capitalism is often associated with two key underlying *legal* principles; that is, private property rights and freedom to contract. As others argue (e.g. Hodgson 2015), capitalism is dependent on social institutions like the law, belying the notion that there is or can be an idealized form of "free market" capitalism in which people are "free to choose" without external interventions of some sort or another (cf. Friedman 1962). In fact, my aim in this chapter was to illustrate just how important contract law is to configuring economic (if not "market") exchange. I focused on contract and contract law in order to problematize a conception of neoliberalism based on or underpinned by notions of (free) market exchange. Rather, I noted in the introduction that: (1) most economic activity takes place within organizations, which are entities defined by contractual relations; (2) contemporary capitalism is driven by a value logic in which future earnings are transposed into present value through contractual relations; and (3) law has largely been neglected in critical perspectives on neoliberalism, especially contract law.

In the rest of the chapter I discussed several aspects of contract and contract law relevant to understandings of neoliberalism, as a way to introduce the reader to the importance of both. I started with definitions of "contract", identifying the differences between economic and legal usage of the term. Then I provided a brief history of contract law, confined to common law jurisdictions – specifically England and the USA. This helped to demonstrate the evolution of contract law from pre-capitalist tenets, followed by a *formalist* revolution in the late 18th and early 19th century and a *realist* response in the early 20th century. Each form of legal reasoning reflects and constitutes political-economic relations of their times. As such, I then sought to examine whether a "neoliberal" form of contract law has emerged. In some senses, it has, been represented by a *neo-formalist* revival in the late 20th century. However, identifying this form of contract law with neoliberalism raises numerous contradictions, of which I focused on two. First, the alignment of neo-formalism with efficiency arguments in the (neoliberal) law and economics movement led some legal scholars to argue that market exchange was less efficient than the legal re-allocation of property rights. Second, equating market transactions with contractual relations is based on the notion that the latter can be replaced with standard form contracts that eliminate aspects of informed consent and reinforce the prevailing interest positions of incumbent market actors, leading to forms of rent-seeking (see Chapter 7). As such, I would argue that these contradictions unmake most individuals as *market* actors and also most transactions as *market* exchange.

Bibliography

Amadae, S.A. (2016), *Prisoners of Reason*, Cambridge: Cambridge University Press.

Aksikas, J. and Andrews, S. (2014), "Neoliberalism, law and culture: a cultural studies intervention after 'the juridical turn'", *Cultural Studies*, 28(5–6), 742–80.

Bebchuk, L. and Posner, R. (2006), "One-sided contracts in competitive consumer markets", *Michigan Law Review*, 104, 827–36.

Birch, K. (2016), "Market vs. contract? The implications of contractual theories of corporate governance to the analysis of neoliberalism", *ephemera: theory & politics in organization*, 16(1), 107–33.

Birch, K. (2017), "Rethinking *value* in the bio-economy: finance, assetization and the management of value", *Science, Technology and Human Values*, 42(3), 460–90.

Bowman, S. (1996), *The Modern Corporation and American Political Thought*, University Park, PA: Pennsylvania State University Press.

Brabazon, H. (ed) (2016), *Neoliberal Legality: The Constitutive Role of Law in the Neoliberal Project*, London: Routledge.

Braithwaite, J. (2005), "Neoliberalism or regulatory capitalism", ANU: RegNet, Occasional Paper No.5.

Butler, H. (1989), "The contractual theory of the corporation", *George Mason University Law Review*, 11, 99–123.

Charny, D. (1999), "The new formalism in contract", *University of Chicago Law Review*, 6(3), 842–57.

Coase, R. (1937), "The nature of the firm", *Economica*, 4(16), 386–405.

Crouch, C. (2011), *The Strange Non-Death of Neoliberalism*, Cambridge: Polity Press.

Davies, W. (2010), "Economics and the "nonsense" of law: the case of the Chicago antitrust revolution", *Economy and Society*, 39(1), 64–83.

Davies, W. (2014), *The Limits of Neoliberalism*, London: Sage.

Eisenberg, M. (1999), "The conception that the corporation is a nexus of contracts, and the dual nature of the firm", *Journal of Corporation Law*, 24, 819–36.

Foucault, M. (2008), *The Birth of Biopolitics*, New York, NY: Picador.

Friedman, M. (1962), *Capitalism and Freedom*, Chicago, IL: University of Chicago Press.

Gerber, D. (1994), "Constitutionalizing the economy: German neoliberalism, competition law and the 'new' Europe", *American Journal of Comparative Law*, 42, 25–84.

Gilo, D. and Porat, A. (2006), "The hidden roles of boilerplate and standard-form contracts: Strategic imposition of transaction costs, segmentation of consumers, and anticompetitive effects", *Michigan Law Review*, 104, 983–1032.

Gordley, J. (2000), "The common law in the twentieth century: some unfinished business", *California Law Review*, 88(6), 1815–76.

Grewal, D. and Purdy, J. (2014), "Introduction: law and neoliberalism", *Law & Contemporary Problems*, 77, 1–23.

Harcourt, B. (2012), *The Illusion of Free Markets*, Cambridge MA: Harvard University Press.

Hart, D. (2011), "Contract law now – reality meets legal fictions", *Baltimore Law Review*, 41, 1–81.

Harvey, D. (2005), *A Brief History of Neoliberalism*, Oxford: Oxford University Press.

Hayek, F. (1944 [2001]), *The Road to Serfdom*, London: Routledge.

Hayek, F. (1960), *The Constitution of Liberty*, Chicago, IL: Chicago University Press.

Hodgson, G. (1999), *Economics and Utopia*, London: Routledge.

Hodgson, G. (2005), "Knowledge at work: some neoliberal anachronisms", *Review of Social Economy*, 63(4), 547–65.

Hodgson, G. (2015), *Conceptualizing Capitalism*, Chicago, IL: University of Chicago Press.

Horwitz, M. (1974), "The historical foundations of modern contract law", *Harvard Law Review*, 87(5), 917–56.

Jensen, M. and Meckling, W. (1976), "Theory of the firm: managerial behavior, agency costs and ownership structure", *Journal of Financial Economics*, 3, 305–60.

Kozolchyk, B. (1991), "On the state of commercial law at the end of the 20th century", *Arizona Journal of International and Comparative Law*, 8, 1–32.

Kreitner, R. (2007), *Calculating Promises*, Stanford CA: Stanford University Press.

Means, G. (1983), "Power in the marketplace", *Journal of Law and Economics*, 26(2), 467–85.

Miller, A.S. (1972), "Legal foundations of the corporate state", *Journal of Economic Issues*, 6(1), 59–79.

Miller, M. (2010), "Contract law, party sophistication and the new formalism", *Missouri Law Review*, 75(2), 493–536.

Muniesa, F. (2014), *The Provoked Economy*, London: Routledge.

Nik-Khah, E. and van Horn, R. (2012), "Inland empire: economics imperialism as an imperative of Chicago neoliberalism", *Journal of Economic Methodology*, 19(3), 259–82.

Nitzan, J. and Bichler, S. (2009), *Capital as Power*, London: Routledge.

Peck, J. (2010), *Constructions of Neoliberal Reason*, Oxford: Oxford University Press.

Power, M. (2010), "Fair value accounting, financial economics and the transformation of reliability", *Accounting and Business Research*, 40, 197–210.

Prasad, M. (2006), *The Politics of Free Markets*, Chicago, IL: University of Chicago Press.

Pratt, W. (1988), "American contract law at the turn of the century", *South Carolina Law Review*, 39(3), 415–64.

Purdy, J. (2014), "Neoliberal constitutionalism: Lochnerism for a new economy", *Law & Contemporary Problems*, 77, 195–213.

Roth, S. (2016), "Why economists don't know how to think about wealth (or profits)", evonomics.com, 3 December, accessed 19 December 2016 at https://evonomics.com/economists-dont-know-think-wealth-profits/.

Slawson, W.D. (1971), "Standard form contracts and democratic control of lawmaking power", *Harvard Law Review*, 84(3), 529–66.

Trakman, L. (2010), "Pluralism in contract law", *Buffalo Law Review*, 58(5), 1031–93.

Treanor, P. (2005), "Neoliberalism: origins, theory, definition", accessed 13 December 2016 at http://web.inter.nl.net/users/Paul.Treanor/neoliberalism.html.

Waddams, S. (1999), *The Law of Contracts*, Toronto, ON: Canada Law Books Inc.

Weinstein, O. (2012), "Firm, property and governance: from Berle and Means to the agency theory, and beyond", *Accounting, Economics, and Law*, 2(2), 1–55.

Zamir, E. (2014), "Contract law and theory: three views of the cathedral", *University of Chicago Law Review*, 81, 2077–123.

Zumbansen, P. (2007), "The law of society: governance through contract", *Indiana Journal of Global Legal Studies*, 14(2), 191–233.

9 Conclusion

Introduction

As I come to the end of writing this book, I have also come to the end of 2016. For many people, especially those of a leftist-bent, this year has been a bit of a disaster. Political moments like the British referendum on leaving the European Union (EU) in June – or "Brexit" – and the US presidential elections in November could represent a significant shift in the geo-political and geo-economic trends of the last few decades. Specifically, a number of commentators have characterized these events as a populist wave of anger against the version of "neoliberalism" pursued by governments in the USA, UK, and EU, especially against past and proposed free trade deals that have left whole communities devastated by unemployment, economic stagnation, and the resulting loss of social safety nets following austerity policies. It looks like global integration, at least in the free trade and open borders mold, is off the cards for a generation, that is if governments want to avoid a prejudiced backlash against immigrants, ethnic minorities, marginalized groups, and others targeted by right-wing political parties (e.g. UKIP) and movements (e.g. "alt-right"). Obviously, this backlash can be further stoked and exploited by the right to further their political ambitions, as has been happening in many European countries ranging from Sweden through Germany and Hungary to Italy and France.

It is perhaps more helpful, however, to think of 2016 as a watershed, rather than the abyss staring back at us. After the global financial crisis, many academics and others wrote about the end of neoliberalism – including myself (e.g. Birch and Mykhnenko 2010) – before the realization hit that not much had really changed. As a result, many scholars then started writing books about how the financial crisis had not really changed much after all, or that neoliberalism continues its march apace (e.g. Peck 2010; Crouch 2011; Mirowski 2013; Dardot and Laval 2014; Brown 2015). Maybe we have finally reached that inflection point when so-called neoliberalism is at an end. What we are left with, though, is the difficult task of working towards a progressive alternative, rather than falling into some form of rabid nativism and ethnic hatred. In some ways, it does not matter whether this alternative comes from the left or right, as long as it does two things: first, it represents a coherent replacement for contemporary political economy (or "neoliberalism"); and second, it does not reduce this transformation to a fight between communities, races, ethnicities, nationalities, and other social groups.

To me, it is evident that neoliberalism, as we understand it at least, is not a viable economic, social, or political system anymore. It is, almost literally, tearing apart countries, communities, and individuals – think of the consequences of Brexit for the UK (e.g. the possible secession of Scotland) and the EU (e.g. the possible exit of other member states). In large part, I would argue, neoliberalism was not viable because, like any system, it entailed a series of contradictions that could not be resolved over the long term. While most people might agree with this, there is, at its core, a central dogma to neoliberalism that makes it so powerful nevertheless. As David Tyfield (2017) notes in his forthcoming book, *Liberalism 2.0*, because neoliberalism is premised on the idea that markets are the *best* mechanism for coordinating *everything*, we may have lost the ability to think beyond the walls of neoliberal epistemology. How can we come up with something "better" than the "best"? I do not propose an answer to this question here, it is something I think others need to address, and they are addressing it as I write. Instead, I want to finish this book with a summary of what I see as the main contradictions in the way people currently understand neoliberalism and how this might explain why we have ended up where we are.

Three contradictions in understanding neoliberalism

In the Introduction to this book I highlighted three contradictions I think affect current understandings of neoliberalism *and* neoliberal principles themselves. These include: (1) the relationship between the corporate entity and corporate monopoly in an era supposedly dominated by markets; (2) the increasing propensity towards rentiership over entrepreneurship in an economy supposedly based on market dynamism; and (3) the importance of contract and contract law, rather than markets, in the organization of capitalism. I do not think I am unique in highlighting these issues in contemporary society and political economy, nor do I think they are necessarily the preserve of a leftist critique of capitalism. As I noted in Chapter 6, for example, the mainstream economics magazine *The Economist* (2016) has castigated the continuing dominance of a number of "dead ideas" in business and management, including the notion that contemporary capitalism is "more competitive than ever" and "that we live in an age of entrepreneurialism". Similar accusations could be made against politicians, policy-makers, mainstream commentators and journalists, and more besides. Dead ideas seem to be all the rage nowadays, perhaps because, as noted earlier, it is so difficult to think of something new when we have had it hammered into our heads for so long that there can be nothing new after market ascendance.

It is therefore worth considering how, after all, the market has not been and never was in ascendance in our societies and economies. Whether this idea of market ascendance, which many critics call "neoliberalism", is a consensual delusion or dominant ideology of the elite, including many of its critics, is an important question to consider, and one I return to briefly later. Others – more competent thinkers than I could ever be – are probably better suited to pursue this issue in the future.

First, it does not seem like there is an either/or choice between markets and organizations in the coordination of contemporary economies – market exchange and corporate monopoly sit side-by-side in most economies, despite the supposed analytical and normative priority given to markets in neoliberal thinking and policy (Crouch 2011). In fact, a significant and even majority of economic activity is undertaken *within* organizations and not markets (Simon 1991; Hodgson 2005), suggesting that markets are relatively less important than imagined or claimed. This has not stopped neoliberal thinkers from trying to theorize away this contradiction. In particular, the work of financial economists like Jensen and Meckling (1976) has provided a fillip to claims that since everything is already a market then business organizations are merely a "nexus of contracts" with no other characteristics (Birch 2016a, 2016b). Moreover, because it is the "owners" of capital (i.e. shareholders) who, by definition, know how best to allocate that capital, the concentration of capital in large or monopolistic organizations makes no difference to its efficient (i.e. "socially beneficial") use. Corporate monopoly, from this viewpoint, is no such thing; it makes no practical difference and can be ignored as a political problem. The analytical hoops that need to be jumped through might put off other people, but all it requires is a faith in the theoretical assumption that everything *is* already a market. Critics who adopt the same assumptions – that everything has been turned into a market – fall into the same trap, however. Consequently, it is important to understand how the differences between markets and organizations are analysed in order to pick apart these arguments.

Second, it seems problematic to conceive of everyone in neoliberal capitalism as an entrepreneurial subject. Again, neoliberals like Ludwig von Mises and Israel Kirzner may argue that every person engages in entrepreneurial thinking and action when they participate in the economy, thereby promoting a particular analytical assumption. But again, that does not mean that von Mises and Kirzner are correct in their epistemic and ontological claims. It is noticeable, however, that many critical thinkers take their claims at face value (e.g. Dardot and Laval 2014; Brown 2015), reinforcing neoliberal arguments with their critical takes on the transformation of individual subjectivities into entrepreneurs of the self. The lack of empirical support for these claims aside, the political consequences of this perspective are troubling – and I return to them later. Rather than entrepreneurship, I sought to examine how contemporary capitalism is increasingly defined by forms of rentiership (Birch 2017a, 2017b; Birch et al. 2017), including the appropriation of value from our "habits of life" (Veblen 1908) through government fiat, monopoly, or the reconfiguration of organizations and markets. It is necessary to understand rentiership as much as it is necessary to think about entrepreneurship, but critical perspectives of neoliberalism largely ignore the former. As such, many neoliberal claims about the benefits of markets (e.g. they produce new goods and services that benefit everyone) are left intact, rather than given the same scrutiny as other claims.

Finally, markets themselves as ontological objects need to be interrogated with more rigour. It is generally accepted that capitalism, including its recent neoliberal variant, is dependent on private property and freedom of contract; two legal and political institutions that are central to the creation and propagation of markets and market-like processes (Birch and Siemiatycki 2016). My aim in this book has been to examine how neoliberalism represents a *contract*-based order, rather than market-based one. This is possible through a dissection of the conception of "contract" in economic and legal terms; the legal definition is a "legally enforced promise" while the economic definition is "reciprocal arrangement" (Eisenberg 1999). In looking at the history of contract law, it is possible to demonstrate that neoliberal capitalism reflects the emergence of *neo-formalism* in contract law, emphasizing the literal interpretation of contracts within a set of norms that assume only certain market actors are "sophisticated" and that markets are only possible with the extension of standard-form contracts, thereby eliminating the very "freedom" on which contractual relations were supposed to be based.

The political consequences of the "neoliberal" peace

Having outlined three contradictions that I see in current critical understandings of neoliberalism and the assumptions underlying neoliberal thinking, I now want to finish the book by considering their consequences in light of recent events. I do not intend to go into detail here, so this will be brief. I leave it up to others to take this further as they see fit.

Writing immediately after Donald Trump's US presidential election victory, Mark Blyth (2016) argues in *Foreign Affairs* that all of this was pretty much predictable in light of the crushing effect that "neoliberalism" has had on most people over the last 30 years. To quote Blyth at some length:

> Over the next thirty years the world was transformed from a debtor's paradise into a creditor's paradise where capital's share of national income rose to an all-time high as labor's share fell as wages stagnated. Productivity rose, but the returns all went to capital. Unions were crushed while labor's ability to push up wages collapsed due to the twin shocks of restrictive legislation and the globalization of production. Parliaments in turn were reduced to tweet-generating talking shops as central banks and policy technocrats wrested control of the economy away from those elected to govern.

In countries like the USA, UK, and Canada, we are left with a political economy in which we are *governed* and *disciplined* by debt (Lazzarato 2015). Debt, especially mortgage debt, became a necessary evil that underpinned a "privatized" pension system in which housing replaced secure pensions. The downside, as Blyth (2016) points out, is that the neoliberal assault on inflation – and resulting deflationary pressures after the 2007–2008 global financial crisis – has meant that the debt burden keeps rising. All the while, average salaries and wages have been falling steadily since the 1970s and crashing since the crisis. We are now in a double bind in which a significant proportion of the population find themselves with a rising debt burden because inflation is no longer eroding that debt, and falling incomes because employment opportunities are constricting due to globalization, automation, and austerity. Unfortunately, there is limited political will on the part of elites to change course since this situation has led to their massive enrichment.

Although the political and economic elites (e.g. politicians, business people, economists, etc.) bear an enormous amount of responsibility for the mess we are in, it is also important to consider the extent to which the rest of the population are also responsible for it. In countries like the USA, UK, and Canada, for example, it is noticeable that the political-economic impacts of neoliberalism did not bring anywhere near the majority of people out on the streets in protest. For example, the Occupy Movement was almost a marginal protest against corporate malfeasance, akin in many ways to equivalent movements on the political right, although considerably smaller (Worth 2013). In fact, most people seem pretty content in these countries with the current state of affairs – at least most of the people who vote; that is, older people, home owners, people with jobs, etc.

The reason why is quite simple in my view. The last 30 to 40 years have witnessed a huge upswing in house prices, especially after the mid-1990s (Birch 2015). Rising housing asset values helped to ameliorate stagnant income levels, or it seems that way. Whether or not rising house prices can replace decent wages is a contentious issue, but one that we need to address head on because the only way I see us getting out of the current neoliberal system crisis is through a massive devaluation of housing and other assets (e.g. fossil fuel reserves). Current fears about the future in light of events in 2016 pale in comparison to the potential anger that could result from even suggesting that we collectively devalue everyone's housing assets. If any government implemented such a plan, it would likely end in a popular uprising of the sort to make a zombie apocalypse seem tame in comparison. However, leaving societies and economies as they are – highly unequal, rising debt burdens, declining prospects for younger generations, etc. – is no solution either.

In light of these troubling conclusions, it seems as if neoliberalism, which we have to remember led us to this point according to many people, has never really been as influential or world changing as many critical thinkers suggest. Claims about the transformation of our identities and subjectivities through the embedding and embodiment of competitiveness, entrepreneurialism, and market-focused thinking do not sit well with the popular response to 2016's politics of "more-of-the-same". On the one hand, and as I sought to show in this book, much of neoliberal thinking and its implementation were never really concerned with the "average" person. Instead, it was about legitimating the actions of the wealthiest (Chapter 6), or promoting entrepreneurial thinking in ("elite") parts of the population (Chapter 7), or reconfiguring what it means to be an (sophisticated) economic actor (Chapter 8), rather than spreading neoliberal ideas throughout the whole population of countries like the USA, UK, and Canada. This is how we have ended up with the situation we are in today. On the other hand, if we assume that Brexit and Trump reflect discontent with the status quo, we have to assume that a large proportion of the population has simply been ignored within neoliberal regimes. In political-economic terms it does not matter, for example, if everyone has the personal or financial capacity to move, as long as the most skilled and credentialed (i.e. an "educated elite") can up-sticks at a moment's notice.

To me, then, neoliberal capitalism is best characterized as an era in which the elite thought they had transformed themselves into go-getting, entrepreneurial, and sophisticated market actors, assuming, in their privilege, that everyone else was doing the same, while ignoring, in their privilege, that everyone else cannot act like "rational" and self-interested individuals – read, "sociopath" – without deleterious social consequences, namely being ostracized by family and friends, losing your social networks, eliminating their financial safety nets to fall back on when "entrepreneurial" ventures fail (as they do all the time), depending on house ownership for security in old age, and so on. The same could be said of the critics of neoliberalism, however. The argument that "we are all neoliberals now", made by people like Dardot and Laval (2014) and Brown (2015) amongst others, sits uneasily with the assumption that this means we must have given up our humanity (e.g. family ties, friendships, religion, community, political beliefs, and so on) in the face of turning ourselves into the perfect neoliberal subject. Understanding neoliberalism is difficult, as this book should have illustrated, but it is vital now more than ever that we try to understand our societies and ourselves, even if we give up on one concept in order to do so.

Bibliography

Birch, K. (2015), *We Have Never Been Neoliberal: A Manifesto for a Doomed Youth*, Winchester, UK: Zero Books.

Birch, K. (2016a), "Market vs. contract? The implications of contractual theories of corporate governance to the analysis of neoliberalism", *ephemera: theory & politics in organization*, 16(1), 107–33.

Birch, K. (2016b), "Financial economics and business schools: legitimating corporate monopoly, reproducing neoliberalism?", in S. Springer, K. Birch and J. MacLeavy (eds), *The Handbook of Neoliberalism*, London: Routledge, pp. 320–30.

Birch, K. (2017a), "Rethinking value in the bio-economy: finance, assetization and the management of value", *Science, Technology and Human Values*, 42(3), 460–90.

Birch, K. (2017b), "Financing technoscience: finance, assetization and rentiership", in D. Tyfield, R. Lave, S. Randalls and C. Thorpe (eds), *The Routledge Handbook of the Political Economy of Science*, London: Routledge, pp. 169–81.

Birch, K. and Mykhnenko, V. (eds) (2010), *The Rise and Fall of Neoliberalism: The Collapse of an Economic Order?*, London: Zed Books.

Birch, K. and Siemiatycki, M. (2016), "Neoliberalism and the geographies of marketization: the entangling of state and markets", *Progress in Human Geography*, 40(2), 177–98.

Birch, K., Tyfield, D. and Chiapetta, M. (2017), "From neoliberalizing research to research-ing neoliberalism: STS, *rentiership* and the emergence of commons 2.0", in D. Cahill, M. Konings and M. Cooper (eds), *The Sage Handbook of Neoliberalism*, London: Sage.

Blyth, M. (2016), "Global Trumpism", *Foreign Affairs*, 15 November, accessed 23 November 2016 at https://www.foreignaffairs.com/articles/2016-11-15/global-trumpism.

Brown, W. (2015), *Undoing the Demos*, New York, NY: Zone Books.

Crouch, C. (2011), *The Strange Non-Death of Neoliberalism*, Cambridge: Polity Press.

Dardot, P. and Laval, C. (2014), *The New Way of the World*, London: Verso.

Eisenberg, M. (1999), "The conception that the corporation is a nexus of contracts, and the dual nature of the firm", *Journal of Corporation Law*, 24, 819–36.

Hodgson, G. (2005), "Knowledge at work: some neoliberal anachronisms", *Review of Social Economy*, 63(4), 547–65.

Jensen, M. and Meckling, W. (1976), "Theory of the firm: managerial behavior, agency costs and ownership structure", *Journal of Financial Economics*, 3, 305–60.

Lazzarato, M. (2015), *Governing by Debt*, Pasadena, CA: Semiotext(e).

Mirowski, P. (2013), *Never Let a Serious Crisis Go to Waste*, London: Verso.

Peck, J. (2010), *Constructions of Neoliberal Reason*, Oxford: Oxford University Press.

Simon, H. (1991), "Organizations and markets", *Journal of Economic Perspectives*, 5, 25–44.

The Economist (2016), "Management theory is becoming a compendium of dead ideas", *The Economist*, 17 December, accessed 20 December 2016 at http://www.economist.com/news/business/21711909-what-martin-luther-did-catholic-church-needs-be-done-business-gurus-management?fsrc=scn/fb/te/bl/ed/management-theoryisbecomingacompendiumofdeadideas.

Tyfield, D. (2017), *Liberalism 2.0: China, Innovation and Beyond the Crises of Innovation*, London: Routledge.

Veblen, T. (1908), "On the nature of capital: investment, intangible assets, and the pecuniary magnate", *Journal of Economics*, 23(1), 104–36.

Worth, O. (2013), *Resistance in the Age of Austerity*. London: Zed Books.

Index